A Cornish Cargo

The untold history of a Victorian seafaring family

Alison Baxter

ISBN 9798670213332

Cover design by Deirdré Gyenes

Cover image: Samuel Phillips Jackson, *The Steam Packet 'Propeller' entering Portishead Harbour, 1850*, Bristol Museum and Art Gallery.
Given by Mrs Collyns, 1982. / Bridgeman Images

Family portraits of the Dupens can be viewed on the author's website https://victorianlives.wordpress.com, where you will also find notes on source material and historical references.

For Tamsin and Eva, the next two generations, with love

*And in memory of my father, who first took me to Cornwall in
search of gravestones*

DUPEN FAMILY TREE

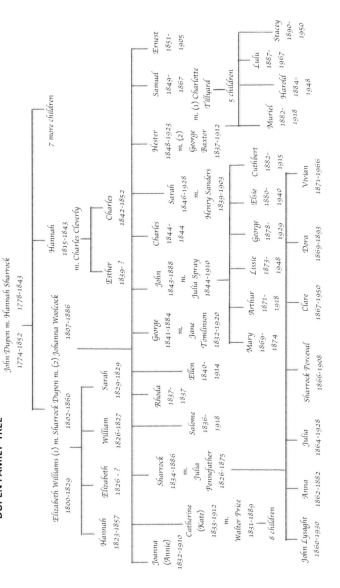

Contents

PART 1 HAYLE

'A family of merchant venturers, mariners and engineers of Huguenot origin with a propensity to wander far over the earth'

Sharrock Dupen of Hayle

1 A Cargo of Memories

A random and irrational sifting process takes place every time someone dies, or a relationship breaks down, or a house move compels us to sort out our stuff. Unbalanced by emotion we make odd choices, throwing away mementos that we later wish we had kept, or preserving things that we will happily take to the charity shop in a few years' time. But the child's sampler that hangs on my living room wall is not something I would ever part with. On a small square of yellowing linen, the alphabet is embroidered twice, in sober shades of dark blue and red. Then come four lines of verse:

The deadliest wounds with which we bleed
Our crimes inflict alone
Man's mercies from God's hand proceed
His miseries from his own

And finally the signature:

Joanna Woolcock Dupen Her work Aged 7 Years A.D. 1839

The letters are made up of hundreds of tiny crosses that must have taken many painstaking hours to complete, but the first line of the verse is too long and there is no space for the 'd' of 'bleed', which sits orphaned above the rest of the line. I wonder if the child who stitched it was mortified by her mistake. Infused in the objects we inherit are emotions that we can never recover.

When I was growing up, the embroidered sampler hung disregarded on the wall of our sitting room. Joanna Dupen was not a person I recognised; I didn't know the maiden names of my grandmothers, let alone my great-grandmothers. Women's names are easily lost. It was only after my parents died and we cleared their house that I started to look for meaning in the objects that surrounded me. Forced to decide what to keep and what to dispose of, my brother and I divided up the books, the pictures, the silver, and the china. He had no interest in needlework so I took away the sampler. Stitching connects women in a way that often excludes men. Put away in a drawer somewhere I still have the tablecloth and napkins adorned with cross-stitched roses that my mother and I completed together, when I was only ten years old and eager to please. It was a time of rare harmony between us, as we shared an activity that my brother could not join in.

Now I wanted to know more about the small alphabet that I had inherited. In sixteenth century England, before the introduction of printed designs, an 'exampler' was a compendium of patterns and stitches for the needlewoman to follow, evolving over the next two hundred years to become a record of a girl's skill. Tranquil domestic scenes of houses and gardens were popular, while some more ambitious needlewomen created embroidered maps. But Joanna's miniature exercise in morality and literacy has no charmingly naïve border of flowers and animals, and no variety of stitches to show off her accomplishments. She was not from a wealthy family who could afford large pieces of fabric or multi-coloured silk threads.

It was the verse that intrigued me. I assumed it must be a prayer or religious text, but the author turned out to be the blue stocking and abolitionist Hannah More. The woman known as 'Holy Hannah' was teaching in Bristol in 1789 when she decided it was her duty to educate the rural poor. She set up charity schools where children learned stories from the scriptures and were taught to read – but not write, in case they got ideas above their station. (In case this makes her sound humourless, I should also mention that she named her cats Passive Obedience and Non-resistance.) More's 'cheap repository tracts', simple tales of Christian morality, were carried by pedlars and chapmen to even the most remote communities and sold in their millions. But to my surprise the verse does not come from one of these. It was written much earlier, when More was still a party-loving young playwright whose work excited the admiration of Garrick and Dr Johnson. *Sir Eldred of the Bower* is a tragic tale that moved Mrs Garrick to tears when read aloud by her husband. It tells of a young nobleman who falls in love with a beautiful young woman and marries her, but on their wedding night he catches her with another knight and stabs them both to death. The stranger, he discovers too late, was no rival but his bride's beloved brother. I was intrigued not only by the child, Joanna Woolcock Dupen, but also by her mother, who selected this verse for her daughter to embroider. She must surely have been an unusual woman if she took her moral messages from romances.

It was time to empty more of the boxes that I had stacked carelessly in the cupboard under the stairs. Amongst the neglected sediment of paper and photographs from my parents' house was a pencilled family tree that my grandfather Harold had started as he lay in his hospital bed, waiting for his heart to fail for the final time. His mother, Hester Dupen, seemed to have had ten older siblings, but there was no Joanna. Fortunately, the internet has made family history accessible in a way that was impossible for earlier generations and I was able to call up a series of census returns that helped me match the child of the sampler with the aunt my grandfather called Annie, Hester's oldest sister. Of course. The affectionate diminutive would have avoided any confusion with her mother, who was born Johanna Woolcock and married Sharrock Dupen, of Hayle in Cornwall.

At the start of Victoria's reign, Hayle was a boom town at the heart of England's Industrial Revolution. Situated at the centre of a complex network of waterways where three rivers, the Hayle, the Penpol and the Angarrack, flowed out through a muddle of pools, creeks, and sandbanks to the coast at St Ives, it was the main port for the tin and copper mines of west Cornwall. Home for a time to the great engineer Richard Trevithick, Hayle boasted a shipyard and the two biggest iron foundries in the world. It was not a textile manufacturing centre like Manchester or Leeds, nor a major trading port like Bristol; it was smaller than Birmingham or Sheffield. But like the great cities of the north and midlands, its growth was driven by the power of iron and steam.

My grandfather spent holidays there as a boy in the 1890s, but by then the town had subsided into a forgotten backwater, its great industrial heritage crumbling away, hidden in plain sight by banks of ivy and a kind of collective amnesia. After he inherited the Dupen family home in the spring of 1918 he must have sold it, holding onto his Aunt Annie's sampler together with a logbook kept by Ernest, the youngest of his sailor uncles, and a handful of other relics. Enough to spark my curiosity but not sufficient to tell me the story of the Dupens. That was something I was going to have to uncover for myself.

I never knew my grandfather Harold Baxter, my father's father, who died in 1948, a few weeks before my parents' wedding. He survives only in a handful of letters and photographs but I imagine him as a quiet, unassuming man, with an enquiring mind and a keen sense of the ridiculous. In the 1930s, the Scottish writer Lewis Grassic Gibbon, who was a close friend, put him into a novel as one of the founder members of a 'Politico-Social' society called the Secular Control Group. A single sentence paints a vivid picture:

> lean, rakish, and middle-aged, with grey-streaked brown hair and grey-streaked blue eyes, a gold-framed pince nez and a gold-mounted petrol lighter, [he] would arrive from Berkshire in a large and impressive touring-car. (*The Thirteenth Disciple*, 1931)

It is the car that gives it away. Gibbon named his own small car 'Harold' after his friend, who owned a garage business and taught him to drive. I hope my grandfather enjoyed his brief appearance in print and was not too dismayed by having radical views ascribed to him such as the

abolition of marriage and enforcement of birth control. I am
fairly sure that he would have been content to endorse the
secularisation of education and the disestablishment of
churches. An admirer of H. G. Wells, he too believed that the
world would be saved by science.

In seeking out my grandfather's forebears I am of course
also looking for him, for the boy who grew up loving engines
and the sea. As I struggle to decipher Victorian handwriting,
masters' certificates, naval service records, and smudgy
newsprint, I wish I could turn to him and say: 'Look, I've
filled in the blanks in your mother's family and added more
names that you never realised were missing, the dead babies
that no one remembered to mourn. This is the truth behind
the myths that surrounded your sailor uncles, and this is what
life was like in Hayle in the heyday of the Industrial
Revolution.'

But first I had to go further back, to the south coast of
Cornwall, where in the early years of the eighteenth century a
French sea captain was shipwrecked off Marazion – although
somewhere down the generations we appear to have
carelessly mislaid the proof: a ship's charter and cargo
manifest in old French bearing the family seal. Captain Jean
Dupen settled in Mylor, marrying a local girl, and it is his
grandson who is pictured in the portrait miniature that I
found wrapped in tissue paper at the bottom of a dusty
cardboard box. I took it and hung it on my dining room wall.
The face of a young man in his twenties looks out from a
gold-rimmed oval set in a rectangle of glossy, black-painted
wood. His short brown hair is parted to one side and he has
fuzzy sideburns. Under his arched brows his eyes are hazel,
and his nose is straight with a slight hook at the end. He
wears the clothes of a gentleman: a dark coat over a white
shirt. His collar rises high to touch his ears, making it
impossible for him to turn his head by more than a few
degrees, and his narrow black tie is knotted firmly under his
chin. This man, the image of the Regency heroes of my

teenage reading, is, according to the handwritten label on the back, my father's great-great-grandfather John Dupen.

All large towns had competent practitioners who produced these portable tokens. Unlike oil paintings, they were private items designed to be realistic rather than flattering; this is my ancestor as he really was. John Dupen's image is protected by glass and held in place at the back by a spiky border of triangular metal strips. These are fragile and snap easily when bent, so I am reluctant to remove the picture to check if it is painted on ivory, but I am fairly sure it is. Similar examples appear in antique dealers' catalogues labelled 'portrait of an unknown gentleman', priced at a few hundred pounds. My however many times great-grandfather may have commissioned the miniature as a gift for his future wife, a keepsake for the long months when he was away at sea.

We all carry with us through life a jumble of inherited objects, photographs, and stories. Like the cargoes in Masefield's poem, they range from exotic ivory and sandalwood to cheap tin trays, but they all tell us something about where we come from. In the islands of the South Pacific, where I lived for a couple of years (another story for another time), a desire for material goods was sometimes confused with the longing for a new Messiah. Our own relics, like my sampler and portrait miniature, can also become a kind of cargo cult, an obsession with the ancestors that we believe will provide us with an identity.

I grew up largely unaware of my Cornish seafaring heritage. It was crowded out by the Scottish story told by my grandmother Jean. Perhaps this is what happens in any family, that one lineage is preferred, one narrative prevails. Jean had the advantage of being a writer, who dealt robustly with her husband Harold's family history. 'He claims it is much more romantic than mine,' she declared as she embarked on her own autobiography, 'but I won't let him speak.' Harold's mother and her host of siblings were, he said, descended from Huguenot refugees. He had fallen under the spell of the

Dupens and so, a hundred years later, have I. It is a well-known if inexplicable condition amongst family historians, wanting to be Huguenot. I suspect most amateur genealogists are looking for a hint of the exotic in their family tree, something to confirm that sense we all have of being special. There was for a time a small Huguenot church in Falmouth and Dupen is a French name, but beyond that all is rumour and legend.

When I learned as a teenager that I had Franco-Cornish sailors in my family tree I thought, like my grandfather, that it was delightfully romantic. I had been reading *Frenchman's Creek* and had a bad case of Daphne Du Maurier. We went, one chilly Easter holiday, to the Fal estuary and spent a fruitless afternoon poking around the churchyard of St Just in Roseland, a village as pretty as its name suggests. By then every other cottage was a second home and expensive yachts crowded the small harbour where fishermen once eked out a precarious existence. We were searching for long-lost headstones, but there was nothing to see. We did not go to Hayle.

A distant cousin, the last of the name to live in England, wrote, 'The Dupens appear to be a family of merchant venturers, mariners and engineers of Huguenot origin with a propensity to wander far over the earth.' From childhood I too yearned to see the world, experiencing an emotion the English have failed to put a name to, but that the Germans call *Fernweh*, a vaguely melancholy wanderlust that can never quite be satisfied. During my childhood we drove all over Europe, to Vienna, Florence, and one memorable summer, across the Iron Curtain to Prague. I had no sense that we were doing anything unusual. As soon as I graduated I set off for French Canada and some years later, when I was offered a job on a remote Pacific archipelago I accepted without a second thought, throwing away an alternative, more humdrum life that would have offered financial and emotional security. It is obscurely comforting to know where my restlessness comes from: that although none of us bear the name, my grandfather, my father and I are all Dupens.

My older self acknowledges the equal and opposite force of a need for roots, for a homeland that I was never going to find in the home counties where I grew up. Many of us, as we grow older and our remaining years accelerate past us at ever-increasing speed, seek a kind of immortality by resurrecting the forgotten lives of our forebears. Irrationally, we hope that unlike them we will not disappear into a mist of garbled memories. We want to anchor ourselves in time and space before it is too late. During the first twenty years of my life I lived in five different places. It made it hard for me to say where I was from. I had no cluster of streets where grandparents, aunts, and cousins lived in close proximity. In seeking out the Dupens I was looking not only for my ancestors but also for a place where I could belong. I was convinced that it had to be by the sea, that saltwater ran in my veins. Perhaps it would turn out to be Hayle. My DNA, I have discovered, is 40% Scottish, but also very markedly Cornish.

For a long time I thought I might write a novel about my Cornish family. I had a few pieces of the jigsaw but many more were missing and there was no box with a helpful picture for me to follow. Surely this story had to be told as fiction. But when I started to research the facts behind my inherited cargo of objects and anecdotes, I realised that they had a different power when assembled into a nonfiction narrative. In an environment where the daily news was becoming more and more fictitious, I had a growing appetite for the tangible, the real. My Victorian ancestors, like almost everyone else's, were ordinary people who lived through extraordinary times, when the world was transformed by the power of steam and Britain's expanding empire. By recovering their story I was rescuing a forgotten version of the past. The events that I write about are documented, the people and places are real. And yet, the more I discovered about my grandfather's mother and her dozen siblings, the more I found myself imagining them back to life, which makes them, in the end, invented characters. The result is a narrative that uses both fact and fiction to get at the truth – or my version of it, at least.

2 From Sail to Steam

The John Dupen of the portrait belonged to the small port of Mylor, on the great Fal estuary, but his second son was baptised in 1802 in St Just in Roseland, the home parish of his mother, Hannah Sharrock. He was given her name. My great-great-grandfather Sharrock Dupen's childhood was spent at war. His younger brother, born just after the battle of Trafalgar, was christened Horatio Nelson. During the twenty hazardous years when the British fought the French, press gangs roamed the streets of Falmouth, snatching unwary lads from their families and carrying them off to serve in His Majesty's navy. These were pugilistic times when boys attacked each other with stones and fists while men gathered to watch boxing matches, dog and cock fights, or badger baiting. Whenever a crowd of intoxicated miners arrived, the cry went up, 'The tin men are coming!' and the shops were hastily closed and shuttered.

Falmouth now feels like a distant provincial town but in those days it was a buzzing hub of news. It had been a Royal Mail packet station for over a hundred years, home to the ships that carried mail and passengers across the globe. Local people were better informed than Londoners about the latest events in distant ports, from Lisbon to the Leeward Islands. The fast, armed brigs that carried His Majesty's mails sailed through the Straits of Gibraltar to Malta and Corfu, crossed the Atlantic to Nova Scotia, Cartagena, and the islands of the West Indies, and made their way south as far as Rio and Buenos Aires. The commanders were the aristocracy of Falmouth. They lived in fine white houses overlooking the harbour and their jackets bristled with gilt buttons and embroidery designed to ape the uniforms of naval captains, much to the irritation of the Admiralty. These men too served in the front line of the wars with the American colonies and the Emperor Napoleon, fighting off attacks by enemy warships, and privateers attracted by their cargoes of gold and silver bullion. Their duty was to protect at all costs the leather portmanteau containing sensitive government despatches. It sat on deck weighted with heavy pigs of iron, ready to be jettisoned overboard rather than captured.

Sharrock Dupen was thirteen and quite old enough to go to sea when peace was finally signed with the French in 1815. I would like to believe that he began his life as a sailor on board one of the famous Falmouth packets, squeezed with some two dozen other crew members into a dank, unventilated space beneath the main deck without even a hammock to sleep in, proud to be part of this historic service. But I have to admit that it is more likely, if less romantic, that he sailed as crew on his father's single-masted cutter. John Dupen, who traded between Falmouth, Spain and Portugal, was not one of the grand commanders who strolled through the town doffing their gold-encrusted hats to the ladies, but he too lived with danger on every voyage. His small vessel could all too easily be swamped by heavy seas, especially if the cargo was not well secured. '*Fortitude* Dupen' says an entry in Lloyds List for 1824, 'Dublin with loss of bowsprit, cargo shifted, and leaky'. He may well have been a smuggler too, making extra money from the illegal trade in tobacco, spirits, and lace. Public opinion held it to be no crime; even the packet service captains were involved.

The wars had brought high taxes, inflated prices, and hardship for the common people. The years that followed were no less difficult, even with the threat of invasion lifted. Too many soldiers and sailors were left without employment, the economy was depressed, and food continued to be expensive. I don't know if John Dupen left the sea to become an innkeeper or if he took on the business to supplement his income, but in 1814 he held the lease of the Lord Nelson, a humble ale house in St Mawes. Dealing in food and drink was to become as much a family tradition as seafaring.

In 1822 John's son Sharrock Dupen married for the first time, but seven years later his wife died, leaving him alone with two young daughters. Widowed and grieving, he must have wanted to keep his children close and the only way to do so was to marry again. Abandoning the precarious life of a mariner, where he had to compete for a berth with the many sailors paid off from the navy, within the year he took Johanna Woolcock as his second wife and set himself up as a confectioner in Penzance. By exchanging the salt air of the Bay of Biscay for the sweet scents of cinnamon, rosewater, and vanilla, he was giving up the hardship of the sea for a softer existence, but a less exciting one. It was probably a choice that his new wife approved of.

My two times great-grandmother, the admirer of Hannah More, was born of yeoman stock in 1807 in Kenwyn, a parish of farmers and miners on the outskirts of Truro. She married Sharrock Dupen in 1830 when she was 23 years old and their first child arrived some two years later. Joanna Woolcock Dupen, my grandfather's Aunt Annie, was born on 31st March 1832 and baptised in the Wesleyan chapel in Penzance. She was followed a year later by a sister, Catherine Sharrock Dupen, known as Kate, and on Christmas Day 1834 by a brother, Sharrock Semmens Dupen. These first three children bore the family names of their mother, grandmother and great-grandmother, a strong cord attaching them to their roots. In those days, women's names were not so easily lost.

The confectionery trade provided a steady living but with a growing family Sharrock Dupen was never going to get rich selling comfits and lozenges. Stirring a boiling vat of sugar was not without risk but hardly offered sufficient challenge to a man used to reefing sails in a force ten gale. He was on the look out for a job with more prospects and when the opportunity arose he did not hesitate to move his family to Hayle, a place where all things were possible for a man of energy and vision.

The town had doubled in size over the previous twenty years, with a population that was approaching 4,000, two thirds that of the nearby cathedral city of Truro. Harvey's foundry, shipbuilding business, and ropewalk employed nearly 800 men while several hundred more were employed by the Cornish Copper Company. The two businesses were long-standing competitors, who had disputed territory and access rights for years, more than once mustering mobs of labourers on the river bank to shout insults and brandish shovels and other improvised weapons at each other. Although they never actually came to blows, there was bad blood between the two sides that persisted long after a legal settlement was reached. Granite boundary stones marked with H on one side and CCC on the other still demarcate territory belonging to the two companies, a reminder of a bitter rivalry that gave the town a lawless edge. Cornwall was in many ways still the wild west.

The first full census (of 1841) tells me that most of the inhabitants of Hayle were natives of the county. They were miners, mariners, carpenters, and masons. Others were employed in the new trades of iron founder, boiler maker, mechanic, and engineer. There were large numbers of apprentices – an apprenticeship at one of the foundries was much sought after. Shipwrights worked in the shipyard, sawyers in the timber mill that supplied the yard, ropemakers in the rope works that produced the rigging. The western end of the town, home to Harvey's works, was known as Foundry, while the eastern side, where the Cornish Copper Company had their business, was called Copperhouse. This was the commercial centre, where tailors and shoemakers lived alongside numerous dressmakers and milliners, as well as a staymaker, a hatter, and a Jewish watchmaker born 'in foreign parts'. It was still a time, I realise, when most people had a job that involved making something, on a relatively small scale and using specialist skills. The men employed in the engineering works never spoke of their factory; it was a workshop and like the blacksmiths of an earlier age, they were artisans.

The sailing ships that tied up at the quay, two-masted brigs and schooners and single-masted sloops, brought Welsh coal for the foundries, timber from New Brunswick and Norway for the shipyard, and hemp, tar, and linseed oil for the ropewalk. On their return voyages they carried copper ore for smelting in Wales and iron goods of every description: massive boilers to power steamships and small portable engines to drain the silver mines of Peru, new-fangled kitchen ranges and weights for sash windows. Other vessels brought sacks of salt to preserve the slippery silver shoals of pilchards that were landed in Newlyn and St Ives, and then carried the fish to the Mediterranean to feed the insatiable demand in Naples and the Kingdom of the Two Sicilies. The Hayle fleet traded across the Atlantic to North and South America, often staying away for years, picking up cargo where they could and delivering it to whatever destination the charterer required. The captains kept up a regular correspondence with their owner, Mr Henry Harvey, who was also the proprietor of the shipyard and one of the foundries.

Harvey had inherited his business from his father John, a blacksmith who, at the end of the previous century, had turned himself into an iron founder and mine merchant, manufacturing the pipes, pumps, and engine parts needed by the nearby copper mines, and shipping in supplies of coal, timber, and rope. Two images survive of Henry Harvey's portly figure seen in profile. In one he is dressed for riding in long pantaloons, a high-fronted coat with cut away tails, and dandified boots with pointed toes. He is bareheaded and carries a riding crop. In the other he is clad in the tailcoat, knee breeches, white stockings and low black shoes reserved for evening wear. A natty stovepipe hat is perched on his full head of hair. His Humpty Dumpty silhouette gives the impression of a jovial Dickensian character and I feel that he should really have been called something more rotund.

Pumblechook, perhaps? But it would not do to under-estimate him.

In 1833 Hayle had been designated an official stannary town; a coinage hall was established on Harvey premises and Harveys made the weights needed to check the tin and copper ingots that were brought for assaying, stamping, and the payment of duty to the Duchy of Cornwall. In the face of ferocious opposition from the Cornish Copper Company, Henry Harvey had constructed a new wharf along the Penpol river and now he acquired land to create a sluicing pool. In December 1834 the 37-acre Carnsew pool was inaugurated, releasing a great wave that scoured the accumulated silt from the shipping lanes and quay. The event was celebrated with a dinner at the White Hart, where Harvey's sister, the widow of the great engineer Richard Trevithick, presided as hostess. When Trevithick disappeared to the silver mines of Peru leaving his wife to fend for herself, Henry Harvey built the hotel to provide a living for his sister and her six children – something that was necessary even after Jane's errant husband returned home with, so legend has it, no more than the clothes he stood up in, a gold watch, a compass, and a pair of silver spurs. By 1835 Henry Harvey could describe himself as 'a Merchant, Founder, Shipbuilder, Grocer, Draper, Ironmonger, Miller and Baker'. Around his foundry clustered other enterprises. He built a smelter to smelt tin from the great Wheal Vor mine, and a lime kiln. He had stables for more than fifty heavy horses that were used to transport machinery from the foundry to the mines and docks. His workers were paid in Harvey's shillings, which they spent in Harvey's emporium on everything from groceries to chamberpots.

A few years earlier, in 1831, a consortium led by Henry Harvey had been formed to establish a regular passenger service between Hayle and Bristol. Captain John Vivian was sent to Glasgow to commission a wooden paddle steamer to replace the unreliable sailing vessels in use on the route. As a

young naval officer in 1803, Vivian had steered Richard
Trevithick's road engine down Tottenham Court Road at the
heady speed of eight miles an hour, and like Trevithick he was
a giant of a man, well over six feet tall. He later made his
name as captain of the Falmouth packet *Little Catherine*, which
was captured by the French in 1813. Held captive on board a
frigate manned by elderly veterans, he was set free on parole
in order to assist the captain during a gale. His honourable
behaviour was recognised when the French captured another
English vessel and handed it over to their prisoner so that he
could return safely to Falmouth with his crew. This was the
man who was entrusted with command of the new steam
packet, the *Herald*.

The newspaper article that accompanied the first
advertisement for the service was effusive in its praise:

> *Royal Cornwall Gazette 1ˢᵗ October 1831*
> The new steam-packet "Herald," recently built at Greenock
> for the Hayle, St Ives and Bristol Steam Navigation Company,
> has taken her station. She performed the voyage from
> Greenock to Bristol, against a strong head wind, in admirable
> style; already she is spoken of as a first-rate steam-packet, for
> strength, beauty & rapidity.

The *Herald* needed a ship's steward, a position that was
one of many new roles created by the age of steam. Even by
1841 there were still only about a hundred of them listed in
the entire census, compared with 100,000 tailors and nearly as
many blacksmiths. It offered a man of entrepreneurial spirit
ample opportunity for profit: the steward was responsible for
providing food and drink on board, buying and selling his
own supplies in addition to pocketing a share of each
passenger's fare as his fee. Sharrock Dupen had proved he
could manage a business as well as a set of sails and Captain
Vivian offered him the job of steward of the *Herald*. They
sealed the bargain over a tankard of ale at the Royal Standard
in Hayle. That, at least, is how I interpret the available
evidence – which does not include the beer.

From the birth records of his children I deduce that Sharrock moved his family to Hayle in 1835 or 1836, hoping perhaps to emulate the success of Henry Harvey. I suspect that his wife was not best pleased; I can only imagine the feelings of a yeoman farmer's daughter at being uprooted to the dirt and clamour of a rough, industrial port. The family most probably came from Camborne, where Kate and young Sharrock were christened, but I decided that if I was going to recreate this critical moment in the family's history I would bring them from Penzance, on a bright spring day, along a route that takes Johanna through the whole town. Her reaction is invented but the sights, sounds, and smells of Hayle are as close as I can get to the reality of the past.

Hayle, March 1835

The big wooden cart rumbles and creaks its way along the rutted, muddy track. Johanna sits uncomfortably wedged amidst the jumble of boxes and baskets, gazing over the hedgerows dusted with creamy white blossom and yellow primroses, to where a few chestnut-coloured cattle are grazing in the fields. She cradles her new baby son on her lap, while her daughters Annie and Kate perch beside her, eyes wide with anxiety, their short legs sticking straight out in front of them. Her husband walks beside the cart with his other two girls, Johanna's stepdaughters Hannah and Lizzie. Leaving behind the market gardens of Penzance, green with the promise of an early vegetable crop, they pass into open countryside. Away in the distance the stone chimneys of the tin and copper mines puff out their black smoke. Wheal Neptune, Wheal Friendship, Wheal Providence, and Great Wheal Alfred: the names are the stuff of myth. Johanna recalls as a child hearing tales of the immense wealth buried beneath the tall granite towers. She used to imagine there were captive dragons to guard this treasure, pumping water from the shafts and straining to lift the heavy buckets of ore to the surface, filling the air with their hot, steaming breath.

She knows better now, of course, but still she feels that there is something monstrous about the great iron engines.

Johanna looks down at the two older girls and wonders how much they remember of the first time they were uprooted. Hannah was six and Lizzie just three years old when their father closed the door of the cottage in St Just for the last time and they left the village where their mother and sister were buried. In the churchyard they also left behind their brother William. Does Lizzie have any memory of her twin? From time to time she gets a blank, far-away look in her eyes, as if she is gazing at something no one else can see. She is doing it now. When Johanna married their father, she knew she would be assuming a heavy responsibility, but she was eager to escape a life spent at the beck and call of her older brothers and sisters. And Sharrock talked with such anguish of the loss of his wife, of his desperate attempts to save the tiny, mewing baby Sarah, and his sorrow when she gave up her fight for life. He was worried that his older daughters, sad and quiet, were growing pale and weak. They needed a mother. Johanna prayed for guidance. In the end the message was clear: it was her Christian duty to accept Sharrock's proposal. He said he would give up the sea and start a business in Penzance, so much more respectable than the rough villages around Falmouth. But now they are moving to Hayle. They have left behind the comforting sweetness of their shop, where sugar sticks and nut-filled comfits sat on the counter alongside the glass jars of lemon drops and herbal lozenges – elderflower for the stomach, soporific poppy to sooth a cough. Johanna's future and that of her children lies in a harsher place, one built on the power of steam.

Late in the afternoon they reach the north coast and smell the ocean again. On the left the river estuary stretches away towards the open sea. Flocks of gulls swoop noisily over the shallow pools and small waders potter on the sands, industriously dipping their beaks in search of worms. A harmless, even a pleasing sight. But Johanna knows how

often an unwary horse and rider has foundered here. Before
the raised causeway and bridge were built, travellers who
wanted to avoid the long journey round by St Erth had to
take a ferry boat across to the Royal Standard inn at high tide
or risk the long ride across the sands. If a horse carried too
much weight, it would sink and stick fast; a rider who
mistimed his passage was lost. John Wesley himself, it was
said, had by the grace of God narrowly escaped the
incoming tide. But today the carthorses trudge steadily over
the causeway, safely out of reach of the water, until they
reach the outskirts of the town.

From the right comes the clattering and hammering of
Harvey's foundry and engine workshops – loud enough,
thinks Johanna, to deafen the men who labour there. Her
husband has explained that it is where they build the high-
pressure pumping engines, the fiery monsters of her
childhood dreams. Cornwall is still the biggest copper
producer in the world. The acrid chemical fumes from the
chimneys and the tin smelter smother the fresh salt breeze
from the bay and catch at Johanna's lungs, making her
wheeze and cough. She covers her baby son with her shawl
and looks accusingly at Sharrock. She remembers the bitter
argument of a few weeks before.

'Do you want your children to grow up breathing soot
and all kinds of filth?' she asked.

'It's the future,' he told her. 'A bit of smoke is a small
price to pay for everything steam can do. Just you wait and
see. In a few years paddle ships will have completely taken
over from the old sailing vessels.'

'But you'll be leaving me alone for half the week.'

'I wouldn't do it if I didn't trust you to manage,' he said.
'You're quicker at totting up the bills than I am.'

He thinks he can flatter me into agreement, she thought. It
was true that she liked the feeling of being in charge of her
own household but she wasn't ready to concede defeat just
yet.

'That's all well and good, but the children need a father's guiding hand.'

'They need new shoes as well. Think of the extra money I can earn. And it's not as if I'll be away for months at a time. My own mother had to cope with much longer absences when my father was off to Lisbon or Cork.'

His sainted mother, of course, as if that was a clinching argument. She could tell from his sheepish expression that he recognised his error. But he said no more to persuade her.

'I've made up my mind and that's that,' he declared firmly.

Johanna sometimes wonders if her marriage was a mistake. She had always dreamed of becoming a farmer's wife, with her own chickens and a clean, scrubbed dairy. But then she remembers the odd feeling in the pit of her stomach when she first met Sharrock. He was different from any other man she knew, not tall, not handsome, but there was something that drew her eyes to him. He didn't boast or swagger but smiled with an air of quiet confidence that convinced her to trust him. That smile can still make her feel like a girl again, even now she is a respectable wife and mother. And truth be told, she is quite looking forward to being her own mistress in his absence.

He is speaking now. She cranes to hear what he is telling the girls.

'Look at the quay,' he says, pointing at the rows of ships, tight-packed along the scalloped edge, their bows pointing outwards. 'Never in all my seafaring days have I seen another such design, not in Cork or La Coruña, Lisbon or Gijon.'

Johanna can hear the eagerness in his voice when he names the foreign ports he has sailed to. How could she ever have imagined he would be content to live a small-town shopkeeper's life, with its petty rivalries and the gossip that accompanies every purchase? She watches as he waves an enthusiastic arm towards the steam packet *Herald*, tied up at the end of the wharf, the reason why he has insisted on moving his wife and children to this brash, smoky port.

The slow-moving cart trundles on over the granite setts of Penpol Terrace, where high on a bank Johanna sees a row of smart new houses, some double-fronted, some not, sitting back from the road behind their strips of garden. They are not big, but nor are they cramped labourers' cottages. They are surely intended for the families of skilled artisans and professional men. From the front windows, thinks Johanna, there must be fine views over the estuary. The residents will be able to see everything that happens on the quayside, which ships are in port and what they are loading and unloading.

'This,' her husband calls up to her, 'is where we will rent a house, next door to Captain Vivian himself, when we have saved some money.'

He walks on at a steady pace while Johanna frets to herself. What if the *Herald* fails to attract enough passengers? The steam packet business is still very new and not always safe; there have been some terrible accidents. They have seven mouths to feed now.

They round the corner by the Royal Standard, passing the iron swing bridge that closes off the Copperhouse Pool. Johanna sees with dismay that the dozens of new houses being built here have turned the ground into an expanse of rust-coloured mud. But then the open land gives way to the respectable shop fronts of Fore Street and she is reassured to see everything here that the family might need: a butcher, a grocer and even a draper. In the distance, across the reed beds of the tidal pool, she catches sight of the stone tower of Phillack parish church. That reminds her and she calls down to her husband:

'Where is the famous brass chapel? The one Mr Wesley praised? Do you remember what the minister told us? That he declared nothing could destroy it, till heaven and earth pass away.'

'I believe Mr Wesley was mistaken,' says Sharrock. 'It has been replaced with a larger building now, more fit for the size of the congregation. You will see how many people attend on Sunday.'

Johanna finds it hard to believe that Mr Wesley could ever have been in error about anything but this is not the moment to start another argument.

The smell in the air now is of roasting malt from the brewery. Barrels are stacked by the road and hammering sounds come from inside the cooperage. Sharrock signals to the carter to turn right by Hooper's inn. They have made good time and will reach their destination before sunset, which is just as well. Although Harveys manufactures the iron lamp standards and retorts needed for street lighting in other towns, Hayle has as yet no gas light.

Johanna knows that her husband has chosen one of the double-fronted residences on the south side of Bodriggy. They are considered more desirable because they are set on high ground away from the noise and fumes of the foundry, but the streets still have a rough, unfinished air.

'Why is our house that strange rusty colour?' asks Lizzie as they stand hesitantly outside their new front door.

'It's the copper,' says her father. 'They make bricks from the waste after they've smelted the ore. A lot of the houses round here are like that. You'll get used to it.'

Johanna tilts her chin and sniffs in disapproval. As Sharrock helps her down from the cart she can see him watching her with an anxious eye. He knows she will soon let him know if the house is not to her liking. He opens the door and the girls run in to inspect their new home. Downstairs is a front parlour, a large kitchen and behind that a scullery.

'See the kitchener,' Sharrock says to his wife, pointing at the cooking range. 'And there's a water pipe on the corner of the street.'

'I should hope so too,' snorts Johanna. 'We don't want to live like savages.'

But she is pleased about the range; many housewives still have to cook on an open fire. The girls have opened the back door and rushed into the garden. It is long, and backs onto open fields.

'Come and see,' Sharrock coaxes, and Johanna follows him outside, clutching her small son firmly to her.

'Plenty of space to grow vegetables,' he says. 'And we can plant a few fruit trees. There's a good drying breeze for the laundry up here too. We're upwind of the foundry most days.'

'Well it's better than I thought,' Johanna admits. 'But I'll need help. You're going to be away for days at a time and I can't do everything. Now let's get a fire going and unpack the kettle.'

3 A Basket of Broccoli

Sharrock Dupen was never going to be content with what he could earn from his steward's fees. He was on the look out for other business opportunities and soon found one that was to live on into the next century as a family legend. The past acquires the fuzziness of half-remembered myth within a surprisingly short space of time. Parents and grandparents tell us bedtime stories that begin 'When I was a child', but as adults we come to believe that these half-remembered anecdotes have no more reality than the fairy tales that started 'Once upon a time'. Just occasionally we are able to disentangle the recorded facts from the Chinese whispers of memory.

This particular example begins prosaically with a vegetable. Broccoli, introduced from Italy in the early years of the eighteenth century, is acknowledged to be a puzzle: while greengrocers and their customers can easily distinguish it from cauliflower, botanists apparently cannot. But I was interested in it for a completely different reason. It was one lunchtime in the 1960s when I first heard the story. My little brother, a fussy eater, was complaining about the vegetables.

'I don't like broccoli,' he declared, pushing it to the side of his plate.

'Well, you'd better learn to like it,' our father told him with a grin. 'Your French ancestors introduced it to England, you know.'

My brother was unimpressed and the broccoli remained uneaten but I was intrigued. It was the French ancestors that excited my teenage imagination. This could explain my obscure sense that I did not belong in suburban Hertfordshire but in some more cosmopolitan setting – a belief I had started to nurture by listening to the songs of Charles Aznavour, reading *Astérix* in the original French, and crossing my sevens in the Continental way. I wanted to know more but there was apparently, in those pre-internet days, no more. And although my father was fond of his broccoli anecdote, the grin betrayed his scepticism.

His own father had been equally disbelieving. It is easy to imagine a similar scene from the 1920s, where my father is viewing the same vegetable with suspicion.

'Eat it up,' says my grandfather Harold with a sidelong glance at his wife. 'Your great-grandfather Dupen brought it from France in his ship. The English had never seen it before. It made him famous.'

Thirty years previously, in the 1890s, Harold and his sister Lulu had also no doubt raised their voices in protest.

'Do we have to eat the broccoli, mama?'

'Of course you do,' said Hester Dupen. 'Your grandfather Sharrock introduced it to England, you know. It made his fortune.'

My great-grandmother Hester was telling a version of the truth but her son, a scientifically minded boy, suspected it was simply a trick designed to encourage him to eat his greens. As an adult he wrote to the editor of the *Morning Post* to say so:

> *Mr Dupen's Grandchild on a Family "Fairy Story"*
> Sir – With regard to your announcement about the Cornish Broccoli industry in Saturday's issue of the "Morning Post", as children we were often told that our grandfather – the Mr Dupen mentioned – first grew Broccoli in England, but I'm afraid we rather regarded this as some subtle kind of fairy story to encourage our appetite for the vegetable! From the announcement it would appear that he really was interested in the broccoli plant, but are there any records to show that he did actually introduce the plant into England, and if so, from where?
> H. H. Baxter Aboyne, Sandhurst Road, Wokingham.

I have no idea if my grandfather received a reply to his enquiry but the online archive of nineteenth-century newspapers now allows me to search for the origins of the story. A commemorative article in the *Bristol Mercury* of 19th

March 1859 tells me that my great-great-grandfather was not the first to grow the plant but the first to transport it from Hayle to Bristol in the 1830s. An initial shipment of four dozen became fourteen dozen the following week and eventually hundreds of heads were being sold in both Bristol and Bath. Sharrock Dupen had a virtual monopoly of the local trade until the growers themselves cut him out. By the time the article was published, the steamer from Hayle was transporting 860 baskets containing fifteen to eighteen dozen heads of broccoli each, destined not just for Bristol but onwards by rail for London, where they would compete with similar shipments from Guernsey.

It was a story that appealed to the imagination of others outside the family. In 1933 the *Cornishman* carried a report of the annual dinner of the Bristol and District Cornishmen, where the Lord Mayor attributed the prosperity of Cornwall to its vegetable trade. In this version, Sharrock Dupen became a sea captain who transformed the economy of his native county:

> *The Cornishman and Cornish Telegraph 19th January 1933*
> CORNISH "EXILES" IN BRISTOL
> In 1837 frost destroyed the cabbage crop in the Bristol district. An old Cornish captain came to Bristol and asked for some greens with his dinner at an hotel. None was forthcoming, and that gave him a "brain wave".
> "I am not surprised" said his Lordship, "as Cornishmen are alert to passing possibilities. This man went back to Cornwall and the next time he sailed to Bristol he brought fifteen dozen broccoli and sold them at 1s each. Next time he brought sixteen dozen and sold them.
> He went back to Cornwall and said, 'You grow broccoli and I will sell them.' That idea of Capt. Dupen and the gullibility of the citizens of Bristol brought about prosperity in Cornwall."

The mayor's picturesque ancient mariner may have been an invention but the economic impact of the trade was a matter of fact, described in the *Cornishman* in another anniversary article that conjured up a vision of a fresh green landscape replacing the rusty slag heaps of the past:

> *The Cornishman and Cornish Telegraph 24th December 1936*
> CORNWALL'S GROWING INDUSTRY
> Many of the older inhabitants of the towns and villages of Cornwall will clearly remember the days, less than fifty years ago, when the livelihood and prosperity of the county of Cornwall, and particularly the "western district", was dependent upon the production of tin and copper. The younger generation know of this but cannot recall the days when mining was the chief industry – they can remember seeing only field upon field of broccoli. The unused mines are there to bear witness to the other days, but today the scene has changed and practically on top of many of the now disused tin and copper mines are fields of broccoli.

As another article put it, 'The miner has become the broccoli grower' – a fate perhaps preferable to that of the northern coalminers fifty years later.

Newspaper coverage continued, although some confusion grew up about the date of the centenary. The *Western Morning News* fixed on 1937, recording that in the last season the dozen or so special express trains dedicated to the trade transported 30,000 tons, more than double the quantity carried in 1928, with more than 580 wagons making the journey to London every night. Six years later, at the height of the war in March 1943, the same newspaper informed its readers that 3,000 acres were under cultivation – making, I assume, an important contribution to feeding the population.

The unlikely tale that I heard as a child turns out to have its origins in fact, although much to my disappointment Sharrock Dupen was not French, and he only introduced broccoli to England if you consider Cornwall in those days to be a different country. In some ways of course it was. The map of England shows the county as nearly an island, surrounded by sea on three sides and divided from Devon to the east by the river Tamar. In the early nineteenth century, according to one historian, there were Cornish people who would tell you they had never been to England. There was limited road traffic between Cornwall and the rest of England until Brunel's bridge over the Tamar opened in 1859, but you could travel by water: from Falmouth along the south coast to London, and from Hayle on the north coast to Devon, South Wales, and Bristol.

Bristol, where Sharrock Dupen spent time every week, had been England's second city until it was overtaken by the new manufacturing towns of the north. Much of its wealth derived from the deceptively neat triangular trade that exported manufactured goods to Africa, shipped cargoes of slaves to the plantations of the Americas, and imported sugar grown by slave labour in the West Indies back to Bristol. The fine Georgian houses in tranquil Queens Square had been built on the profits from this traffic in human misery. After years of fierce campaigning, in 1807 the slave trade (if not the use of slaves) formally ended, but Bristol remained a commercial hub for goods from across the world. It had never been the easiest of harbours to access. The expression 'all shipshape and Bristol fashion' originated in the days when any ship making its way up the Avon needed to have all its contents well-secured; if it was caught in the river when the tide went out, it would ground and tip over on the muddy bed, sending everything that was not fixed in place crashing to one side. But in 1809 the Floating Harbour was opened, bypassing the river and its notorious tides of seventy feet or more. The entrance to the new Cumberland Basin was safely protected by a sturdy set of lock gates and once ships passed through, the water level never changed by more than six inches. The port continued to thrive throughout the first half of the nineteenth century, despite increasing competition from Liverpool and Southampton, which had direct access to the open sea.

'Footstepping' is what biographers call the process of following the trail of their subjects to the places where they

lived and worked. Family historians do the same for their
ancestors, walking the streets of distant towns, mentally
demolishing buildings, trying to visualise a bygone world. But
to see through the eyes of an earlier generation we sometimes
need to do more, to make a disorienting shift in perspective
from land to sea. In this redrawn map of the early nineteenth
century, London is no longer the central point for a starburst
of radiating road and rail lines. Instead, shipping routes spin
out from western ports like spider's silk thrown across the
oceans, while a fine web connects Bristol, Cardiff, Dublin,
and Liverpool, servicing the new manufacturing centres with
coal and raw materials, and transporting consumer goods to
market. The Irish steamers brought oats, potatoes, salmon,
and fragile Waterford glass to Bristol, along with squealing
pigs, bales of linen, and barrels of Guinness. But it was a
young man's game. None of the old merchant ship owners
were prepared to invest in the new steam packets; it was too
much of a gamble. The ships were owned by partnerships of
multiple shareholders, who pocketed the dividend if the year
ended in profit but were personally liable for any losses. In
moving to Hayle my great-great-grandfather was abandoning
his allegiance to the old trade routes out of Falmouth to make
his way in this brave new world.

When Sharrock Dupen first started work on the Hayle to
Bristol service, travel by steamship was an uncertain and risky
experience. Thirty years after the launch of the first
commercial steam-powered vessel in 1802, there were some
500 paddle steamers conveying goods and passengers on
short journeys around the coast of Britain or up and down its
major rivers. Although most journeys passed without
incident, accidents could happen and when they did, they
were often dramatic. Sharrock may well have read an account
of one such disaster. The boiler of the *Union* steamship, which
plied the route from Gainsborough along the River Trent to
the Humber estuary, exploded just before the vessel left Hull,
blowing half the 150 passengers into the air. The death toll

was estimated to be at least sixteen, with many others suffering broken limbs, gashed heads and ripped clothing. The passengers in the cabin, mostly ladies, were drowned before they could escape:

Royal Cornwall Gazette 16th June 1837
Many persons were blown on shore. One young man was blown on the roof of premises, three stories high. Several persons mounted to his assistance, but he was quite dead. Another man was blown on board the steamer Albatross, and literally smashed to pieces.

Space in the four-page newspaper was always at a premium and the editor decided that there was no need to include the names of all the victims since they would hardly be of interest to his readers. More lives not only lost, but lost to history.

But despite the risks, Sharrock was no doubt grateful for steady employment. For most of the country, 1837 saw the start of a depression that lasted until 1844 and led to the death from starvation of an estimated one million British people. In the year when *Oliver Twist* was first serialised, reports from the factory cities of the north and midlands told of depressed trade, scarcity of employment and low wages. The desperate economic situation was given a human face in the story of a labourer from Smethwick who, at his wits' end after losing his job, stabbed his two young sons and then hanged himself. The children had been crying for bread.

Sharrock Dupen was not going to let his children starve. The *Bristol Mercury* carried regular advertisements for the *Herald* and from these I picked a likely date of 18th April 1837 for the launch of his new business.

COMMUNICATION
BETWEEN BRISTOL & CORNWALL
The Public attention is respectfully called to the facility and economy with which the Land's End, the Mining Districts, and the most picturesque parts of the County of Cornwall, may be visited; and also to the certain and early Conveyance

of Goods, from every part of the United Kingdom, to ST.
IVES, HAYLE, CAMBORNE, PENZANCE, MARAZION,
HELSTON, PENRYN, FALMOUTH, TRURO, REDRUTH,
also calling at ILFRACOMBE going and returning.
That Fast Sailing Steam Packet HERALD With Engines of
100-Horse power, John Vivian, Commander
A Stewardess on Board
WILL SAIL
From Cumberland Basin, Bristol:
FRIDAY, April 21 6 ½ morning
From Hayle and St Ives
TUESDAY, April 18 2 ½ afternoon

Cabin Passage, including Steward's Fees, £1. 5s; Deck ditto
10s 6d; Children under 12 Years of Age, Half-price. Large 4-
wheel Carriages £3. 3s; small and 2-wheel ditto, £1. 15s;
Horses, £1. 10s; Dogs 5s
Horses, Carriages, Luggage, and General Merchandise,
carefully conveyed.
Refreshments of the best description may be had on Board.

I also had a much later newspaper article that I was
longing to use. It was written in 1856 by a commercial
traveller who weathered a terrifying storm on the same route
under the stewardship of 'portly, rubicund and courteous
Dupen', in company with a 'falling to pieces young man', a
brave, sunburned missionary, and a child-like Frenchwoman
with her sickly-looking husband (referred to as '*mon cher
Edouard*'). But I could find no way to improve on the drama
of the original, which concludes with the passengers falling to
their knees on the rain-soaked deck as the clergyman
heroically declaims a psalm. So I abandoned the French
couple and the missionary, and allowed just a few elements of
the real-life scene to inform a fictional portrait of my great-
great-grandfather at a turning point in his career.

Hayle to Bristol, 18th April 1837

The wind is whistling in the rigging as Captain Vivian casts
an assessing glance towards the west, where dark clouds are
rolling in over the bay. It is 2.30 on Tuesday afternoon and
the *Herald* will be leaving Hayle with the tide. Sharrock
Dupen reassures the doting mother of young gentleman
entrusted to his care, who is returning to Rugby school,

'Have no fear, we shall have a voyage as calm as a sail in
a duck pond.'

The lad looks somewhat disappointed.

An older man totters on board asking everyone around
him if there is going to be a gale. He confides that he has
never been to sea before.

'I won't go if there's to be a storm,' he declares.

'One of those,' thinks Sharrock, smiling courteously as he
escorts his passengers down to the saloon. Their fare includes
the services of the steward, but he sometimes wonders if it is
sufficient to compensate him for the aggravation.

'Even if we have a bit of a blow there's nothing to fret
about sir. We do this run every week come rain or shine. The
Herald is a good, modern vessel and Captain Vivian one of
the best.'

The crew hurry to finish stowing the cargo and
passengers' luggage in the hold, swing the winches away,
and swiftly cast off the ropes mooring the ship to the quay. A
shout of 'Go ahead' to the engineer rings out. The paddles
start turning and the *Herald* steams slowly past the wharves
and into the channel marked by buoys that will take her
safely over the sandy bar and into the bay.

In the saloon, the nervous gentleman who has never been
to sea before is dozing on a sofa until the movement of a
great wave jerks him awake. He cries out,

'Oh no! Steward! Help me! Help me!'

Sharrock is there at his elbow, calmly assisting him to
settle himself once more.

'Let me fetch you a tot of brandy, sir. We'll soon be past
the worst.'

'How much longer will this continue?' groans the
traveller.

'Not too long, sir. It'll be smooth sailing once we're past
Hartland Point. Would you like a rug, perhaps, to make you
more comfortable?'

Sharrock does not explain that the treacherous, rocky
shore of the point is still some hours away. It is going to be a
long night. He thinks back to his early seafaring days and
wonders how some of these people would have managed in
the Bay of Biscay. But his expression remains imperturbable
as he hands out refreshments and reassurance.

At midday on Wednesday, 150 nautical miles later, they
are approaching their destination. They have made good
time, hugging the coast of Cornwall and north Devon,
turning east after Ilfracombe into the wide estuary of the river
Severn, and finally making the tight right-hand turn into the
mouth of the Avon. The little paddle steamer, her single
funnel puffing out acrid smoke, churns her way up the
winding river towards the port of Bristol. A chill spring
breeze ruffles the muddy brown waters. They are passing
through the wooded gorge where Mr Brunel's suspension
bridge is to be built; the foundation stone was finally laid last
year but there is as yet nothing more to be seen.

Standing amidst the clutter of baskets and bundles
belonging to the deck passengers, the young schoolboy grins
cheerfully.

'That was something like, wasn't it steward?'

'I'm glad you enjoyed it, young sir,' replies Sharrock. 'But
I'm not sure all your fellow travellers would agree.'

Indeed, the cabin passengers in his charge did not stop
complaining all night. Made queasy by the smell from the
hold, where the cargo of fish was being slowly kippered by
the heat from the engines, they slept little, continuing to be
anxious and fretful. The steward will be relieved to see the
back of them. His mind is on other things. He has invested

money he can ill afford in a new venture. His friends have mocked him, but the baskets stacked in the hold will, if all goes well, enable him to supplement his income and help provide for his growing family.

Sharrock Dupen helps his charges gather their belongings and prepare to disembark as Captain Vivian brings the *Herald* carefully into the lock. It is a long wait while the men slowly wind the heavy paddles that open the sluices to bring the ship up to the level of the inner harbour. To the left the basin is lined with small shops and public houses while on the right stand the open-sided wood-drying sheds of the Canada wharf. If the passengers care to look up beyond the trees on Clifton Hill, they can admire the fine white curve of Royal York Crescent where the wealthy merchants of Bristol have their houses, well away from the stench of the docks. Finally the ship draws up to the quayside. The crew make her fast with ropes, the ramp is lowered, and the steward holds out a steadying hand as the passengers make their way cautiously onto the muddy bank, the ladies in bonnets and warm shawls holding up their skirts to avoid the puddles, the gentlemen keeping a wary eye on the ragged boys who flock to carry bags and valises in the hope of earning a penny.

The crew will spend Thursday in Bristol and leave again for Hayle with the early morning tide on Friday. They start unloading the cargo of tin plate, rolls of copper, and iron bars from Harvey's foundry. There are boxes of shovels too, bound for the navvies at work on the new railway track that will link Bristol to London. On her return journey the *Herald* will carry supplies for the shopkeepers of Hayle: chests of coffee and kegs of lard; firkins of butter and boxes of soap; needles, buttons, candles, bales of feathers, and sacks of beans. It is too early for summer visitors in search of the salubrious air and picturesque scenery of St Ives, but there will doubtless be one or two mining engineers or businessmen on their way home.

Sharrock steps back onto the ship to collect his own cargo. He inspects his baskets nervously; a lot depends on

the freshness of the contents. He beckons to a lad with a
handcart to come and help him and they set off for the St
Nicholas market. Their route takes them past open
pastureland to the wharves where dozens of sailing vessels
are moored. A faint aroma of treacly molasses pierces the
thick sewage stench of the river, underlaid with the resinous
scent of Baltic timber, and the occasional sharp topnote from
the oranges and lemons that are carried from Marsala along
with barrels of sweet Sicilian wine. There are emigrant ships
too, big copper-bottomed brigs taking on passengers for New
York and Quebec, shabby men with an air of determined
cheer, anxious-looking women hugging their children to their
sides. Sharrock wonders if he would ever uproot his family
and cross the ocean in order to save them from penury. He is
determined that he will never have to face that choice.

He quickens his pace. There is no time to stop at the
shipbuilding yard where Mr Brunel's *Great Western* is taking
shape, its galley fitted out by Harveys of Hayle with the most
up-to-date iron cooking range. Like the *Herald* she is a
wooden hulled paddle steamer but she is big, some 235 feet
long, and broad too. She is going to prove that it is possible
for a steamship to cross the Atlantic without running out of
fuel. If Sharrock were ten years younger, before Johanna and
the children, he might have been tempted to sign on for that
voyage. But he has other business in mind.

He crosses the wide, green space of Queens Square,
where ladies stroll and children bowl their hoops under the
watchful eye of their nursemaids. It is a peaceful scene but
the building work on the north side is a reminder of a time
six years earlier when the elegant Georgian terrace was
reduced to rubble during the Reform Bill riots. Sharrock has
no time for politics; he would rather have hard cash than a
vote. Votes don't feed a family. Beyond the square he comes
to the Welsh Back where the ships from Swansea and Cardiff
dock with their cargoes of coal. He turns the corner into the
High Street and finds himself in front of the stone pillars of
the covered market. Picking up one of his baskets, he signals

to the boy to follow with the others and goes inside. Under
the high glass roof with its brightly painted plaster
decoration, the meagre offerings of potatoes, turnips and
cabbage look unappetising. A late frost has spoiled the early
vegetable crop in Gloucestershire and Sharrock Dupen is
hoping to fill the gap with fresh Cornish produce. The local
housewives will pay good money for his four dozen heads of
bright green broccoli.

CENSUS 1841

The first complete census of the population of England and Wales was taken in 1841. It was an exercise that was to be repeated every ten years, offering family historians a regular snapshot of their ancestors, briefly fixed in time and space. Now that it is searchable online you don't even need to leave your own home to summon up the records that tell you who made up the household on that one night in March: the family members, lodgers, servants, and assorted hangers on. By examining the surrounding entries you can also start to build up a picture of the neighbourhood. Sharrock and Johanna Dupen are living in the Bodriggy area of Hayle. There is no street address but I imagine they are renting one of the 200 new dwellings constructed by the Cornish Copper Company in the early years of the century, on land that ran from the old manor house down to the waterfront. Sharrock's occupation is given as 'Steward of Herald', the use of the vessel's name an indication of its importance to the town. The presence of two female servants aged 15 and 55 tells me that the family is doing well. Their neighbours are miners, engineers, sawyers, and blacksmiths, members of the skilled upper-working and lower-middle class.

There are new additions to the family. Salome Emma was the first baby to be born in Hayle, in 1836. Little more than nine months later, Rhoda Louise was born, lived for two short months, and died two days after Christmas 1837. She lies in the churchyard of St Felicitas, high on the hill across the bay, but no headstone marks the place. Baby Rhoda had disappeared so completely from my jigsaw puzzle that for ten years or more I was not even aware of her as a missing piece, but I am glad that she can now take her place in the emerging picture. It is impossible to know how long and how deeply her family grieved for her. I don't even know if her death at Christmas was more painful than it would have been at any other time of year. We cannot project our emotions back into another time but it is false to imagine that the high rate of infant mortality meant parents were less attached to their children than we are. When another baby girl was born in 1840, she was given her dead sister's second name: Ellen Louise. Rhoda's burial details and some simple arithmetic help me to date the birth of Salome, who seems to have slipped through the net of all the online parish records. It is at times like this that a fascination with family history shades into an obsessive compulsion to find unimportant facts that will not change the shape of the story. Although I don't need to know Salome's birthday it remains an uncomfortable gap that niggles like a missing tooth.

Johanna's oldest stepdaughter, Hannah, has left home by 1841, while sixteen-year-old Elizabeth is working as a draper's assistant, a job that required a good standard of literacy and numeracy to be able to measure lengths of ribbon and lace, count out buttons, and calculate change. The girls of the family are being educated to earn their own living. It is the beginning of a new age, one that, although the family did not know it, would come to be defined as Victorian.

In June 1837, shortly after Sharrock carried his first cargo of broccoli to Bristol, came news from the court in London. The king, who had been suffering from intermittent attacks of inflammation of the lungs accompanied by a teasing cough, had started to display more worrying symptoms that made his doctors advise him to 'abstain from conversation on topics of an exciting description'. His planned removal to Brighton was postponed and the health of his devoted Queen, who was spending each night in a chair in the ante-room, was also giving cause for concern. Two weeks later William IV, the jovial red-faced sailor king, was dead. The *Royal Cornwall Gazette* published the 'particulars relative to the illness and death of his late most gracious Majesty', gave a short outline of the king's life that tactfully ignored his early nickname of 'Silly Billy', and concluded with appreciative words for the 'promptness, courtesy and decision displayed by our late monarch'.

It was unsettling for William's subjects to realise that his successor was a half-foreign, eighteen-year-old girl. The next column, headed 'Accession of Queen Victoria', reprinted in full the 'gracious declaration' of the new queen, who made sure to emphasise that in spite of having a German mother and governess, she was British to the core: 'Educated in England, under the tender and enlightened care of a most affectionate mother, I have learned from my infancy to respect and love the constitution of my native country.' She presented a touching picture as, attired in deepest mourning, she appeared at a window in St James's Palace:

> *Royal Cornwall Gazette 30th June 1837*
> The spectacle at that moment was singularly beautiful and affecting. In the centre stood a female monarch of tender years suddenly summoned to assume the difficult and perilous office of earthly ruler and preserver of interests of a great nation – in this position stood a youthful Queen bathed in tears, and nearly overwhelmed by the circumstances of her station.

The young queen's new subjects would have been understandably anxious about what the future might hold. The Jacobite rebellion was after all still a living memory: in that same issue of the *Gazette* the death was reported at the age of 104 of a Chelsea Pensioner who had been a drummer boy at Culloden in 1745.

A year later, on 16th June 1838, the *Bristol Mercury* carried a full account of the arrangements being made for the coronation, together with a portrait of Victoria especially engraved for readers of the paper, who would have had no other way of knowing what she looked like. Immediately below her image was an advertisement for Brunel's *Great Western*, which had been successfully launched in March and was sailing every month between Bristol and New York for a fare of 40 guineas. ('Children and servants half price. No Second Class or Steerage passengers taken.')

On 28th June the young queen was crowned in London and in Hayle, Harvey's workers were treated to a celebratory feast where a whole ox was roasted on a spit at the foundry. The *Bristol Mercury* filled three columns with a description of the coronation procession and the illuminations. Public buildings, the gentlemen's clubs in St James, and private residences competed to display the brightest and most elaborate designs, which included crowns, laurel leaves and the initials V. R. This time one of the advertisements that appeared alongside the news was for the steamship *Herald*, reassuringly equipped with 'New and efficient Boilers, constructed on the safest and most approved principle'. National politics and steamship services were both of critical importance to the men who had access to newspapers. These were not only members of the professions and gentlemen, who could afford to buy their own copy, but also artisans and tradesmen with aspirations, who read them in coffee houses, taverns, and the public reading rooms that proliferated in every port, men like the steward of the *Herald,* Sharrock Dupen.

4 A Methodist Past

B y the summer of 1843, the world looked very different. The queen, married in 1840 to her gifted and intelligent cousin Prince Albert of Saxe-Coburg Gotha, had settled into her role. She had given birth to three children and survived three bungled assassination attempts. Her much-loved Prime Minister and mentor, Lord Melbourne, had been voted out of office and Sir Robert Peel had finally formed a Tory government. In the world of steam, Brunel was preparing for the launch of the *SS Great Britain*, the largest ship in the world. Twice as powerful as the *Great Western*, the huge iron-hulled vessel was described as 'the greatest experiment since the Creation', since she was driven not by inefficient paddle wheels but by new technology in the form of an Archimedes screw. On land, railway mania was beginning; the Great Western railway between Bristol and London, another of Brunel's projects, had opened in 1841, and in May 1843 the line linking Hayle and Redruth was inaugurated:

> *Royal Cornwall Gazette 26th May 1843*
> OPENING OF THE HAYLE AND REDRUTH RAILWAY FOR PASSENGER TRAFFIC – On Monday last, this important line, the benefits of which have hitherto been exclusively confined to the carriage of ore and coal for the mines in its neighbourhood, became for the first time available as a conveyance for passengers through the populous districts with which it communicates. This desirable result is we understand attributable to the enterprise of an individual at Hayle, who has at his own expense fitted up two convenient railway carriages, holding from twenty to thirty persons each, to start twice a day from each of the termini, and we hope the result will be such as to repay him for his trouble and risk. The principal benefits arising from this arrangement are the increased facilities it affords of communication between the important districts of Truro, Falmouth, Hayle and Penzance, between which the mail and

stage vans have hitherto been the only conveyances. To persons sailing by the Hayle steamers it will be found extremely convenient, the difficulty of the journey to Hayle having been in many cases the chief objection to that route to London.

Two weeks later, on Whit Monday, 1,500 people were transported to Redruth in four trains to enjoy the annual preaching at the Gwennap Pit.

Cornwall had been an early stronghold of Methodism. It was a hundred years since John Wesley first rode across the empty expanse of Bodmin moor towards Redruth, heading for St Ives, where he had heard of a religious meeting. The members were to become the first Methodist society in the county. This was just five years after the spiritual experience that convinced Wesley of his salvation through Jesus Christ, a revelation that he wanted to share with the world. There were 4,000 Methodists in Cornwall at the time of Wesley's final journey there in 1789 and fifty years later the number had grown to 26,000. In this, as in other ways, the county set itself apart from the rest of England.

I cannot be sure that the Dupens attended the Whit Monday preaching in 1843, but it seems likely that Johanna, who had named her latest baby John Wesley, would have wanted to be there. She was a young woman at the time of the last great Methodist revival, and could have experienced the ecstasy of conversion at a love feast, a version of the early Christian *agape* that had been reintroduced by Wesley. I imagine her joining other youthful worshippers at a service where they sang, clapped, and jumped for joy, bearing witness to their faith before sharing water from a distinctive two-handled cup. And I keep other evidence of her Methodist inheritance on the shelf above my desk.

The miniature volume, measuring no more than three inches by four and a half, is small enough to be tucked into a pocket. It is bound in faded leather the colour of oxblood and stamped with a gold border. Printed in Oxford at the

Clarendon Press in 1824, the title page declares that the text, 'translated from the original Greek', is 'Appointed to be read in churches'. It is the New Testament of my childhood, of every school assembly and Religious Education lesson – or 'Divinity', as it was called in the timetable, hinting at its transformative powers. We were not a churchgoing family but I attended a Church of England high school, and can still recite passages of scripture by heart. Two years after I left school, the New English Bible was published. It was intended to make it easier for everyone to read and understand Christ's teaching, but as an unbeliever I retain an attachment to the language of the King James version, which over the course of more than three centuries was woven into the fabric of our lives, and connects us directly to a time when a life without faith was inconceivable.

The front and back covers and the spine of the little book are decorated with tiny gold images of the Lamb and Flag, a pairing more familiar to us these days from pub signs. Traditionally the lamb is depicted holding a banner that bears the cross of St George, but this one is carrying a large crucifix. He steps out with a military bearing that is slightly at odds with the large daisy-shaped halo floating above his head. A familiar phrase hovers at the edge of my memory and I retrieve it from the gospel of St John (I:29), where John the Baptist welcomes Jesus, saying: 'Behold the lamb of God, which taketh away the sin of the world.' The lamb and flag was the symbol of the Moravian or 'German' church that had so impressed Wesley on his voyage to America in 1736. But its significance is not just religious; it is also the emblem of the town of Redruth, which adopted it from the Cornish tin mines. The ingots of tin were stamped with a lamb to indicate purity, a device possibly inherited from the woollen trade of medieval times.

On the first page is an inscription:

Sarah Wesley Sanders 1900
Given to my mother Johanna Dupen by her cousin
Frederick Trestrail on her marriage to my father
Sharrock Dupen on the 5th of July 1830

When Sarah, the tenth of their children, added this
handwritten note fifteen years after her mother's death, she
ensured the survival of another fragment of family history,
although it raises as many questions as it answers. It sent me
off in a flurry of online research to find Frederick Trestrail,
who was indeed Johanna's cousin, four years her senior, the
son of her mother's younger brother, and with a few clicks I
find I have added another twenty people to my family tree. I
don't want them, I don't need them, they are just so much
genealogical clutter, but the website designers know how to
keep us hooked. Hint after hint appears on my screen as I
follow a trail that leads further and further from the Dupens,
until in the National Archives I find Frederick's son
registering a patent for a carpet design in 1861. The
temptation to go in search of that carpet is as irrational as it is
powerful, but I resist and go back to the census returns.

Frederick Trestrail was not just an affectionate relative but
also a well-known minister. His family background was
Wesleyan, but he was studying at the Baptist College in Bristol
at the time of Johanna's marriage. Baptists were a minority in
Cornwall, making up just 1% of the population, so I deduce
that Frederick was a particularly committed Christian, with
strong Nonconformist beliefs. After his ordination he moved
around England and Ireland to various livings until he
became secretary to the Baptist Missionary Society. One of
the benefits of living in Oxford is that I can order up long-
forgotten books from the depths of the Bodleian Library. I
spend an afternoon in the quiet light of the Upper Reading
Room skimming Frederick's memoirs, in the hope that he
might mention his cousin. He doesn't, but he paints a vivid
picture of their mutual grandmother, Mary Vincent Trestrail,
a striking woman with dark, piercing eyes and a determined

spirit. Women, unlike in the Anglican church, took an active part in Methodist worship, and Frederick recorded that his grandmother was a staunch Wesleyan throughout her long life. I like to think she took her children, including Frederick's father and Johanna's mother, another Mary, to listen to Wesley's message. This second Mary Trestrail, who lived to the age of ninety, must surely have held her daughter's New Testament in her hand. When I rest the little book in my palm I seem to feel, light as a dried leaf drifting across my fingers, the touch of a woman who heard John Wesley preach.

There are certain places that have an almost magical power to evoke the past. The Gwennap Pit, hidden at the end of a winding road about a mile and half outside Redruth, is one of them. On the grey autumn day when I visited the site it had a deserted, eerie feel, lost between high hedges and shrouded in light drizzle. I had a sense that I had travelled much further from Redruth than the map or the time on my watch suggested. John Wesley first preached there when it was just an overgrown sunken hollow formed by the collapse of some old mine workings. It was said that more than 25,000 people flocked to listen to him in 1773 and although the figure is physically impossible, there was undoubtedly a congregation of several thousand crammed into the amphitheatre, with more outside. In total Wesley spoke at Gwennap eighteen times, taking advantage of the natural acoustics to reach a huge audience on each occasion. But it was not until 1807, the year of Johanna Woolcock's birth, that a band of loyal tin miners and their helpers cleared the encroaching vegetation to create a grassy amphitheatre about 125 feet across and 20 feet deep at its centre. They enabled the preaching tradition established by Wesley to continue and services are still held there each summer.

Whit Monday 1843 must have been a day that, with its heady mixture of steam power and religious fervour, lived on in the memory of all who took part. The child of the embroidered sampler, Annie Dupen, was eleven by this time, old enough to notice and remember, still young enough to be frightened by the strangeness of it all. Sixty years later her nephew Harold may have taken her for a drive in his motor car. By then she would have seen the experience of travel change out of all recognition, as steam replaced horse power and was in turn superseded by the internal combustion engine. In one of those disorienting moments where time seems to telescope, I realise that the elusive ghost of my grandfather has the power to bring me within touching distance of a remote past that was, for him, just a single generation ago. It was a moment that demanded to be told from Annie's point of view.

Gwennap Pit, 5th June 1843

The Dupens are preparing to catch the train from Hayle to Redruth. The new railway has been open for two weeks and extra trains are going to run today to give the townspeople a chance to experience this exciting new mode of transport. For the first time Annie, her sister Kate, her brother Sharrock, and half-sister Lizzie can go with their mother to the annual Whit Monday preaching at Gwennap Pit. The little ones, Salome, Ellen, and George, are to stay at home with the servants. Fortunately the steam packet is not due to sail for Bristol on its regular weekly voyage until the following day so their father is free to accompany them. Annie heard her parents arguing the previous evening. She has noticed that her mother often has the last word on such occasions.

'You're not going to take the baby, are you?' her father asked.

'Of course he must come. Don't forget that my own dear mother heard John Wesley preach at Gwennap when she was just thirteen years old. She talked about it all her life. He was a great man and our baby carries his name. Besides, who is going to feed him if I leave him at home? Just answer me that.'

Annie fidgets anxiously in her Sunday frock, her hair
neatly tied with white ribbons, her stout black boots tightly
laced over her woollen stockings. She is not sure she wants
to travel on a train; she has seen the wooden carriages rattle
along the track beside Penpol Terrace and they look very
unsteady. The family walks the short distance to the
terminus, jostled by the throng of people all determined to
make the journey to Redruth. Annie clings desperately to
Lizzie's hand. Finally they reach the second of the two
carriages and she catches a glimpse of the team of heavy
horses hitched to the front. Her father elbows his way
forward and lifts his children in. Her mother follows and
settles baby John on her lap. It is very warm in the crowded
carriage and Annie is feeling a little dizzy. A stout lady sitting
next to her takes out a handkerchief drenched in eau de
cologne to discreetly wipe the perspiration from her face. The
smell makes Annie queasy and she presses her lips firmly
together. Her ears are buzzing with the noise; it is as if a
swarm of giant bees has settled on the railway track. Her
brother wriggles his way to the open window and cranes his
head to see.

'There are four open wagons hitched behind us, and
hundreds of people piling in. Some of them will have to wait
for the next train.'

'Do come and sit down, Sharrock,' scolds their mother.
'And mind where you put your feet. I'm so sorry,' she
apologises to the lady whose skirt he is crushing.

A shout from the driver signals their departure and the
horses heave and strain until the string of wagons begins to
move. Creaking and rattling, they are off. The train crawls for
half a mile at a slow walking pace as far as the bridge, where
it halts. Sharrock hangs out of the window.

'The horses are being unhitched. Oh I say! They're
attaching the steam engine. You should just see her puff!'

Clouds of smoke drift into the carriage and black smuts
settle on Annie's clean frock. The pungent, sulphurous smell
from the burning coal catches at her throat. Then they are on

the move again and picking up speed. They pass the great
Copperhouse Pool on their left and soon afterwards slow to a
standstill.

'Why have we stopped, papa? Is it a hill?' demands
Sharrock.

'Yes, indeed. It's the Angarrack incline. This part of the
line is so steep that they need an extra engine fixed at the top
to pull the train up the slope and let it down safely on its way
back.'

'How can they do that? Surely the rope will break?'

Annie shudders at her brother's cheerful question,
imagining them all crashing down in a great heap of bodies
and metal. But her father says,

'It's an iron rope, of course. Don't frighten your sisters like
that.'

Once they reach the top, the train runs along a high
embankment and Annie watches the surrounding landscape
of green hills pass by at an astonishing speed. She feels light-
headed and faint and buries her face in her mother's
shoulder. They may reach, says her brother knowledgeably
but unhelpfully, as much as thirty miles an hour.

At Camborne the train stops to set down a handful of
passengers and their places are immediately taken by as
many again. It sets off once more and, after passing the
massive engine house and turrets of Cook's Kitchen Mine,
halts at the depot to take on coal and water. From there they
pass through a succession of cuttings until they reach another
high embankment surrounded by open countryside. Annie
has plucked up the courage to look out again. She finds that
she is becoming accustomed to the sensation of speed. At
last, more than an hour after leaving Hayle, they pull into the
station at Redruth.

Annie's father lifts her down from the carriage. She is hot
and sticky and her hair curls damply around her ears. The
family push their way to the edge of the crowd and her
mother rummages in her basket to find a stone bottle of
barley water. After they have each taken a refreshing

mouthful they are ready for the next stage in their journey.
They start to walk, following a slow-moving horse-drawn
omnibus along a narrow track between high hedges. After
about half an hour they arrive at the Gwennap Pit. Outside
the six-foot high wall hordes of cheerful people dressed in
their Sunday best cluster round half a dozen cake stalls. The
spicy scent of gingerbread fills the air. Scruffy boys jostle to
hold the bridles of the horses belonging to the more well-to-
do worshippers. The family make their way past shabby,
barefoot beggars with outstretched hands, through the gate
into the great open amphitheatre, and find a space on the turf
seating. Clouds scud across the sky, casting fast-moving
shadows over the seated crowd.

'One, two, three…' Annie's brother is counting. 'There
are thirteen rows of seats,' he declares. 'How many people
does that make? Ten thousand?'

'At least a thousand, maybe two,' says Annie, whose
arithmetic is rather better than Sharrock's. She has never in
her whole life seen such a big crowd. She is not sure she
likes it.

Her mother is handing out chunks of bread and cheese
from her basket. Baby John has started to wail and she holds
him to her breast under her shawl. Suddenly the buzz of
excited chatter stops. The air is still. People are holding their
breath in anticipation. The preacher appears in the centre of
the grassy hollow beneath them. To Annie, struggling to see
over the heads of the crowd, it is as if he has dropped from
the heavens. An unassuming-looking white-haired man,
soberly dressed, he begins in a soft, melodious voice,
reminding his audience of John Wesley, who was the first to
preach the gospel in this very place. In the hushed
atmosphere his words reach to the far corners of the natural
amphitheatre as he speaks of the coming of Jesus, of sin and
repentance. Then his voice rises to an ecstatic shout as he
raises his arms, opens his hands and tips back his head to
gaze at the sky, enjoining the congregation to turn their
backs on temptation and seek salvation through the Lord.

Annie half-expects him to float up into the clouds like the picture of Jesus in her scripture book. Her mother is quietly weeping and even her brother has fallen silent. Around them some of the congregation are bowing their heads while others are reaching up and calling out. The preacher draws his sermon to a close and announces that they will sing. The multitude of worshippers rise to their feet and the words of Charles Wesley's hymn ring out:

> *Praise the Lord who reigns above*
> *and keeps his court below;*
> *praise the holy God of love*
> *and all his greatness show*

5 A Free Gardener

S harrock Dupen, with the safety of his immortal soul secured, could focus his energies on the path to worldly success. This involved not only hard work but also the careful cultivation of influential acquaintances. In Hayle, Henry Harvey's business was continuing to thrive and diversify. Harvey was canny enough to recognise the need to protect himself from the ups and downs of the mining industry and in 1838 he sold an unwanted mine engine to provide power to the new East London waterworks, opening up a whole new market. A year later he commissioned a new boring mill capable of producing iron cylinders fifteen feet long and wide enough to drive a horse and cart through (there is a photograph to prove it). At the other extreme the foundry was turning out fancy goods, 'Hayle toys' that resembled the better known Birmingham toys: finely wrought items for personal use including snuff boxes, nutmeg graters, vinaigrettes, and children's rattles.

In 1843 Harveys won a commission from the Dutch government to construct an engine to drain the seventy square miles of Haarlem Mere and protect the cities of Amsterdam and Leiden from the risk of flooding. There was considerable hostility to the plan in Holland, where people were strongly attached to the tens of thousands of windmills that had been part of the landscape for so many years, but the Haarlemmer Mere Commissioners were forward-thinking men who undertook careful research before settling on their bold and original solution. The Leeghwater engine was to be the biggest steam engine in the world, with a cylinder twelve feet in diameter and a piston nineteen feet long. 'It is truly gratifying to us to observe,' declared the *Royal Cornwall Gazette* on 24th March 1843, 'that Cornish engineers still keep so far in advance of all the world, and not less gratifying to see, that Foreign Powers know and appreciate their excellence.'

After the success of the *Herald* another larger steam packet of 400 tons, the *Cornwall,* was commissioned to respond to the increased demand for the service when the Great Western Railway finally reached Bristol from Paddington. Harveys made the engines for the new vessel, which was a third bigger than the *Herald.* The two ships would continue to run alongside each other, competing successfully with a new rival, the *Brilliant,* until 1849 when the *Herald* was scrapped. Captain Vivian's son, another John Vivian, took command of the *Cornwall* when it went into service in May 1842, and Sharrock followed him. As ship's steward and vegetable exporter he would have been a prominent figure in the economy of Hayle.

When Sharrock began his weekly voyages to Bristol, the city still bore the scars of its radical past. In 1831 only 6,000 men out of a city population of 104,000 were able to vote, for just two Members of Parliament; Cornwall, with a population no more than three times the size, elected 44 MPs. That autumn, after the House of Lords rejected the Reform Bill, which would extend the franchise, the city saw some of the worst riots in the country. The gaol burned down, as did a good half of Queens Square – the blaze fuelled by the fine wines and spirits in the cellars. A force of dragoons, the 'Bloody Blues', was called in and cut down hundreds of unarmed men and women in what was said to be the worst massacre on British soil since the battle of Culloden. The madness of the French Revolution had not yet faded into history and harsh penalties including hanging and transportation were used to deter any further incitement to rebellion. But the battle for reform had achieved an unstoppable momentum and in 1832 a bill was passed that gave one in seven Englishmen the right to vote.

It is against this background that Sharrock Dupen became active in public life. The franchise was still extremely limited; eligibility depended on property value and I doubt if the annual rent for his house in Hayle was above the threshold of £10 a year. But he acquired status and influence in other

ways. Sharrock Dupen, like his father John and several of his
uncles, sons, and nephews, was a Freemason, a fact that I
register with intrigued dismay. My grandfather and my father
would, I think, have shared my disquiet. They were not
Masons, but my father-in-law was. After he died, we found an
innocuous little briefcase stashed at the bottom of his
wardrobe, and I remember being overcome with a
momentary, irrational panic. The act of opening it felt like a
subversive act. What were we supposed to do with the
contents? However much I deplored his participation in what
I understood to be a quasi-religious ritual that excluded
women, it felt disrespectful to throw his regalia away. In the
end we identified a member of the local Lodge, who took it
off our hands to be dealt with in whatever way he deemed
appropriate – perhaps there is a trade in second-hand Masons'
kit, as there is for school uniform.

Public attitudes to Freemasonry were quite different in
1826 when, as a simple mariner, Sharrock was inducted into
the Lodge of Love and Unity in Falmouth, one of half a
dozen lodges in western Cornwall. The growing movement
was a way for the aspiring middle and upper-working classes
to build networks of influence in an unfair society where
advancement still depended largely on birth. Naturally there
was no place for women and the men who ran the Lodges
would have been puzzled by any charge of misogyny.
Respectable middle class women were expected to remain
within the domestic sphere and if they participated in
philanthropic organisations, these were largely separate ones.
For reasons that remain obscure, the records show that in
1838 the Lodge of Love and Unity was disbanded and in that
same year a new lodge, the Cornubian, was registered in
Hayle. The first signatories included the landlord of the White
Hart, William Crotch (who had taken over from Jane
Trevithick when she retired), Henry Harvey's nephew
Nicholas, three others designated as 'gentlemen', and ship's

steward Sharrock Dupen. My great-great-grandfather had
successfully established connections to the elite of the town.

But after a number of the original subscribers moved
away, the Cornubian remained inactive for the next ten years
while Sharrock extended his network of business contacts by
joining the Olive Lodge of Free Gardeners in Bristol. This
Order is thought to have originated in East Lothian in
Scotland in 1676 as a result of an interest in landscape
gardening amongst owners of the new country mansions. The
professional gardeners who laid out the parks around the
houses came together – so the story goes – to form an
association, following the example of their fellow workmen,
the stonemasons, but adopting horticultural names such as
Rose, Myrtle, and Cedar of Lebanon for their lodges.
Through his trade in broccoli Sharrock would have done
business with the men who ran the market gardens around
Penzance. This would no doubt have been enough to
recommend him to the members of the Olive Lodge.

Free Gardenry was part of a nationwide movement to
create Friendly Societies, associations that provided a safety
net of mutual aid to working men. In return for a small
subscription, members benefited from sickness and death
benefits. The very poor were of course unable to afford even
a modest contribution but the percentage of potentially
vulnerable families who were covered was surprisingly high.
In an age when respectability (or at least its outward
appearance) was a condition that both middle and working
classes aspired to, Friendly Societies provided protection
against the final shame of a pauper's funeral. As people
moved to urban areas away from family networks and the
patronage of the country landowner, the numbers joining
swelled to more than a million in the early part of the
nineteenth century, with the largest numbers in the industrial
north and midlands. Eventually they had four times more
members than the Trade Unions. They adopted rituals,
symbols and regalia that were similar to those of the

Freemasons, as well as coded greetings and hierarchies, but
with one crucial difference: the main purpose of Masonic
lodges was the creation of bonds between members rather
than mutual insurance. Like the medieval guilds of skilled
artisans, the Friendly Societies shared a commitment to
collective self-help, accompanied by a tradition of elaborate
costumes and feasting. It was their social activities, or in the
popular term 'conviviality', that distinguished them from
other insurers. Portly, red-faced Sharrock Dupen no doubt
enjoyed many a convivial evening on his overnight stays in
Bristol:

Bristol Mercury 2nd September 1843
The Bristol Olive Lodge of Free Gardeners celebrated their
eighth anniversary by dining together at their spacious lodge-
room, Cat and Wheel Tavern, Castle-Green, on Wednesday
last, when upwards of eighty of the brotherhood sat down to a
plentiful board of viands consistent with the season, and
which did credit to the taste and judgment of the host, Brother
Hedges. The wines were of superior quality, and the dessert,
part of which was presented by Brother T. Pym, was of first-
rate quality. On the removal of the cloth, the R.W.G.M. of the
lodge gave "Her most gracious Majesty the Queen, and long
may she continue to be the choicest flower of Old England's
garden!" (Loud cheering, followed with Mr. Alford's
celebrated national song and chorus, "Huzza! May the queen
live for ever"). The rest of the usual loyal toasts were given,
and responded to in succession; after which the chairman
addressed the brethren in a very impressive and appropriate
manner, relative to the utility and propriety of adhering most
strictly to the principles of the order, exhorting the company
to remember that brotherly love and philanthropy have much
to do with free gardenry. [...] The "Olive Lodge" having been
given in the usual way, the grand master observed – he had
yet another duty to perform, not less important than those
already aimed at: he meant to call to their attention to another
and younger subject – namely, the offspring of the Olive
Lodge – her first-born- "the Cornubian Lodge of Free
Gardeners, at Hayle, Cornwall" (loud cheering). The

R.W.G.M. Brother Dupen, of that lodge, being present with several of his office bearers, rose to return thanks, which he did in a manner at once calculated to stamp the prosperity of free gardenry wherever he may have the opportunity to expound its principles.

Membership of Friendly Societies was almost exclusively working class but leadership positions were often taken by skilled workers and small businessmen. As far as I can work out from this news item, Sharrock must have taken the lead in attaching the name of the dormant Hayle Freemasons' Lodge to a new branch of the Free Gardeners, becoming its Grand Master. It may be unfair of me to suspect my great-great-grandfather of joining a Friendly Society solely for the business and social advantages of membership. The Societies also played a significant role in changing attitudes towards collective action. The 1840s were an unsettled and anxious time for the ruling class, when the country was still adapting to the idea of a young female sovereign. The Chartists, not satisfied by the concessions of the Reform Act of 1832, were agitating for a 'People's Charter' that would abolish the property requirement and introduce secret ballots, annual elections, and salaries for MPs. The suspicion of trade unionism tainted any kind of independent association of workers, including Friendly Societies. It was a dilemma for the gentry. On the one hand they welcomed the notion that working men were organising themselves to keep their fellow workers out of the poor house and reduce the amount that needed to be levied by the poor rate; on the other hand they were drinking in pubs – and using their societies' funds to do so – thus demonstrating their manifest unsuitability for the task of managing themselves.

Friendly Societies defended their choice of venue on the grounds that public houses were often the only place where men could meet outside of their long working hours. Like the better-known Oddfellows and Foresters, the Free Gardeners laid claim to a biblical heritage in order to counter the charges of immorality that might arise from clandestine meetings and secret rituals. The Free Gardeners' version was based on Genesis Chapter 2 verse 15, 'And the Lord God took the man, and put him into the Garden of Eden to dress it and keep it'. Adam, unsurprisingly, and somewhat less obviously Noah and Solomon, were acknowledged as gardeners and associated with the three degrees of membership: apprentice, journeyman, and master gardener.

I cannot be sure how far my great-great-grandfather was in favour of reform; I imagine him as a pragmatist rather than a radical. Like Henry Harvey, Sharrock Dupen seems to have been a deal maker. An ambitious man who set out to better himself, he would probably have spoken out in favour of individual self-help while making the most of the opportunities available through his business and social networks. Rather than political power he sought indirect influence. If he could not vote or stand for election, he could still look like a community leader as he marched down the street in an elaborate costume and was applauded by the public.

The annual parades and feasts were designed as spectacles to be enjoyed by the local population as well as the participants and were reported with enthusiasm by the local press. In the same week that the Cornubian Lodge was toasted in Bristol, members celebrated its first birthday with a procession in full costume to the parish church of St Erth in Hayle, where the vicar preached a sermon, there being apparently no conflict between membership of the Order, with its eccentric interpretation of the bible, and the established church. The members then paraded through the principal gardens of the parish, where many of Harvey's foundry managers and directors lived, before adjourning to the new White Hart, a stylish white, neo-classical building with a pillared portico to rival anything to be seen in Penzance or Truro, for an excellent dinner. A year later the celebration was repeated in even more elaborate fashion.

Sometimes the possessions we most wish we could have inherited are long gone. I would have treasured the regalia of Sharrock Dupen, Master of the Cornubian Lodge of Free Gardeners. Who wouldn't want to inherit a dark blue apron embroidered with Noah's Ark and a border of flowers and foliage? Or a tiny silver watering can pinned to a satin ribbon? Despite the lack of surviving relics, my imagination was captured by the decorative symbols; it would have been a colourful scene however I chose to tell it. But this was Sharrock Dupen at the height of his success, and to invest it with an appropriate sense of pride and awe, I decided to visualise it through the eyes of his oldest daughter.

Hayle, 8th July 1844

The town of Hayle, basking in glorious sunshine, is on holiday. Annie's father left the house very early that morning to join his Brothers at the railway station. Sixty-five members of the Cornubian Lodge, he said, were going to take the first train of the day to Redruth, the same train Annie remembers taking on the memorable day last year when they went to hear the preaching at Gwennap Pit. The Lodge is celebrating its second anniversary and the whole family is going to see their father lead the procession that will march the eighteen miles from Redruth through Tuckingmill and Camborne to Copperhouse and Hayle. Annie is proud of her father. When she walks with him to chapel on Sundays she sees how the men of the town stop and salute him as the Grand Master. He knows everyone and they all know him. The Lodge is a mysterious place; in fact it isn't even properly speaking a place but a group of men who meet at the White Hart once a month. Her father comes home from those meetings smelling of beer and even redder in the face than usual. But it doesn't do to criticise. After all, the members of the Lodge are bound to take care of each other if they fall sick or are in financial need; that is its purpose, or so Annie has overheard her father declare when her mother complains.

It is mid-afternoon when the family leaves the house. Dozens of townspeople have already gathered in Penpol Terrace but Annie's brother Sharrock wriggles his way to the front of the crowd.

'Wait!' calls Annie breathlessly. 'George is following you. Catch him before he gets knocked down.'

Three-year-old George chuckles fearlessly as he darts between people's legs to reach his brother. As usual he is determined to prove that he can keep up with Sharrock. Annie is carrying John. He is getting far too heavy for her these days, but he started to cry when she tried to leave him with their mother, who is holding the grizzling new baby, Charles Wesley, in her arms. Charles is a fretful child. No one seems to know what ails him but he is not thriving like his brothers. So many babies, thinks Annie. So much worry. She knows they are precious gifts from God but she is not sure she wants to get married if the Lord is going to insist on such generosity. She has reached the front of the crowd with Kate close behind, Salome and Ellen clinging tightly to her hands. They gaze wide-eyed at the ships in the harbour, flying their colours in honour of the day. Sharrock names them one by one; he spends so much time loitering around the wharf that he knows them all.

'There's the *Nancy*, and the *Jane*, and the *William*. And see, Annie, that's the *Joanna*.'

He'll be off to sea himself just as soon as he's allowed, he says. His father has promised to take him on the *Cornwall* if he works hard at school but it has made no difference; he is as idle as ever. You would think he would be ashamed that his sisters are so much better at reading and reckoning than he is.

Annie is hot and uncomfortable. Despite the weather, she wears thick, itchy black stockings and layer after layer of chemise and petticoats. There is no escaping the obligations of respectability; the eyes of the town will be on her father, and she must be a credit to him. Standing by the dusty roadside in the heat, her arms start to ache and she sets John on his feet. He clings to her skirt for a minute and then sits down with a thump.

'Just let me rest for a moment,' she tells him as he raises his arms wailing, 'Up! Up!'

After what seems like hours of waiting, but is probably less than half an hour, the procession rounds the corner from the Copperhouse Pool. Her father is in the lead mounted on a fine white charger and attended by two pages on ponies. It is just like a fairy tale; he could be a knight riding out to slay a dragon and rescue the princess. But Annie wonders if she is the only one to notice how stiffly he sits. He is no horseman and has been in the saddle for at least six hours. He is preceded by a trumpeter, also on horseback, a Brother who carries the big blue banner depicting the Garden of Eden, and two others bearing a triumphal arch of fruit and flowers. They are all wearing dark blue ankle length aprons, embroidered with colourful images from the bible: Adam and Eve and the serpent, Solomon and the gardens of the Holy Temple. There are carefully stitched vines with bunches of purple grapes, dusty green olive trees, and pink flowers. Annie can see some of her own proud handiwork adorning her father's robe. She nudges Kate.

'Look,' she says, 'those are my grapes.'

The crowd applauds the men as they pass by carrying wands, china vases of flowers, globes, a silver salver, and a bible on a rich purple velvet cushion. Miniature crossed spades and rakes hang from wide sashes worn across the chest or as V-shaped collars. Annie's father also displays the Master's Jewel: the Order's insignia of a square and compasses with an open pruning knife. He looks over to his watching children and acknowledges them with a grave nod. Annie holds John up to see, George jumps impatiently up and down, while Ellen and Salome let go of Kate's hands to wave, and Sharrock stands stoutly to attention. Annie hopes that Papa is as proud of them as they are of him; he looks magnificent.

6 Debt and Disease

The optimism of the glorious procession was short-lived. By 1845, Sir Robert Peel's Tory government was under increasing pressure to repeal the Corn Laws that protected the interests of Britain's landowners. Politicians of all parties were anxiously watching the weather; a poor harvest would push up prices and make it harder to hold out against those who argued for the abolition of punitive tariffs on foreign imports of grain. Disaster struck when the potato blight arrived from America, destroying a staple food of the rural poor. The ensuing famine did much to change Peel's mind about free trade. The *Bristol Mercury* accused him of 'placing the barrier of unnatural laws between food and a famishing population', quoting a Wiltshire man who stated:

Bristol Mercury 15th November 1845
What our people in this parish be to do I know not, they live on potatoes. Some families where there are children have them three times a day – if they have anything three times a day; all the people have them for breakfast and supper, and the rot is getting so bad now that most of them have not many potatoes left. With bread getting so high, and the wages not getting up, and the potatoes gone, God above only knows what is to become of the poor people.

The following year, with support from the Whigs, the hated laws were repealed, splitting the Tory party and ending Peel's own career.

Cornwall was one of the worst affected areas. Even after the abolition of tax on imports, hard winters and bad harvests meant a doubling in the price of grain, while to the fury of the local population, wheat and barley continued to be exported from Cornish ports. During the winter of 1846–1847, bands of miners armed with picks and shovels laid siege to the towns of Redruth and Penzance. After twenty years of erratic openings and closures the mines were in decline – this time,

so it seemed, for good. The 'rage for emigration' that had
begun in the agricultural areas in the 1830s spread. Cornish
miners also started to emigrate in large numbers to seek their
fortune in Chile, Peru, and Malaya.

But it was in Ireland that the people were most dependent
on potatoes and suffered the worst hardship. In Bristol,
where ships continued to arrive from Dublin and Cork,
Sharrock Dupen would have been aware of the desperate
situation. When the 1846 crop failed completely, a
correspondent from County Cork warned, 'I venture to
predict that if large and continued grants are not made by
government, or works of a large scale undertaken, the people
will be in a state of starvation and insurrection.' The mayor of
Bristol launched a charitable appeal for money, food and
clothing to send to the destitute Irish and in February 1847 a
letter was received from the commander of the steam sloop
that had transported a shipment of food from the city. He
painted a harrowing picture of naked, emaciated women lying
in hovels on beds of straw next to the corpses of their loved
ones and predicted an outbreak of pestilence since, 'They
have ceased to put them into coffins, or to have the funeral
service performed, and they merely lay them a few inches
under the soil.'

Not everyone was as sympathetic however and on 2nd
April, under the heading 'What is to become of Ireland?' the
editor of the *Royal Cornwall Gazette* accused the starving people
of Ireland of laziness and ingratitude. The fractious
relationship was to persist throughout Victoria's reign: two
countries trapped like those ill-matched spouses of the period
who found it impossible to live together on civilised terms
but were unable to divorce. Eventually legislation was passed
to allow married couples a means of escape, but the British
government remained unwilling to let Ireland go, afraid of
how any show of weakness might play out in the lands of the
empire.

By 1848 thousands were still dying of starvation and in the rest of Europe the ever-present spectre of revolution was becoming a reality. In January Harvey's ships would have brought news from the Mediterranean that the inhabitants of Palermo in Sicily had taken up arms against their Spanish Bourbon rulers. Unrest soon spread to the north of the Italian peninsula, where Garibaldi returned from exile in South America to join in the fight to free Lombardy and Venice from Austrian rule. In February Louis-Philippe of France was overthrown. Uprisings spread to the German states, Prussia, Poland, Hungary and other parts of the Hapsburg empire. The British government was nervous as the Chartists continued to agitate for reform. On 10th April 20,000 of them assembled on Kennington Green on their way to petition Parliament. But they were outnumbered five to one by the police, and 85% of these were special constables, an indicator of the comparatively weak level of popular support for radical action. Britain, to the surprised relief of many, did not have a rebellion and the rally marked the end of Chartism as a significant force in British politics.

By September 1849 the French had elected a new president, Louis-Napoleon, nephew of Napoleon Bonaparte, and peace was restored to the Italian peninsula, with Garibaldi reported to be under arrest in Genoa. In August the British government judged that the time was right for the Queen and Prince Albert to make a state visit to Ireland, where they were accorded an enthusiastic reception and provided with a railway carriage that was said to have cost £5,000. Sharrock Dupen, scanning the account in the *Royal Cornwall Gazette*, would not have known that the population of Ireland had by that time declined as a result of starvation and emigration from over eight million to a figure closer to six million.

In Hayle, Henry Harvey was ailing, left semi-paralysed by a stroke. His portly figure was no longer seen perambulating around the streets of the thriving foundry quarter that was his creation, but his business was still the mainstay of the town's

economy. The Harvey empire was now managed by Henry's
nephew (and Sharrock Dupen's fellow freemason), Nicholas
Harvey. After the Leeghwater was successfully installed and
tested, orders followed for two more engines, to be built by
Harveys and by Fox and Co. at Perran. The size of the task
was almost inconceivable. It was estimated that even when all
three were in place it would take thirteen months to pump the
billion tons of water from Haarlem lake. In 1849 when the
Cruquis, a proud descendant of the original Newcomen beam
engines used to drain the Cornish mines, was finally
completed, it surpassed the Leeghwater as the biggest steam
engine in the world.

By the following summer there were fourteen people
squeezed into the Dupen home, if you counted the maid. I do
a rapid calculation to make sure I am not exaggerating. The
babies kept coming at roughly two-yearly intervals; after
George Semmens, John Wesley, and Charles Wesley, came
Sarah Wesley. All except Charles survived. He lived for just
six months and died in the autumn of 1844, one of some fifty
babies and children under the age of five to be buried in
Phillack that year. But the tally was no worse than that of any
other twelve-month period; the mortality rate for under-fives
remained stubbornly close to one in three throughout the
century.

On 22nd January 1848 my great-grandmother Hester Ann
Rogers Dupen was born: a child, I like to think, of the year of
revolution (and, of course, the Communist Manifesto). I
wasted a lot of time trying to identify where her name came
from: a family member, I assumed. I should have just googled
it, and eventually I did. Hester Ann Rogers (1756–1794), who
appeared at the top of the search results, was the daughter of
an Anglican clergyman. She defied her parents to join the
Methodist church and became a close friend of John Wesley,
a class leader, and visitor of the sick. Her *Spiritual Letters*,
published together with extracts from her diary, were popular
devotional reading for Methodist women. Johanna Woolcock

would have been familiar with the book and must have
chosen her name for her youngest daughter as a change from
the preceding three children, but after Hester she reverted to
the Wesleys for her twelfth baby, born in the summer of 1849
and named Samuel Wesley, after the father of John and
Charles.

Sharrock had to ensure the whole family was clothed, fed
and educated. His oldest son was now his assistant on the
Cornwall, Kate and Lizzie had positions at a draper's shop, and
Annie was teaching, but their father was still the main
breadwinner. It was an expensive business; food was
estimated to take up at least half the income of an average
family. But he could only be glad when his children turned
out to be strong and healthy. Unlike the poor of the town,
who had barley gruel for breakfast, a barley pasty for lunch,
and barley cake for supper, they would have thrived on
generous portions of bread, porridge, potatoes and a good
meat stew on Sundays. Dressed in neatly mended hand-me-
down clothes, they attended Sunday school every week. By
this time the Dupens had moved to Penpol Terrace, the fine
row of houses that overlooked the quay. The family's position
in the ranks of the respectable middle class seemed assured,
living as they did amidst households of mining and shipping
agents, engine fitters and shopkeepers. These neighbours, like
the Dupens, kept maidservants and charwomen – although
only the surgeon employed a groom and drove out in his own
gig. Sharrock perhaps hoped that one day he could do the
same; nothing seemed impossible to a man prepared to work
hard and take calculated risks in pursuit of profit.

But cholera was once more sweeping through Cornwall. In
those days the course of any illness was frustratingly
unpredictable and one disease was not always distinguished
from another. A cough, sniffle, or raised temperature could
presage a simple cold or a deadly case of measles, influenza,
typhoid, or scarlet fever. Diarrhoea was almost too common
to be remarked on. The remedies at the disposal of surgeons

and apothecaries were limited and sometimes downright dangerous. Sharrock and Johanna Dupen no doubt tried to be vigilant but in the end they had to put their trust in God. They could not live their lives in a constant state of anxiety over one or other of the children. Cholera was another matter. It was alien, outlandish, monstrous.

The couple would have had clear memories of 1831, when the disease first reached the shores of Britain with an outbreak in the northern town of Sunderland. From there it spread to London and throughout the country, including Cornwall, where the first cases appeared in the parish of Phillack in August. By the time the epidemic subsided two years later it had killed 52,000 people. During the same two-year period, two major outbreaks of influenza caused the deaths of many tens of thousands more. It was commonly believed that fatal diseases were airborne and spread through the noxious and invisible miasma that hung over rivers and marshland. Henry Harvey believed the stagnant, filthy Penpol Pool next to the original White Hart inn to be the main source of infection. To his credit he wrote to the parish authorities in St Erth urging the formation of a Board of Health to tackle the problem but neither the magistrate nor the vicar was keen to intervene, apparently for fear of offending the landowner. Harvey next tried to buy the land so that he could drain the pool and fill it in but his offer was turned down. It was this refusal that led to his even more ambitious plan to construct a new tidal pool at Carnsew, the one that was inaugurated in 1834. The cholera eventually subsided as mysteriously as it had appeared and when Henry Harvey finally purchased the Penpol Pool in 1837, he drained it not, so it seems, out of concern for public health but in order to build his fine new White Hart hotel.

The latest pandemic had struck England in the autumn of 1848 at the end of a dreadful period. After typhoid carried off many victims in the hot summer of 1846, the new 'Irish fever' arrived with people fleeing the potato famine. At the same time old-fashioned influenza and dysentery continued to claim thousands of victims. By the summer of 1849, although there were still those who tried to dismiss it as the famine fever that prevailed in Ireland, the cholera had reached Cornwall. In Hayle the disease was largely confined to the poorer parts of town, where a soup kitchen was set up to feed 250 of the most needy. A month earlier the *Royal Cornwall Gazette* had set out the precautions to be taken, although those most at risk would have no access to the newspapers and would remain unaware of the warning. Readers were recommended to wear warm flannel next to the skin, avoid getting their feet wet, and eat solid starchy foods and meat, not vegetables that were likely to promote looseness of the bowels:

> *Royal Cornwall Gazette 17th August 1849*
> The chief causes of Cholera are, damp, filth, animal and vegetable matter in a rotting state; and, in general, whatever produces foul air.
> Householders of all classes should be warned, that their first means of safety lies in the removal of dung heaps, and solid and liquid filth of every description, from beneath or about their houses and premises.

Before flush toilets and mains drainage, ash, sawdust or garden soil was thrown into the outdoor privy to help the contents rot down and control the smell. The result was either a heap that accumulated behind the open back of the privy or a bucket that had to be emptied. Both systems produced compost for the garden, unless the town had a 'night soil' man who would collect the euphemistically named product and take it away. Sharrock no doubt made arrangements to have the cesspit behind his house emptied, hoping this would be effective. It was to be another five years before Dr John Snow was able to prove his theory that cholera was in fact a water-borne disease.

Death from cholera could be frighteningly swift: a newspaper report told of an aged barber taken ill in the morning and dead by the afternoon. But the disease was not invariably fatal and the newspaper also reported that a young man who had been pronounced dead was found sitting up in bed just minutes before the arrival of his coffin. He was able to partake of some nourishing beef tea and was soon fast recovering. Others were less fortunate and those who assisted in caring for the sick and laying out the bodies were often the ones to be next taken ill:

Royal Cornwall Gazette 21ˢᵗ September 1849
REDRUTH.— Up to Saturday evening, there having been no deaths for the week, the Board of Health were in hopes the worst had passed over. During that night and following day, however, there were 7 deaths, viz., a woman known as "old Margaret"; the wife of Thomas Vincent, a vendor of fish, who had attended Redruth market on the Friday, and St. Day on Saturday; two persons, north of the town, named Broad and Maddern; a man at the western end named Rogers; John Goldsworthy, a chandler in Foundry Row; and a woman named Francis in Cocking's-court, all of whom neglected to apply for timely medical assistance. Jenny Cocking, the nurse, who had attended "old Margaret," and had been poorly 2 days, died on Wednesday.

It was a time when human nature was seen at its best; local people not only prayed for the sick but also donated money they could often ill afford. The workmen at Harvey's foundry collected a generous financial gift for the doctor in recognition of the risks he ran.

In September 1849 just as it appeared that the epidemic was abating, Sharrock was faced with a new danger:

London Gazette 31ˢᵗ August 1849
WHEREAS a Petition of Sharrock Semmens Dupen, for the last fourteen years residing at Hayle, in the parish of Phillack, in the county of Cornwall, but all the above period a Steward and Provider on board the Herald and Cornwall Steam-packets, trading between the city and county of Bristol and Hayle, in the said county of Cornwall, an insolvent debtor,

having been filed in the County Court of Cornwall, at
Redruth, and an interim order for protection from process
having been given to the said Sharrock Semmens Dupen,
under the provisions of the Statutes in that case made and
provided, the said Sharrock Semmens Dupen is hereby
required to appear before the said Court, on the 13th day of
September next, at ten o'clock in the forenoon precisely, for
his first examination touching his debts, estate, and effects,
and to be further dealt with according to the provisions of the
said Statutes; and the choice of the creditors' assignees is to
take place at the time so appointed. All persons indebted to
the said Sharrock Semmens Dupen, or that have any of his
effects, are not to pay or deliver the same but to Mr. Francis
Paynter, Clerk of the said Court, at his office, at Redruth, the
Official Assignee of the estate and effects of the said
insolvent.

My grandfather's grandfather benefited from important
and controversial changes to the law in the 1840s. Prior to the
new legislation Sharrock would have had to be imprisoned
first before he could apply to the court and his fate would
have depended to a large extent on his creditors. The *Bristol
Mercury*, commenting on the Insolvent Debtors' bill of 1844,
was in no doubt that it was entirely proper to have ended this
practice:

Bristol Mercury 31st August 1844
There are two very different classes of debtors: the honest and
the dishonest – those who cannot and those who will not pay.
Nothing can be more cruel and absurd than the imprisonment
of the honest but unfortunate debtor, for not only is the chance
of liquidating his debts thereby destroyed, but his family are
frequently reduced to beggary and starvation, and numerous
and shocking are the well-authenticated cases of ruin and
misery which have resulted from a stretch of power on the
part of the creditor.

The County Court judges tasked under the new law with
examining small debtors had a large measure of discretion and
a responsibility to uphold morality quite as much as the law.

They took into consideration not only the behaviour of the debtor but that of his creditors too, and could write off debts if they thought credit had been extended unwisely. An 'innocent' man was unlikely to be gaoled, and dishonest traders who lured unwary customers into buying goods they could ill afford were publicly criticised for unacceptable business practices. There was concern, however, that in the rush to remedy injustice the balance had tilted too far in the other direction. Working and lower-middle class society functioned on credit, with shopkeepers who extended 'tick' to their customers owing money in turn to their suppliers. One person defaulting on his rent, grocery bill or other obligation could cause a whole row of dominos to collapse. The *Bristol Mercury* went on to paint a dramatic picture:

> "Unfortunate debtor" and "hard-hearted creditor", have become stock terms in the language. Nor is this to be wondered at, for nineteen-twentieths of our light literature creates and gives currency to such impressions. On the stage your debtor is generally a melancholy genteel gentleman, in faded black, with an angel in white muslin for a daughter, both of whom are persecuted by some "fiend in human form", in the shape of an imperative, hard-hearted creditor [...] Creditors, too, have families as well as debtors: and many an honest man is compelled at times to adopt apparently harsh measures, in order to support his own family, and to be able to meet his own creditors.

As a result of representations made to parliament, the legislation was amended in 1845 to reinstate the possibility of gaol as a penalty for debt. Sharrock was ineligible to take his case to the bankruptcy court, since only traders who made their living from buying and selling, or those owing more than £20, could apply to be freed from their debts in this way. Instead he must be examined by a local court and agree a schedule of payment by instalments. If he failed to convince the judge that he was not to blame for his predicament, he could go to prison. It was a perilous moment for the man who, just a few years earlier, had paraded through the town in his robes, mounted on a fine white charger. My image of the courtroom owes much to Charles Dickens, who recreated his father's experience of the Insolvent Debtors' court in *The Pickwick Papers* some ten years earlier, but it was not a remotely comic occasion.

Redruth, 13th September 1849

It is a Thursday morning when Sharrock Dupen leaves his house to take the train to Redruth and keep his appointment with the court. For this journey he has dressed carefully in a plain dark coat of worsted cloth, a respectable waistcoat and a neatly tied cravat. It is important for him to look like a blameless victim and not a foolish spendthrift. How has it come to this? For more than ten years his earnings from the steam packet service grew along with the increasing numbers of passengers. His vegetable business prospered too. But now, despite all his attempts to stave off the shameful moment, his name has been printed in the newspapers in the list of insolvent debtors.

Although the court order protects him for the time being, he is still at risk of being put in gaol. The consequences are unthinkable. If he loses his job his family will have to rely on the earnings of the older children to survive. Between them they should be just about able to manage but it will be a close run thing. Under the harsh conditions of the New Poor Law, any further misfortune could see the family broken up and sent to the workhouse in Redruth. Thirteen-year-old Salome could be put out to service but that is not the life he wants for his daughters. There is no help to be had from his brothers; George disappeared from their lives when he emigrated to America, John and Horatio are dead, and Robert away with his ship. Their widowed father is himself struggling, too old now to go to sea.

As he sits on the hard bench in the cramped wooden carriage of the train, Sharrock's mind turns to his other

Brothers, the ones from the Cornubian Lodge. They are at the same time a source of his difficulties and his best hope of relief; surely they will offer loans or other assistance to extricate him from his present circumstances. After ten years with no activity, the Lodge finally had finally come to life the previous year, partly thanks to the efforts of Sharrock himself. It was all very well being Grand Master of the Free Gardeners but everyone knew it was the Masons who held the real power: men like Nicholas Harvey, Henry Harvey's nephew. As one of the founding members Sharrock has a position to maintain but it costs money to entertain the gentlemen of the Lodge. His reputation as a generous and open-handed drinking companion has been purchased at a price he can ill afford. The market gardeners of Penzance no longer need him to sell their produce; they have made other arrangements that cut out the middle man. His earnings from the *Cornwall* are reduced too, reflecting the uncertainty in the local economy.

For months Sharrock has tried to juggle his financial affairs but the nature of the victualing trade makes it difficult; cash flow is always tight. Finally he has run out of both time and money. There is not enough left at home to pawn. He has filed his petition to be recognised as an insolvent debtor to avoid the imminent threat of arrest. During his journey to Redruth he goes over and over his actions of the past year. Was there anything he could have done to avoid this?

The train puffs slowly into Redruth station and draws to a hissing halt. Sharrock gets down onto the platform into a cloud of steam as dense as the fog that fills his head. He makes his way up the hill to Andrew's hotel. Unusually, that is where the county court is sitting for the two days it will take to work through the month's list of cases; the usual courtroom is out of use because the body of an unfortunate man killed in an accident lies there awaiting the coroner's inquest. The dark and stuffy hotel parlour smells of beer, stale tobacco and sweat. The judge is seated opposite the door, a small wooden writing desk on the table in front of him. He

wears dingy black robes and a grubby white wig – or it may
be the lack of natural light that makes it appear so. The clerk,
Mr Francis Paynter, is a solicitor from Penzance, a man in his
late fifties whose well-cut coat and gold pocket watch
proclaim his own condition of comfortable solvency.
Sharrock is directed to a wooden chair that is slightly too
small for his bulky form, next to the other man who is due to
be examined that day. His name, he confides in a low voice,
is George Austen and he is a confectioner and grocer by
trade. He is some ten years younger than Sharrock and looks
anxious and underslept. A motley bunch of shabbily dressed
spectators are settled in for the morning's entertainment,
several of them clutching lumps of bread and cheese or a
pasty wrapped in a grimy checked handkerchief.

Sharrock presents the full tally of his debts and the limited
schedule of his assets.

'You must understand, sir, that my earnings as steward of
the *Cornwall* are my only source of income,' he declares.
'My debts have been incurred, I assure you, through no fault
of my own. I swear that I am not a gambler or a drinker. I am
a victim of the hard times that are affecting so many
businessmen, as I am sure you know, sir. I have to buy my
supplies for the steam packet without any certainty of being
able to sell my full stock of refreshments. It is very hard to
predict what I will need. People are not travelling as much
because of the cholera.'

'And your assets, Mr Dupen?' enquires the judge.

'I have surrendered all my personal property to Mr
Paynter here. There is nothing left in my home but the
necessary furnishings for my family. I have eleven children,
sir, and only four of them of an age to earn. Believe me, I
have no silver plate or valuable china, no fine embroidered
linens. Just the bare essentials of life.'

The judge looks at him sternly and gives his instructions.

'Mr Paynter here will sell your watch and chain and other
personal items to repay at least a percentage of what is owed
to your creditors. You will pay off the rest at a rate of three

shillings a week. And try to be more prudent in future. I will I
expect to see you back here for a final hearing on Thursday
11th October.'

With a sigh of relief, Sharrock steps back and sits down.
As soon as Mr Austen's case is dealt with, he will invite his
fellow debtor to join him in a consolatory glass of ale.

7 Laundry Day

I have always been fascinated by large families, coming as I do from a very small one. I grew up, like so many women of my generation, reading about the improbable numbers of children born to the Chalet School girls. For years I believed that two or three sets of twins were normal, even desirable, and I am still slightly surprised that my daughter is an only child. There were no other households in Penpol Terrace with as many children as the Dupens; six or seven was a more common number, although that may have reflected a lower survival rate rather than fewer conceptions. Late marriage, prolonged breastfeeding, and abstinence were the only means available to respectable women from the lower and middle classes to limit the size of their families. Johanna Dupen must have spent the best part of twenty years either pregnant or breastfeeding. It is a physical state that I find almost impossible to imagine. The constant fatigue and interrupted sleep, the aching legs and sagging, leaking breasts, the nausea, indigestion and incontinence, all these must have taken their toll. But her constitution was robust and she was to live for another thirty years after the birth of her final baby.

I know that but she did not. In the nineteenth century death in childbirth was common, mainly as a result of infection transmitted by doctors and midwives with no concept of hygiene, but also from complications that are now unlikely to prove fatal. My daughter, monitored throughout my labour and hauled out urgently with forceps, would possibly not have survived if she had been born a hundred years earlier – and nor would I. If Johanna was afraid every time that the next baby would be the one to cause her death, she left no record to tell us. As a devout Methodist she would have submitted to the will of God and if she was ever tempted to protest we will never know. Rightly or wrongly I see her as a matter-of-fact, sensible woman who got on with the tasks of daily life without questioning her lot. It is the fate of women who cope to be underestimated; they make the difficult look easy.

Like most people, the Dupens were no doubt renting their home; very few men of Sharrock's class bought their own property. I have found it impossible to work out exactly which house was theirs because the census schedules do not match the current street numbers and I suspect they may have moved more than once. But none of the likely candidates has more than two rooms downstairs and three bedrooms: one for Sharrock, Johanna and the babies, one for the girls, and one for the boys. The maid must have slept in the kitchen. Some families took in lodgers to help make ends meet but that was not a solution open to my grandfather's grandparents. My own late-Victorian house was built with four bedrooms, two downstairs rooms, and a kitchen at the back. In my head I try to people it with another dozen family members and fail completely. Where did they all sit, let alone sleep? Could they possibly all have eaten Sunday dinner at the same table? How many pounds of potatoes and loaves of bread did they consume each week? Even families who, because of their income and occupation, counted as middle class lived in conditions that most of us would find intolerable, with beds shared between two or three children and sometimes more. It was not a problem that they would have identified themselves, at a time when occupying a whole house rather than just a room was already a marker of privilege. Personal space was not a concept that they would have recognised. I doubt if Johanna Dupen or any of her daughters ever spent a single moment alone.

Keeping everyone clean, clothed, and fed required a monotonous round of gruelling daily activity. The endless dinners cooked and dishes washed, the beds made and carpets swept, day after day in an unvarying routine, leave no trace. The stuff of women's lives is ephemeral and unconsidered. The Dupen washing would have been done by hand, quite possibly without even a mangle, and it would have taken a full day or more. With six adults and seven children there would have been unending piles of chemises, petticoats, nightgowns, babies' napkins, and the flannel binders that protected them from taking a chill in the stomach or bowels. In a family of growing girls there were no doubt bundles of bloodied rags each month too, although history has little to say on that subject.

A typical Monday began before dawn, when the housemaid, sixteen-year-old Ann Mitchell, got up even earlier than usual, to light the fire under the boiler. The water needed to be hot by the time breakfast was over. The metal cylinder that sat in a corner of the back kitchen held about twenty gallons. Made of cast iron, the 'copper' stood on the flagged floor with its own narrow chimney pipe that came out at a right angle from the back and then went straight up inside the wall of the house, passing close to the rafters of the main roof. Ann would have opened the small door in the front and lit the fire with a few bits of kindling. Once the cinders were ablaze (no one wasted best coal to heat the copper) it was time to stoke the kitchen range and put the kettle on for breakfast. This was the only hot meal of the day because as soon as it was over, big pans of water would be put on the range to boil for the laundry; the copper could not supply enough for the quantities of linen produced by such a large family.

When the charwoman, Jane Bryant, arrived she must have gone straight to the back kitchen to take the sheets out of the water they had been soaking in overnight. Then she would have opened the tap in the side of the copper and drawn off hot water into the wooden washtub. As she rubbed and beat the heavy sodden masses of white cloth with a wooden dolly, Johanna made a soapy jelly with shavings from a big bar dissolved in hot water. Stained items of clothing were scrubbed with this slippery goo before being dunked in a tub of soapy water, wrung out, rinsed, and put into the copper to

boil. Ann was kept busy refilling the copper and feeding the
fire to make sure there was enough water for load after load.
Finally it was the turn of the dirty cloths used for cleaning to
be soaped, scrubbed, and boiled. At last the fire under the
copper was allowed to go out and Jane Bryant went home. It
would be all to do again the following week.

Just one laundry day in the thousands that took place in
the Dupen household is remembered by history:

Royal Cornwall Gazette 27th September 1850
On Tuesday last about 12 o'clock, smoke was seen issuing
from the dwelling-house of Mr Sharrock Dupen, Steward of
the Cornwall steamer, at Penpoll Terrace, Hayle. Alarm was
instantly given, and a large concourse of people soon
assembled to ascertain from whence the smoke proceeded,
when it was discovered that the back part of the roof was on
fire. Fortunately it rained hard at the time, and the wind was
not high; and the fire was speedily extinguished. It is
supposed that the fire originated in the back kitchen by the
washing furnace chimney which had been used the preceding
day, taking fire, which communicated to the rafters of the
dwelling house, these having been very improperly permitted
by the builder to be placed so contiguous to danger.

Hayle was probably too small to have one of the new
public fire engines but there was one at the foundry that
could have attended the scene. Another newspaper report
tells of a fire that broke out the previous September in the
new boring mill engine house, situated at the very centre of
the site. A fire there could have had disastrous consequences
but most fortunately it was discovered in time:

Royal Cornwall Gazette 7th September 1849
[Captain West] immediately rang the fire bell for assistance,
which was promptly attended to. Fortunately there is an
excellent fire-engine belonging to the firm, which was soon
put to use, with a plentiful supply of water, which soon
extinguished the fire.

Not a week passed in 1850 without a report of a blaze
somewhere destroying a house, a haystack or even part of a
railway station. Flying sparks on board ship were a constant
cause for concern while clothing that caught light was a
regular cause of death and injury in the home. Fire, like
disease, was one of the unavoidable risks of daily life.

This was a time when the notion of separate male and
female spheres was taking hold. The working lives of men
and women diverged as activities like weaving and spinning
moved out of the home, where they had traditionally taken
place alongside baking, brewing and preserving, and into the
factory. Although women and children made up a large
proportion of the industrial workforce, it became a badge of
respectability for middle class wives not to go out to work.
Disregarding the hard labour required to keep a large family
clean, clothed and fed, mothers were seen primarily as
guardians of morality within the home, where their role was
to educate the next generation in religious faith and virtuous
behaviour. The doctrine must surely, I think, have had a
different force in maritime communities, where the father was
absent for long stretches of time. Seafaring families could
never have counted on the presence at important moments of
the man of the house. There would always have been
decisions to take and business to transact that could not await
his return. Johanna Dupen would have shouldered
responsibilities that were unknown to wives whose husbands
came home each night to the sanctuary of their own fireside,
learning early in her married life to deal with household
emergencies like the one recorded here. It felt important for
me to capture a sense of how a woman like Johanna
experienced the daily burden of her life.

Penpol Terrace, Hayle, 23rd–24th September 1850

Monday is everyone's least favourite day, when the house is
turned topsy-turvy and no one comes home for dinner.
Johanna knows she is lucky to have help but it sometimes
feels as if one laundry day is no sooner over than the next
one begins. The men's shirts quickly become filthy with the
soot from the ship's engines and it would not do for the
steward to appear with soiled linen, while Lizzie and Kate
have to be neatly turned out with clean collars and cuffs for
their work measuring out dress fabric and ribbon, and cutting
lengths of lace. When it rains, as it is doing today, there is
damp washing hung all over the kitchen. But at least the
clothes stay relatively clean when they are dried indoors; on
fine days when they are taken outside they quickly become
covered with smuts from the foundry chimneys if the wind is
in the wrong direction.

The house has never been more full, and although Lizzie
is planning her wedding for the spring and will move away
with her young engineer, Johanna is already swollen under
her stays with the unmistakeable signs of another baby on the
way. She uses both hands in the small of her back to
straighten from bending over the washtub, and wonders if it
will ever end, this constant cycle of weaning and births, or if
this next will be the death of her. It is unlike her to be morbid
but her arms and legs ache at the end of another long day of
scrubbing and wringing. She is so very, very tired.

Annie and the older children have come home from
school and the boys have joined the little ones, who are
playing with their peg dolls in the dining room. It is too wet
to go in the garden so they take out their wooden blocks and
the precious box of lead soldiers.

'No, Sam,' she hears John saying sternly. 'Not in your
mouth. See, here are the blocks. Let's make a tower.'

Such a kind brother, her John, she thinks. It's wrong to
have favourites but John is such an easy child compared with
his brothers. Perhaps it is having Mr Wesley's name that has

kept him on the right path. With a pang she remembers
Charles. Would he too have been gentle and biddable if he
had been spared? Annie's voice breaks into her reverie.

'Let me make you a cup of tea, mama. Sit down. Salome
and I will do the rest.'

Johanna sinks onto a hard kitchen chair with a sigh,
ignoring the drips from the sopping fabric suspended above
her head. She watches while her daughters sponge and brush
the woollens and delicate coloured prints that cannot be
boiled, to remove the worst of the grime.

'I remember,' she says, 'when you were born, Annie, and
we lived in Penzance. The air was so clean and fresh.'

'Didn't it smell of fish, mama?' asks Annie. 'I'm sure that's
what you said before.'

There is precious little sympathy to be had there. She
knows why Annie is sharp with her. She is afraid – afraid of
being left to care for her brothers and sisters if her mother
does not survive the next birth, to be the family cook and
washerwoman instead of spending her days in the
schoolroom. Who can blame her for being anxious? The lot
of an oldest daughter is never easy, and Annie's work gives
her no opportunity to meet eligible young men. Not that she
shows the slightest interest in such things. She is too fond of
her own authority to willingly relinquish it to a husband.
Johanna knows how often she herself has to bite her tongue
when Sharrock comes home and expects her to be at his
beck and call; it is in many ways easier when he is away. She
gives herself a mental shake and finishes her tea.

A little later the children are given their bowls of bread
and milk and put to bed. Kate and Lizzie come home from
the draper's shop when it closes at eight o'clock and the
menfolk return from the wharf at about the same time. After a
cold supper of bread and cheese, everyone sits wearily in the
dining room. Johanna and the girls are busy with the never-
ending piles of mending. Every washday shows up more
ripped seams and holes that need repairing. At last it is time
for evening prayers. Another Monday is safely over. No one

gives a thought to the still-glowing cinders in the back kitchen.

Tuesday is sailing day for the *Cornwall* and Sharrock and his eldest son set off for the quay in good time the next morning. At home the laundry is still dripping from the airer over the kitchen range, filling the room with steam and feeding the mildew on the walls. By midday Johanna is standing by the stove, ignoring the ache from her varicose veins, stirring a pot of starch, while Ann has set the flat irons to heat, ready to begin smoothing some of the lighter items that by this time are merely damp rather than sopping wet. Jane Bryant is upstairs washing the bedroom floors. Suddenly they hear hammering at the front door and shouts of fire. Johanna rushes outside and sees their neighbour Mr Glasson standing in the rain and pointing at the back of the roof. A thin but worrying stream of smoke is rising into the air.

'Quickly, Ann,' cries Johanna. 'Run to the foundry for help.'

She hurries back indoors to collect the three little ones, who start to cry as they are herded out into the drizzle.

'Jane,' she calls on her way out of the door, 'come down! Come down right now!'

As they stand in the front garden Jane Bryant puts her arms round Sarah and Hester, who are wailing with fright, while Johanna gathers up baby Sam and hugs him to her.

'There, there, me lover,' she hears her charwoman say to Hester. 'Don't ee be frightened. Fire engine'll be here dreckly. Your brothers'll be jumpin' when they find out what they missed.'

Johanna sends Jane to her neighbour's house with the children while she waits outside, hugging her sodden shawl around her, watching anxiously for any flames. But all she can see is the sinister plume of smoke. A curious crowd has started to gather, gawping helplessly as half a dozen of Harvey's men arrive, pushing the company's fire engine, hung around with buckets, ladder and hosepipe.

'Don't ee be feared, ma'am,' calls the foreman. 'Us'll soon have that out for you. Looks like the chimney of your copper's caught.'

'But I only skyed it just a month ago. It should still be clear. It certainly made a loud enough bang when I set the gunpowder off.'

But a spark must have flown up and ignited the soot that so easily clogs the narrow pipe, spreading flames to the rafters, which have caught and are starting to smoulder. Fortunately the heavy rain that makes the washing impossible to dry also acts to douse the fire and once a bucket of water is thrown down the chimney of the copper the worst of the danger is over.

The firemen depart, brushing aside Johanna's thanks.

'Bain't going to let Mr Dupen's house burn down,' says the foreman with a grin. 'Just you tell him to buy us a beer next time he sees us in the Royal Standard.'

In the smoky kitchen Johanna sits down heavily on a wooden chair. Where is Sharrock when he's needed? Half way to Bristol, as usual. What if no one had seen the smoke? They are fortunate that Mr Glasson has retired and is at home most days. She is wet through and chilled to the bone but Sam is grizzling and starting to cough. Before she goes to change her dress she must get him dry and give him a little warm milk with honey to stop him catching cold. He is a delicate child who needs constant vigilance. How on earth will she manage once the next one arrives? Is it wrong to hope this will be the last? I have always tried to do my duty, Lord, she thinks, but enough is surely enough.

CENSUS 1851

At the time of the next census, that of 1851, Sharrock's father John Dupen is lodging in a coffeehouse in the Foundry area of Hayle. But six months earlier, around the same time as fire broke out in Penpol Terrace, his name appears in the workhouse admissions register for Redruth. Nothing could better illustrate the harsh truth that anyone in Victorian Britain could become poor. The fine gentleman of the portrait miniature was by then 76 years old, his wife had been dead for seven years and he was no doubt unfit for work. In general a larger proportion of elderly men are listed in the workhouse records than women, who are more likely to be found living with their adult children and contributing to housework and childcare despite their infirmities. The Redruth workhouse, a long, low building of grey stone with a slate roof, big sash windows and a central archway leading to an inner courtyard, had been constructed at Carn Brea just outside the town as part of the rolling out of the New Poor Law. The fact that John was taken in here rather than Falmouth suggests that he had moved to be near his son.

The old parish-administered system had provided flexible payments to the elderly and incapacitated, widows, and men (but not women) temporarily out of work. Money was made available to pay doctors' bills, buy food, or support illegitimate children, while under the Speenhamland system (a kind of eighteenth-century Universal Credit) relief was granted to any man, employed or unemployed, whose income dropped below a certain level. Population growth made all this increasingly unaffordable. By 1830 the poor rate represented 20% of all national expenditure (in the Redruth area it cost an average of 4s 5d per head of population) and it was clear that something had to change. The outcome was the New Poor Law of 1834. Over 15,000 parishes were grouped into some 600 'unions' and in the five years that followed 350 new workhouses were built to accommodate an influx of paupers, who would no longer be eligible for the 'outdoor relief' that allowed people to stay at home and receive basic financial aid. This, at least, was the theory.

Thirteen unions were created in Cornwall. The one for the area of Redruth covered eight parishes, including Phillack in Hayle. In 1837 the sum of £6,000 was approved for the construction of a workhouse to accommodate 450 people. Inmates were separated by age and gender and put to work in the kitchen, laundry or garden. They emptied the cesspit, took care of any livestock, and maintained the fabric of the building. They chopped wood, ground flour, wrecked their backs breaking stones to mend the roads, and shredded their fingers picking oakum from old hemp ropes to be used in caulking the hulls of naval vessels. These mindless and physically draining tasks were designed to make workhouse life so unpleasant as to deter able-bodied claimants. The principle of 'less eligibility' is today known as 'better off in work' but the mind-set is the same. For the first time a distinction was being made between the impotent (sick, elderly, and widowed) and the indolent, encouraging the popular perception of deserving and undeserving claimants that persists to this day.

Given that the buildings were more weather proof than the average slum dwelling and the diet no worse than that of the labouring poor, people were not necessarily reluctant to apply for 'indoor relief' because of the physical conditions. It was the indignity of submitting to an arbitrary regime of degrading rules that made it something to be avoided if at all possible. On arrival the new inmates had their bundles and pockets searched, they were stripped of their own clothes and bathed; their hair was cut short and they were issued with a rough cotton uniform and ill-fitting slippers. It was a process that robbed them of individuality and self-respect.

The new law succeeded in reducing both poor rate expenditure and the number of 'outdoor' paupers but coverage was incomplete and inconsistent. Although nearly a fifth of the workhouse population was aged over 65, the majority of elderly paupers were still allowed outdoor relief. The records suggest that John Dupen went into the workhouse for just six months, from September 1850 to March 1851. The census describes him as an annuitant, which presumably means he had by that time been granted a pension from the authorities. True to its outlier status in the far and sometimes wild west, Cornwall had a distinctly less generous approach to eligibility than the south and north east, and paid smaller pensions, towards the bottom end of a range that went from 3s to 1s 6d a week. Sharrock's father would have enough to cover his board and lodging but little money to spare for small luxuries such as tea and tobacco. I can only hope that the ageing sailor was able to take a daily stroll to the quay, to watch the ships and smell the sea air during the year that was left to him before he died. I imagine his grandsons sometimes came to sit with him and begged for dramatic tales of his seafaring days, of storms and shipwreck, and outrunning the dastardly Frenchies.

But there were two further casualties of John Dupen's descent into penury: Esther and Charles Cleverly, the children of his daughter Hannah, who were aged ten and eight in 1850. Hannah had married a sailor named Charles Cleverly, who was serving on *HMS Delight,* a ten-gun brig-sloop that was used on the packet service. This was one of the 'coffin brigs', so-called because of the large number that were wrecked, and it is possible that Charles was lost at sea. I can find no record of his death or burial. Hannah and her daughter were living with her parents at the time of the 1841 census but she died in 1843, a year after the birth of her son. The children must have stayed on with their grandparents and appear to have entered the workhouse at the same time as their grandfather, but unlike him they did not leave. Their names appear in the sixteen long pages of paupers, twenty on each page, resident in the Redruth workhouse on the night of the 1851 census.

Servants, labourers, washerwomen, housekeepers, and
orphaned children, each with a story of desperation that will
never be known.

Workhouse life followed a fixed routine, changing only
with the seasons. In summer the rising bell rang at 6 a.m. and
at 6.30 a ration of bread and gruel was served in the dining
hall. Dinner was at midday and consisted of broth or pease
pudding, with a meat (or meat-flavoured) stew or suet
pudding at the weekend. The regulation diet, carefully
calculated for the different categories of inmate, was not
ungenerous but there was plenty of scope for the master and
matron to falsify the accounts and skimp on the rations.
Esther may have glimpsed her brother and grandfather in the
dining hall but she would not have been allowed to speak to
them. They were allowed at most an hour together on a
Sunday after chapel. Strict segregation was enforced between
younger children, older girls and boys, and men and women,
to avoid moral contagion. It is unlikely to have prevented
either physical brutality or sexual abuse, but the victims were
never going to report it.

Children were supposed to have three hours of schooling
each day, consisting of basic reading, writing, arithmetic and
religious knowledge, although there was some debate about
writing. No one wanted pauper children to be better educated
than those belonging to respectable families. The teaching
was of a generally low standard because no competent
schoolmaster or schoolmistress wanted to live in a workhouse
and earn a pittance. In the afternoon the girls knitted or did
needlework and domestic chores while the boys sometimes
had the rudiments of history and geography presented to
them. There was no recognisable recreation period, no toys or
games of cards, and little or nothing to read beyond the bible
and the occasional moral tract. Esther would have been
trained for domestic service and I imagine that was her
eventual fate when she disappears from the records at the age
of thirteen. Hester and Esther are two variants of the same

name, thought to derive from the Persian word for 'star'. The
story of my great-grandmother's cousin is one that in an
alternative reality could easily have been hers.

I hope Esther survived. Her brother Charles did not. I
could write a touching deathbed scene where a thin, pale boy
lies feverish in the infirmary, at the mercy of a dishevelled and
drunken nurse. But this feels intrusive and unfair to the
memory of a child who was not a storybook character but a
real boy, who never knew his mother and after being
separated from his big sister, survived just two years of the
rough and tumble of the boys' ward. Other real-life
workhouse inmates have written about the teasing and
bullying, the meagre portions of disgusting food, the filthy
sanitary arrangements, and the brutal regime of the
schoolroom. So I prefer to record simply that Charles Henry
Cleverly, aged ten, died in 1852 and was no doubt buried in a
pauper's grave. His uncle did not arrange for his body to be
brought to the parish church in St Erth where his grandfather
was buried in February of that same year; his only memorial is
the official register of deaths and what is written here.

Meanwhile, in Penpol Terrace, the census of 1851 is the
only time that we find the entire Dupen family at home,
including Johanna's final baby, born just one month earlier
and named Ernest Vincent. The household, which takes up
almost a full page of the record, is made up of Sharrock and
Johanna, their daughters Annie, Kate, Salome, Ellen, Sarah
and Hester, their surviving sons Sharrock, George, John,
Samuel, and baby Ernest, as well as a charwoman and a house
servant. It was no wonder that Sharrock could not take in his
widowed father, still less his orphaned niece and nephew.
Although Lizzie had married the previous year and moved
away to Plymouth, there was no room in Penpol Terrace to
squeeze in even one more person. Sharrock is described a
'Provider on board the Cornwall steamer', and his oldest son,
aged sixteen, is the assistant steward on board the same
vessel. Annie is a school governess and Kate a draper's

assistant. It may say something about the value the family
attached to education that the others, from fifteen-year-old
Salome to three-year-old Hester are 'scholars', with only the
babies, Sam and Ernest described as 'children at home'.

The presence of servants in Penpol Terrace is an
indication that Sharrock must have bounced back from his
temporary insolvency, and indeed, the population in general
was experiencing a mood of national optimism. Britain had
become the acknowledged world leader in manufacturing
thanks to plentiful supplies of good quality coal and the
associated ability to forge iron and generate the steam that
was needed to run every type of machinery. British people
were more and more mobile, migrating in large numbers to
the new industrial cities and taking day trips out to the equally
new seaside resorts. Around a quarter of them had a family
income of more than £300, bringing them well within the
definition of middle class. They lived in a country that was
becoming ever more connected: by 1850 the railway network
extended to over 6,000 miles and Greenwich time, which had
been adopted by the Great Western Railway, was soon to
spread to the whole country. (Except in Oxford, where the
university allowed the railway to come no closer than Didcot
and stubbornly retained Christ Church time. To this day
services in the cathedral begin five minutes after the hour.) A
reliable and frequent postal service carried twice as many
letters in 1849 as in 1839 and the first electric telegraph
service was established in 1846. New ways of making paper
and printing brought down the cost of newspapers and
increasing numbers of periodicals (often illustrated) were
being launched. On 1st May 1851 Queen Victoria opened the
Great Exhibition in Hyde Park, in the glass cathedral that was
the Crystal Palace. It was the world's first trade fair and the
realisation of Prince Albert's vision, to showcase his adopted
land as a politically stable industrial giant.

Britain itself occupied half the exhibition space, while the
rest was filled with the greatest wonders that foreign countries

could supply: an ivory throne from India, furs from Canada, French porcelain, Russian sledges, and Swiss (naturally) watches. There were some 100,000 objects, ranging in size from a massive hydraulic press to the Koh-i-Noor diamond, locked in a display case like an exotic bird in a cage. The *Royal Cornwall Gazette* published a special report of the Cornish Department on 9th May to accompany the account of the opening. There was a fine display of tin, copper and iron ore accompanied by mining apparatus, specimens of china clay, granite and porphyry, various model boats, a sample of 'maranated' [*sic*] pilchards and two knitted sailors' frocks from Polperro. Harveys, surprisingly, seem not to have been represented but Mr J. Pool of the Copperhouse foundry supplied a 'well executed model of a Paddle Wheel for a steamer'.

In the six months from May to October six million visits were made by up to 40,000 people at a time. They dawdled happily along the ten miles of aisles in temperatures that reached 95° F on the warmest days, wondering at the displays of art and architecture, industrial and domestic machinery, carpets, velocipedes, and stuffed kittens taking tea. For the first time ladies could literally spend a penny in private, making it possible to stay all day and safely enjoy the (non-alcoholic) refreshments provided by Messrs Schweppes. From 24 May the weekday price for the exhibition was reduced to one shilling with the aim of making it affordable to the masses, although on the whole it was still the middle and artisan classes that took advantage of the opportunity. They travelled on excursion trains arranged by Thomas Cook and were, it was reported, 'far more critical and discriminating in their mode of examining the treasures of the Exhibition than the more wealthy sight-seers who had preceded them'. On one of these one-shilling days the queen walked unprotected amongst her subjects, stopping at the central fountain that had been constructed from four tons of pink glass. 'It was,' reported the newspapers, 'in point of fact, the first extempore walk of the Sovereign in the presence of her people without other guards than themselves.' The relationship between monarch and people had been transformed from the uneasy early days of her reign.

It is unlikely that any of the Dupen family made the journey to London to view the Great Exhibition but the boys may well have heard accounts of it from their schoolmates, some of whom were Londoners. The Hayle Mathematical and Commercial Academy, a large institution on Foundry Hill 'in an open and elevated position, within a few Minutes' walk of the Sea', was where Sharrock Dupen chose to send his sons to school. Whatever the financial difficulties Sharrock had experienced, he somehow found the money to pay the fees, which must have been less for day pupils than the £20 charged for boarders, but still a significant sum. The Dupen brothers had as their companions boys from the best families in town, the sons of professional men, doctors, ship's masters, and engineers, as well as a dozen or so boarders who came from further afield. They included Captain Vivian's grandson John, and Nicholas James West, a great-nephew of Henry Harvey and future manager of the works. Competition was fierce but the Dupens seem to have thrived in the rough and tumble of the big schoolroom, where three classes were grouped by age. In the 1st class in June 1853, Nicholas West carried off prizes for Grammar, Geography, History, and Mapping, but in the 2nd class it was George Dupen who took the prizes for Composition and Geography, while in the class below, his ten-year-old brother John was awarded prizes for Grammar and Scripture.

HAYLE ACADEMY, CORNWALL
Mr. James Hosking, Principal.
Greek Master MR. EDWIN PETTERS DAVEY
Latin MR. W. TAYLOR
French, Spanish, & Italian Mons. Thomazie
School Duties to be RESUMED on MONDAY, July 18th.

Cornwall has long been celebrated for the salubrity of its atmosphere. Many young gentlemen from London, Bath, and Bristol (educated at the above establishment) have derived such a large amount of benefit as to elicit from their friends the warmest expressions of grateful satisfaction.

Only one Vacation during the year, viz., four weeks at Midsummer.

TERMS FOR BOARDING &c. :-

Pupils under 10 years of age £16 per annum

Above 10 and under 18 £20

Above 18 £26

These terms include Washing, Use of Books, Charges for Stationery, and Instruction in the following branches:-

Writing, English Grammar, Composition, Book-keeping, Mensuration, Algebra, Trigonometry, Euclid, Use of Globes, Mapping, Drawing, Natural Philosophy, & c.

A Quarter's notice is required before the removal of a Pupil. Greek, Latin, Spanish, French, and Italian, each £2 per annum. Steam-packets leave Bristol for Hayle every Tuesday, Thursday, and Friday.

Dated, June 24th 1853.

I imagine the Dupen boys as a boisterous bunch, full of energy and curiosity, always getting into scrapes. The quay was no doubt where they spent most of their time when they were not at school, watching the ships arriving and leaving, helping to carry boxes and bundles that gave them an excuse to go on board and explore the mysteries of the hold. They and their friends must have spent many hours in summer jumping off the dock into the harbour, ducking and splashing each other. Sometimes perhaps a friendly sailor would show them how to tie a hitch, or demonstrate the proper way wield a marlinspike. They would scramble into the rigging like a tribe of annoying monkeys or shin up the mast as far as the crow's nest – until they were shooed down by an irate master or mate. It was almost inevitable that lads from Hayle would choose to be sailors.

In 1854 the oldest of the Dupen brothers, Sharrock, left the *Cornwall* and struck out on his own, departing from London on a sailing vessel called the *Adelaide*. At least, his relieved parents must have thought, he has not gone to fight. The general air of optimism was badly dented that spring when Britain went to war in Europe for the first time since her victory over Napoleon at Waterloo. The Turks had been fighting the Russians for six months in a dispute over, ostensibly, who was in charge of protecting the Christian subjects of the Ottoman Empire and their sites in the Holy Land – Catholic France or Orthodox Russia. Britain and France, anxious about what they saw as Russian expansionism, sided with Turkey and on 28th March declared war on the Tsar. The battles are remembered now in street names across both countries – Place de l'Alma, Rue Inkerman, and numerous terraces called Sebastopol. But rather than a series of glorious victories the Crimean War was in reality a sorry tale of bungling ineptitude. The troops were poorly equipped, sanitary conditions were appalling, and cholera and dysentery rife.

A joint force landed north of Sevastopol on the Black Sea in September 1854, and after defeating the Russians at the Battle of Alma, set out to take the city. The next major battle, Balaklava, which has gone down in history because of the gallant but catastrophic Charge of the Light Brigade, did little to advance the campaign. In November the British were victorious at Inkerman, where a certain General John Lysaght Pennefather made his name. The Crimean War was the first to be recorded in photographs and a contemporary portrait shows the moustachioed general seated outside a tent surrounded by his staff, his long legs in their striped uniform trousers crossed as elegantly as if he were in a polite drawing room rather than a landscape ravaged by war. Twenty-year-old Sharrock Dupen may have heard the name but he was not to know that his future was linked to that of the Pennefathers:

it was another five years before he met and married the
general's niece.

The siege of Sevastopol continued through a freezing
winter that led to thousands of deaths from exposure and
near-starvation, until in September 1855 the Russians finally
evacuated the city. Six months later peace talks concluded
with a treaty that established the Black Sea as a neutral zone
and protected Turkey from further Russian interference.
While the Freemasons of Bristol gathered to celebrate the fact
that 'The people of all countries could now cross the Black
Sea without the defiance of Russian war vessels', the
newspaper reaction was on the whole more cynical. *Trewman's
Exeter Flying Post* reprinted in full a broadside from the *Sun*: 'A
war, of two years and two days, bright with promise, has
ended in disaster disappointment, and shame. [...] the sad end
is just like the traitorous beginning, with this proviso, that we
have lost all and gained nothing.'

The label 'Crimean' ignores the fact that it was also a
Baltic war, with significant battles along Russia's coastline in
the Gulf of Finland, where the shortcomings of the British
fleet soon became apparent. The great sailing ships of the line
were ineffectual in the shallow creeks and inlets of the Baltic,
a vital source of timber, pitch and cordage that must not be
allowed to fall into the hands of the Russians. What was
needed was a completely new design of ship: short and tubby,
flat-bottomed and steam-powered, the gunboat was born out
of necessity. The intention was that gunboats should rely on
their engines rather than using them as auxiliary power, but
there was no room to carry enough coal for a voyage of any
great length, so they had a hinged funnel that could be
lowered out of the way of the sails and a screw that could be
lifted. 'Down funnel and up screw,' went the command. They
struggled on long ocean voyages, skittering, so it was said, like
tea trays over the surface of the waves, but came into their
own in the Baltic, as well as the Black Sea. They operated off
the shore of the Crimea and in the Sea of Azov around the

mouth of the Don, where they attacked the Russian supply routes, destroying crops of wheat, boats, and fisheries. Such was their success that by 1856 when the war ended, the navy had well over a hundred of them, just three years after the launch of the first one. Nearly twenty years later they were still in use when, as a young naval engineer, John Dupen was posted to the China station.

8 Cutting for Stone

Shortly after the end of the war, a small item in the newspaper provided me with another domestic story about the Dupens, one that brought home the reality of illness for Victorian families:

Royal Cornwall Gazette 31ˢᵗ October 1856
HAYLE.—On Thursday last week, the operation of cutting for stone in the bladder was performed by James Mudge, Esq., on a child just past his seventh year, son of Mr. S. S. Dupen, of this place. The operation was completed in ten minutes, the stone weighing upwards of four drams.

The seven-year-old child was Sam Dupen. When another Sam, Samuel Pepys, was operated on, he had a special case made to display his stone, which was said to be the size of a tennis ball. There is no record of Sam Dupen's stone and I don't know if he kept it, along with a boy's collection of shells, feathers, and other curiosities, to show off to his brothers. It was certainly not one of the heirlooms that I inherited.

The age-old process of lithotomy has been practised since the time of the ancient Greeks, when wandering cutters travelled from place to place performing the operation. Hippocrates knew that it required specialist skills, writing in one translation of his Hippocratic oath: 'I will not cut for stone, even for patients in whom the disease is manifest; I will leave this operation to be performed by practitioners, specialists in this art'. Bladder stones virtually disappeared in Europe in the course of the nineteenth century, possibly as a result of the new railway networks that made milk widely available to all – stones have been linked to calcium deficiency. Now they occur most frequently in children in poor rural communities of Africa and Asia, where the diet is restricted to a single cereal and no dairy products. Boys, for

anatomical reasons, are more likely to develop them than
girls.

James Mudge, who performed Sam Dupen's operation,
was a surgeon apothecary. There were many thousands of
these, who were gradually morphing into what we would
recognise as general practitioners. The Apothecaries Act of
1815 had made the licensing of dispensing practitioners the
responsibility of the Society of Apothecaries and a three-year
apprenticeship was mandatory. Candidates generally followed
the tradition of 'going up for College and Hall', presenting
themselves for examination by the Royal College of Surgeons
at the same time. This required a period of study at an
approved hospital, where students studied anatomy by
dissecting corpses – no longer, thankfully, supplied from
graveyards by the infamous 'resurrection men'. Mudge would
have followed this dual route. There were other medical
practitioners in the town, including Dr Millett, who was a
member of the elite caste of physicians. As a graduate of the
prestigious King's College, Aberdeen, and brother of a landed
proprietor, Dr Millett was solidly entrenched in the middle
class, while Mr Mudge worked with his hands and was not
considered a gentleman. But in this instance he was probably
better qualified.

The operation performed by Mr Mudge was a lateral
lithotomy, popularised in the eighteenth century. It was the
preferred method well into Victorian times, with a mortality
rate of under 10%. (A definite improvement on the much
earlier practice of a certain Dominican friar, said to be the
sleepy Frère Jacques of the nursery rhyme, who operated on
5,000 patients, gradually improving his survival rate after
losing seven in a single day.) Pepys would have undergone a
more invasive procedure in 1658, and without anaesthetic.
You can see images of the instruments used on the website of
the Royal Museums in Greenwich but I don't recommend
them to the squeamish. According to Pepys's biographer,
Claire Tomalin, he would have been prepared for the

operation with a special diet and a series of warm baths, then on the day of the procedure he would have been trussed with linen strips to hold his limbs in place, as well as being held down by four strong men. Afterwards, the usual practice was simply to dress the wound with a plaster of egg yolk, rose vinegar and oil rather than stitching. If the patient survived the shock of the operation there was always the danger of sepsis; Pepys was fortunate not to develop an infection, perhaps because he was the first case of the day and at less risk of bacteria carried from patient to patient on the unwashed hands of the surgeon. Chloroform and ether were both available from the late 1840s, when pain-free surgery was welcomed as a miracle by a generation who had experienced the everyday agony of tooth-drawing, bone-setting, or even, like novelist Fanny Burney, mastectomy. But the use of anaesthetic was itself not without risk. It was implicated in a number of deaths and calculating the correct dose for a child was something of a gamble. If Sam was deemed too young to be safely anaesthetised he may simply have been sedated with a tincture of opium. In either case the surgeon would have had to act fast.

Becoming a parent makes you vulnerable in a way that is well-nigh impossible to imagine until it happens. The fears of Victorian mothers were more frequent and well-grounded than ours, and despite the faith that sustained women like Johanna Dupen, she must have found it hard to reconcile herself to the possible loss of a beloved child. It would have been easier for me *not* to imagine this episode in too much detail (and I have to say that the procedure also reminds me rather too vividly of the cutting and stitching of childbirth), but I felt that I owed it to the spirit of Johanna to convey something of the courage and self-discipline required for her to hold her child still under the surgeon's knife.

Penpol Terrace, Hayle, 26th October 1856

Seven-year-old Sam has never been robust and for the past
few weeks he has been in pain, clutching his abdomen and
weeping uncontrollably when he tries to urinate. Sometimes
at night he wets the bed that he shares with Ernest, much to
his younger brother's disgust. The urine is dark in colour and
stained with blood. His mother doses him with Godfrey's
Cordial, which calms him for a while, but she is frightened.
The memory of baby Charles is a constant reminder of the
fragile thread that binds her children to this world. Sam is
refusing to eat and grows thin and pale, his skin translucent
over his blue veins. She knows that there is a way to end his
agony, but he may not survive the procedure. Her husband
says they have no choice; without intervention their son may
die of the pain. On the day Sharrock finally sets out to seek
help, Johanna steels herself for the inevitable decision and
prays for the strength to see it through.

Mr Mudge, a medical practitioner with an impressive set
of letters after his name, lives in a fine villa in Foundry.

'He is quite a young man,' Sharrock tells his wife when he
returns home, 'recently married and with a baby daughter of
his own, so he understands the anxieties of a parent. But he
has an air of confidence about him that cannot fail to
impress.'

'An air is all very well,' says Johanna grimly. 'But is it
justified? That's what I want to know.'

Sharrock patiently recites once more all the reasons they
have to trust Mr Mudge. Dr Millett has recommended his
colleague, who studied at St Bartholomew's hospital in
London and is well-versed in all the latest surgical
techniques.

'He says that if he operates Sam has a good chance of a
complete recovery,' concludes Sharrock. Johanna bites her
lip and falls silent.

On the morning of Thursday 26th October Mr Mudge
arrives at the Dupen house with his apprentice, who is

introduced as Mr Wolf, and his bag of instruments. Annie's pupils have been told to stay away – they don't want anyone outside the family in the house – but she is keeping her sisters and Ernest busy with lessons in the parlour, while Kate has gone to work and John has been sent off to the academy as usual. It is a grey autumn day; in the kitchen the oil lamps on the dresser have been lit to brighten the room but the surgeon calls for extra candles. It is important that he can see exactly what he is doing. Sam's father carries his son downstairs in his nightgown and lays him on the sheet that covers the big wooden table. He has been given two large glasses of water to drink to make sure his bladder is full before the operation. Wide-eyed with fright, he clutches at his mother's hand and struggles to sit up as she smooths back the hair from his clammy forehead. Mr Mudge smiles kindly at him and tells him that his pain will soon be over. He takes out a sponge and a glass bottle. Silhouetted on the wall a dark shadow flickers, the Sandman on his way to put a child to sleep.

'I will anaesthetise the lad with chloroform,' the surgeon tells Johanna, 'just like the queen when she gave birth to Prince Leopold. It is perfectly safe.'

Johanna grips her son's wrist. She can feel his bones under the skin, light as a sparrow. Is this the day that he will fly away from her? She starts to pray:

God of Love incline thine ear
Hear a cry of grief and fear
Hear an anxious parent's cry

Charles Wesley lost five of his own children; he knew what it was to fear for the life of a beloved son.

Mr Mudge holds the sponge to Sam's face and his eyes start to close. Johanna can smell the sickly sweetness. The surgeon raises the hem of the white cotton gown and draws the bony little knees up towards the chest. He instructs the child's mother and father to hold him firmly, one on each side. It is essential that he should remain as still as possible. Mr Wolf holds a narrow, grooved stick against Sam's body to open up the space between the tiny genitals and the anus. Mr Mudge adjusts the candles, then with his left hand he pulls the skin tight and with his right uses a slender silver blade to make a horizontal cut into the bladder. Urine seeps out onto the sheet. Joanna mutters the same few lines of Wesley's prayer over and over as the surgeon inserts a narrow pair of metal forceps into Sam's bladder, removes a tiny stone and drops it into a bowl on the table. He dresses the wound, Sam's legs are lowered to the table, and his small body is covered with the nightgown again.

The whole procedure has lasted just ten minutes, although to the anxious mother it felt much longer. Mr Mudge takes out his apothecary's scales and weighs the stone.

'More than a quarter of an ounce,' he declares. 'No wonder the child was suffering.'

He packs away his instruments and says,

'For the next week you must keep him in bed, watch for any sign of fever and check the dressing regularly. Encourage him to take a little gruel or broth. He needs to build up his strength.'

'Surely he will have pain from the wound?' asks Johanna.

'If it troubles him you can let him have a few drops of the laudanum mixture that I will leave with you. I will return tomorrow to check on my patient.'

Sam starts to stir. He is confused and says that his head aches. Mr Mudge is reassuring. Chloroform can have that effect but it will soon pass. He must be a good boy and lie quietly so as not to disturb the dressing.

Sharrock carries his son back upstairs and settles him in the truckle bed in his parents' room. Johanna sits down and takes out her testament. She reads a few verses aloud and Sam's dismal wailing dies away, quieted by the sound of his mother's voice. Although the operation appears to have been successful it will be some weeks before they know if he will make a complete recovery. On Sunday she will ask the minister to pray for him.

9 Starting at the Foundry

The newspaper article concluded with the news that the child was doing well, with every prospect of a perfect recovery, but I have a suspicion that Sam remained too delicate to join his older brothers at school. His name certainly never appears in the newspaper as a prize winner, unlike those of George and John. John Wesley Dupen lived up to the promise of his name; he was a studious boy, and to judge by his prize for scripture, a devout one. He was also the first in the family to study engineering, leaving school at the age of fourteen to enter Harvey's foundry. It was the start of a tradition that would be followed by his youngest brother, his oldest son, his nephew Harold, and my father, who was Harold's son – all, I imagine, meticulous men who enjoyed the craft of construction, taking accurate measurements, fitting components together, recycling materials to create new solutions to tricky problems.

Sometimes our family possessions, particularly much-loved toys, survive only in memory. The model ships *Jenny* and *Snowdrop* that were part of my childhood are now long gone. I am fairly sure *Jenny* (or was it *Snowdrop*?) was painted green and cream and her sister ship black and white. My grandfather built them for his sons – and named them after the family's two chickens. Boats and hens alike featured in the bedtime stories my father told in answer to the plea, 'Daddy, tell me about when you were a little boy.' I consult my brother, who tells me that one model was steam-powered by means of an ingenious contraption that burned methylated spirit and the other had an electric battery, but he cannot remember which was which. By the time we knew them, they were rarely sailed and could not be relied upon to perform to order. Later still, they were banished to the attic and must have been disposed of when my parents moved house for the final time, retiring to the mild climate of south Devon, where my father set up a workshop in the garage and took brisk walks along the seafront. Although he had never been a sailor, he was drawn to the water in a way that mystified my mother, who was miserably prone to seasickness on the smoothest channel crossing.

The model ships are a reminder of how the power of steam transformed the experience of going to sea. Only two years separated John from his brother George, who was to choose the old world of clippers and barquentines, but in future the men of the family would have a choice, deck or engine room, two tribes that eyed one another with a mixture of respect and suspicion. Sharrock Dupen's decision to pay for an apprenticeship for his third son was a forward-looking one, designed to allow John to take full advantage of the opportunities offered by the new age. The world was coming to depend on steam power for everything from pumping London's water supply to manufacturing kitchen ranges. A young man who understood the workings of an engine had a skill comparable to the ability to write computer code today. He could take his pick of well-paid jobs in the factories, on the railways, or at sea. John's indenture as an 'Apprentice in the Art of an Engine Fitter' would bind him for four years at a wage of a few shillings a week, increasing with each year of experience – not quite enough to pay for his keep but a useful contribution to the family budget. While Harveys undertook 'by the best means that they can [to] teach and instruct', John made a solemn commitment:

> The said Apprentice his Masters faithfully shall serve their secrets keep their lawful commands everywhere gladly do [...] He shall not commit fornication nor contract Matrimony [...] He shall not play at Cards or Dice Tables [...] He shall not haunt Taverns or Playhouses nor absent himself from his said Masters' service day or night unlawfully.

The working day was probably not very different from that described by Nicholas Harvey in 1841, when he gave evidence to the historic commission on the employment of children. Scandalous findings in the coal mines, where tiny children laboured half-naked, operating trap doors and pulling carts in pitch darkness for twelve hours at a time, led to changes in the law over the next ten years. The employment of under-tens was ended and working hours of older boys and girls limited. In contrast, conditions in the foundries of the west of England were judged to be largely acceptable, with little evidence of accidents or ill health. The official hours for all indoor workers were six till six in summer and seven till seven in winter and if overtime was worked, it rarely extended beyond eight or nine o'clock at night and was paid as a quarter day. Harvey assured his interviewer that if boys were required to work through the night, they took those that had not worked during the day. They were allowed half an hour for breakfast and an hour for midday dinner, when most went home to eat, and they had two annual holidays, on Christmas Day and Good Friday. Harveys had an excellent safety record, with only two fatal accidents in twenty years, thanks to the care taken by the foremen and the overseer in charge of inspecting the machinery. Most of the boys had only a Sunday school education, limited to reading and catechism, but the inspector found evidence of an active book club run by the workers. He also noted a tendency for them to spend their wages on showy clothing for themselves and their children, making it worthwhile for London tailors to travel into Cornwall on a regular basis.

All his life John would have watched the smoke rising from the foundry chimneys, heard the loud hammering, and seen the massive engine cylinders being moved to the wharf. Sometimes it took twelve great horses, working in teams of four, heaving obediently as their drivers shouted to them, 'Steady, Daisy! Come on, Captain! Whoa there, Betsy!' Their coats gleamed with sweat as they struggled to shift the

massive load, their clattering hooves striking sparks from the
granite setts. I imagine that if John wanted to see how these
iron monsters were forged, he was even more eager to
understand how steam engines worked. He would have
started his apprenticeship in the deafening clamour of the
casting works, before being promoted to the pattern shop,
where he would study the essentials of draughtsmanship,
drawing and cutting out the wooden designs used for the
moulds. He would then have been taught to work with
wrought iron, heating the metal and hammering it into shape,
turning the lathes that cut the cylinders, until finally he was
judged ready to tackle the delicate process of assembling
engine components. I can't be sure exactly when he started at
the foundry; it was possibly just after he turned fourteen in
1857, but I have chosen 1858, to match the launch date of
not only Brunel's *Great Eastern* but also the new coastal
steamship *Cornubia*. I wanted to capture John's pride and
excitement at becoming even a minor player in the making of
history.

Harvey's Foundry, Hayle, summer 1858

John Dupen has wanted to be an engineer for as long as he
can remember. He has pestered his father to allow him on
board the *Cornwall*, to observe the engines being made ready
for departure and interrogate the engineers until they lose
patience and send him packing. He once tried asking his
brother Sharrock, but Sharrock didn't care.

'Just so long as they get us to Bristol,' he says.

George too thinks he's a fool.

'Steam will never replace wind power,' he declares. 'It's
far too expensive and unreliable.'

George is in Jamaica now. Or up a mast somewhere in
the middle of the Atlantic. John has never had any desire to
swing on a yard sixty feet in the air. He can climb as well as
any Hayle boy but he is more interested in solving puzzles

than in performing acrobatics. Now at last he has been given his chance to learn exactly how engines work.

His heroes are Mr Brunel and Mr Trevithick. Captain Vivian is always willing to entertain the academy boys with tales of the glory days of the past and his friend, known as the Cornish giant. Mr Trevithick, who was brother-in-law to old Mr Harvey, was the first to use strong steam. The model boiler that he boldly tested on his kitchen fire, as if it were no more dangerous than a tea kettle, was made by Mr William West, grandfather of John's schoolmate Nick West. The new engine turned out to be so efficient at draining the mines that the depth of the shafts was doubled. That's what John likes about engines – they have the power to change things. Mr Trevithick invented the steam-driven carriage too. Captain Vivian had the good fortune to drive one of them himself in London, but his favourite story, one that he never tires of repeating, is of the time his cousin Andrew and Mr Trevithick set out up Camborne Hill one Christmas Eve. That, of course, is where the song comes from, the one the boys mustn't let their mothers and sisters hear them singing.

'But the best of it was,' says Captain Vivian with a gruff chuckle, 'that after the engine broke down they went off to the hotel to enjoy a fine dinner of roast goose and completely forgot about it. So it went on merrily boiling away until it blew itself to shivereens. They were lucky no one was killed!'

Then there is Mr Brunel. He built the viaduct that soars 45 feet above the foundry buildings. John remembers the day when the first railway engine steamed across the rattling wooden structure. That was when he was nine, still just a little boy. He didn't really understand how clever it was to build it on stone pillars so that they wouldn't catch fire. Mr Brunel's famous screw steamer *Great Britain* was launched in the same year that John was born and now work is nearing completion on his *Great Eastern*, after her monster hull was finally floated sideways into the Thames in January. Last year his father brought home an old copy of *Household Words*, with an article that John devoured and then repeated endlessly to his brothers and sisters. The little ones were infected with his excitement but his big sisters were unimpressed.

'A leviathan,' said Annie dismissively, 'is sea monster not a ship. Read the Book of Job.'

At last John is about to follow in the footsteps of these two great men. On this bright summer morning he picks up his morning crib of bread and jam, turns aside from his mother's kiss, squares his shoulders and pulls himself up to his full height of just over five feet. He is no longer a child but a working man. He walks proudly beside his father on his way to his first day as a Harveys' apprentice.

When they arrive at the foundry offices Mr Nicholas Harvey himself is there to greet them, shaking hands with John's father and nodding benevolently at John.

'Good to have one of your boys with us, Dupen,' he says. 'Here, lad, you know my nephew, young West, don't you? You do as he bids you and you won't go wrong. Now, Dupen, I wanted a word with you about the Lodge meeting...'

The two men walk away and John is left standing in front of Nick West. He shifts uneasily from foot to foot, aware that he has been singled out by Mr Harvey's attention and unsure how his old schoolmate will react. But West grins at him in a friendly fashion.

'Come on,' he says, 'follow me.'

The two boys make their way into the dark, echoing space of the casting works, where men and boys wheel barrow-loads of coal to feed the fires, work bellows, rake out ash, pack sand around wooden patterns to make moulds, and pour molten iron into the hollow left after the pattern has been removed. The stink of sulphur catches at John's throat and his eyes start to water, but he looks around eagerly. This is where he belongs.

The morning passes in a blur of fetching and carrying. The foreman keeps his apprentices hard at work and John feels the sweat trickling down his face and soaking into his neckerchief. But there is something magical about the sight of glowing liquid being transformed into solid iron. At eight o'clock they stop for half an hour and John takes his breakfast out into the yard with the other apprentices. Hayle is still a small town and he has known many of them all his life. The talk is all of the new steamship that is going to replace the *Cornwall* on the Bristol run. The *Cornubia* is sitting at the Carnsew quay being fitted out with her last furnishings before she goes into service.

'Proper job, her be. Remember when they launched she back in February?' asks John Bawder, a neighbour from Penpol Terrace. 'Must have been five thousand people come along to watch. And they let that little girl cut the rope,' he snorts.

'I know, I was here in the foundry with my pa. Us could see everything,' replies John, trying not to sound as if he is boasting. But he can't resist adding, 'Pa was invited to the dinner, seeing as how he's going to be the steward.'

'Just to think,' says Bawder, 'that her made sixteen miles an hour round to Penzance. How fast do ee reckon her'll be to Bristol?'

'Could do it in twelve or thirteen hours, my pa says,' John replies. 'It'll be on one tide, that's for sure.'

'Don't ee want to go with your pa? Could've got a job on board, I reckon, if ee wanted.'

'Aye,' admits John, 'I could, but I wouldn't want to do what he does. Having sixty passengers fussing around me. "Oh steward, is it going to be very rough? I'm such a martyr to seasickness,"' he squeaks in the tones of a timid lady traveller. Then he continues in his own voice, 'I'd go in the engine room if they'd let me. But she's still a paddler, the *Cornubia*. Screw steamers now, them be the ones to watch.'

'Ee reckon?' asks another boy that John doesn't know. 'Her be a right beauty though. Us could go take a look at she after work.'

John is about to refuse, knowing that he will be expected home. But then he thinks, why not? I'm a working man now. I can please myself.

CENSUS 1861

When the next census was taken in 1861 the house in Penpol Terrace had emptied. Johanna is listed as a widow and head of the household. Annie is a governess, John an engineer, and Sarah, Samuel and Ernest scholars. The other brothers and sisters are missing. There are a thirteen-year-old boarder and a nineteen-year-old visitor, but no servants. Where had everyone gone?

The oldest son, Sharrock, is living in Bristol and has taken as his wife the well-born Julia Pennefather – on the face of it a surprising match. Genealogy is a frustrating occupation. The research is like watching a damaged reel of old film. People and events flicker in and out of focus and the screen goes blank at the start of a particularly interesting scene. I can only speculate about why Julia was married by special licence from her aunt's house in Reading and not from her home in Gloucestershire, and why her uncle by marriage was the only family witness. I find it hard to believe that Sharrock and Julia moved in the same circles. Julia's father was Irish and it seems possible that they met on the steamer from Bristol to Dublin, when Sharrock was serving as the steward. Julia was 33 years old and by the standards of the time firmly on the shelf. The marriage register states only that both were 'of full age', but two years later, when Sharrock as head of the household completed the 1861 census, he gave his wife's age as 28. Julia would not have been the first woman to discreetly postpone her birth by half a dozen years. Sharrock must have calculated the advantages to be had from allying himself to a niece of the hero of Inkerman. Sir John Lysaght Pennefather was credited with winning what became known as 'the soldier's battle' and was now commanding Her Majesty's troops in Malta. He had only one stepdaughter and no sons; it would not have been unreasonable to hope that the distinguished military man might stand godfather to a future child of Julia's. She and her family must surely have known her future husband's occupation and status and yet, on the marriage register, Sharrock mendaciously declared his profession and that of his father as 'Gentleman'.

Kate was the next to marry, shortly after her brother, but she chose a man of her own station in life. A Bristol man and the son of a tailor, Walter Price was in trade. In 1851 when he was twenty, the census records him as a tallow chandler (making and selling the evil-smelling candles that were only just being replaced as the main source of lighting in most homes), and a grocer in 1861. Perhaps he was one of Kate's father's suppliers, or a fellow mason, or both. He may have travelled to Hayle on business and been invited to dine with the family, or it could be that the young couple met at chapel, or in the shop where Kate worked. She would have been a very suitable match for an ambitious tradesman, who would be able to use her skills in his business.

Western Daily News 17th November 1859
At the Wesleyan Foundry Chapel, Hayle, Cornwall, on the 17th inst., by the Rev. Edward Watson, Mr Walter Price, of Thomas Street, Bristol, to Catherine Sharrock, fourth daughter of Mr S. S. Dupen of the Cornubia steamship.

Once Kate had moved away to Bristol with her husband, the house in Penpol Terrace was less full than it had ever been. The family was more secure financially too after John secured his apprenticeship at Harvey's foundry and his three elder sisters had all become teachers. But in September 1860 everything changed. Their father, never particularly agile, started to hobble. I imagine that he complained of a painful foot, fever and a general malaise. His foot and leg would have become red and swollen, until eventually he was obliged to take to his bed and send for the surgeon. The doctor dressed the leg, which must have been covered by then in pus-filled blisters, but Sharrock grew weaker and weaker. Eventually the doctor declared that he would have to operate to cut out the diseased tissue. On 5th September the operation took place at home, as Sam's had done all those years before, but unlike his son, Sharrock Dupen did not survive.

The death certificate tells me that he died after an 'achiropedic' operation, an adjective that does not exist in even the most comprehensive medical dictionary but probably refers, like 'chiropody', to the foot. Erysipelas, on the other hand, which was also confirmed as being present in the foot and leg, was a common cause of death. Known in the Middle Ages as St Anthony's fire, it was a streptococcal infection that would have been almost impossible to treat without antibiotics. It killed the philosopher John Stuart Mill amongst many others. Sometimes it was the result of an injury but in the case of stout, red-faced Sharrock Dupen, it could have been connected with heart disease or diabetes:

> *Bristol Mercury 8th September 1860*
> *Deaths*
> Lately at his residence, Hayle, Mr Sharrock Dupen, 25 years in the service of the Hayle and Bristol Steam Packet Company, deeply deplored by his bereaved and sorrowing family. His end was peace.

Sharrock died intestate, leaving an estate worth less than £200, or around £8,000–£9,000 in today's money. While he had clearly restored his position after the disastrous insolvency of 1849, he had not accumulated enough savings to leave his widow free from financial anxiety. He was buried in Phillack churchyard, high on the hill between the quiet waters of the Copperhouse Pool and the drifting sand dunes that conceal the wild surf of the bay. On 12th December Johanna was granted Letters of Administration that described her late husband as a 'Mariner not in Her Majesty's Service'. Whatever business ventures he launched and social status he acquired along the way, as far as officialdom was concerned Sharrock Dupen ended his working life as he had begun, a simple sailor.

The only image that I possess of my two times great-grandfather is a hand-tinted photographic print. The artist has

added a soft brown colour to his fuzzy receding hair and
made his eyes light hazel. He is seated at ease, leaning slightly
backwards, his roomy coat with wide lapels open over his
waistcoat, which is carefully unbuttoned to show his
gentlemanly white shirt front. His dark silk tie is knotted in a
bow under his upturned shirt collar. This is the style of the
1850s, or the late 1840s. The colourist has given him rosy
cheeks and pink tinted lips and although he is not exactly
smiling his expression seems benevolent. It is hard to judge
his age; he could be anywhere between, say, 45 and 55. He is
clean-shaven and his sideburns are modest. A gold pocket
watch hangs from a chain across his substantial paunch, a
display of comfortable prosperity. I wonder if this is before or
after the unhappy episode in 1849 when he was made an
insolvent debtor.

A photograph is a moment arrested in time, where the
immobility of the sitter conceals as much as it reveals. But as
Sharrock Dupen looks out of his frame at me and I look back
at him, I have the illusion that in this portrait there is still life.
I have endowed the man in the photograph with the same
placid good humour that I have always thought to be
characteristic of Sharrock's grandson, the grandfather I never
knew. Perhaps I just want him to be a man who weathered
both real and metaphorical storms with grace. Twenty-four
years later, a regular traveller was to record his impressions of
the steam packet service in a reminiscence of the old days. It
is a fitting epitaph:

The Cornishman Thursday 7ᵗʰ February 1884
Some mention must be made of Mr Sharrock Dupen, the
steward of the Herald, who followed his officer, Capt. Vivian,
into the Cornwall. He was a rather short, extremely stout man,
but withall very active. He victualled the boats well and the
passengers had always good reason to be satisfied with the
table.

PART 2 THE WORLD

Log-Book

Borne upon the ocean foam
Far from my native land and home

E. V. Dupuis
London.
September 22nd 1873.

10 An Expanding Empire

The *Queen of the Avon*

One by one Sharrock and Johanna's children set out from Hayle to seek their fortunes across the world. I imagine long periods without news, punctuated by an occasional salt-stained letter that arrived at the house in Penpol Terrace to reassure Johanna that one of her sons was still alive, at least at the time of writing. George is a particularly shadowy figure who is missing from the census returns for thirty years, between 1851 and 1881. When he reappears, it is as a planter, with a wife born in India. His is clearly a tale of adventure and transformation, if I can just piece it together.

Searching for evidence of this unexpected connection to Britain's imperial past, I eventually found what I wanted in a pretty, glass-fronted cabinet, hidden behind my grandmother's Crown Derby coffee service: two ornate silver bangles and a pair of brass beakers pitted with the small irregularities of hand-beaten metal. In her will, Annie Dupen left her 'Indian silver bracelet' to one of her nieces. I expect all the sisters had them, gifts from their brother George. The beakers are not mentioned but they also could have been brought home from India. Uneven bands of engraved geometric patterns frame a series of images of Hindu gods, six seated figures on one cup and seven standing or dancing on the other. The only one that I recognise is Ganesha, with his unmistakeable curled trunk that conjures up affectionate memories of Babar the elephant – so the other figures are possibly not deities at all, but his attendants. Although the black outline has started to disappear in places, the design has not been rubbed away by constant handling. I doubt if the cups have been used very often, if at all.

I wonder what Johanna Dupen thought of these heathen objects that her son brought home. Holding one of the beakers in her hand, perhaps she was transported to an alien place of unfamiliar words: bungalows and bazaars, chutney and chintz, kedgeree – and coolies. To write about empire is to confront some unpleasant truths about our ancestors. George and his fellow Victorians employed 'coolie' as a blanket term that covered not only Indian plantation workers but also Chinese dockworkers, Malay pilgrims and pretty much any non-European manual labourers. It denoted an inferior breed of men and women, who could be treated accordingly. If I am to render the reality of my family's past, I will not be able to avoid language and attitudes that today we find offensive. I realise with a jolt that despite the growing affection I feel for my imagined characters, the Dupen siblings, I may have found these people hard to like if I had met them. But it doesn't stop me from wanting to get to know them better.

I began with low expectations of what I could find out. George's sister Hester was only seven years old when he left home and she barely saw him after that; her son, my grandfather, never knew him. Throughout the second half of the nineteenth century the rage for emigration continued unabated. Miners and farmworkers were joined by boys of the lower-middle class, who took up posts as merchants' clerks and government administrators across the east, from Calcutta to Singapore and Hong Kong. Nearly half of all young Cornishmen aged between 15 and 24 left the country, while another third moved to other counties of England. George was just one of countless thousands who left. And yet he was originally, according to my research, not an emigrant but a sailor, who must have expected to return.

Those of us with ancestors in the merchant navy are fortunate that it is one of the best-documented of all occupations. I enjoy the combination of logic and inspired guesswork that you need to solve a cryptic crossword clue. A similar combination of research and serendipity allowed me to follow George around the world. Once I had his certificate as second mate, I had a record of all the ships he served on, his dates of service, and his rank. Knowing the names of the vessels gave me access to the shipping registers, lists of passengers and crew, and newspaper columns full of shipping movements. Whole websites are maintained by enthusiasts who have done much of the necessary transcription of Victorian handwriting. You could spend a lifetime (and some people do) studying the different types of sailing ships and their rigging, the complex systems of trade winds, and the roles of the different crew members. But the joy of research also lies in discovering new writers. I never shared my brother's enthusiasm for C. S. Forester and Patrick O'Brian, but I now I found myself enjoying the works of Richard Dana, a well born Bostonian who went to sea in the 1830s in what sounds like a rather drastic attempt to restore his health. Seventy years later Joseph Conrad, another novelist I struggle with, mourned the passing of the great days of sail in his memoir *The Mirror of the Sea*. I read it alongside the recollections of a former midshipman, a wealthy ship owner, and the wife of a master mariner. I am grateful to all these voyagers for the insight they gave me into their world and can only apologise to their ghosts if, despite their best efforts, I muddle up my barques and barquentines, mainsails, royals, and topgallants.

George's ocean-going world was not very different from the one his father, grandfather, and even great-grandfather would have known as young men. Although Sharrock Dupen had taken advantage of the opportunities opened up by the advent of the steam packet, the vessels built in Harvey's shipyard and others that used the port of Hayle were still wooden sailing ships: sloops and brigs, schooners and brigantines. In the early years of the nineteenth century it was by no means a foregone conclusion that the future of maritime trade lay with iron and steam: coal took up a lot of space that could more profitably be used for cargo. George was a few days short of his fourteenth birthday when he first went to sea in 1855, in a small three-masted barquentine of 150 tons, registered in Bristol and trading to and from Ireland and the Mediterranean. It was not unusual for a lad of that age to be taken on as an apprentice (whose father paid a fee for him to be trained) or simply as a 'boy' (the term for a greenhorn of any age), but the record shows George starting as an Ordinary Seaman. I wonder if he nagged his parents to let him go, or even ran away without their permission in search of adventure. Surely with his record of academic achievement his father had other hopes for him.

The young sailor must from the start have shouldered the full responsibilities of a crew member, tarring, greasing and caulking in the constant battle to control leaks; hauling on the sheets and picking up the words of the shanties the men sang to keep time – 'Cheerly men' for a slow rhythm, 'Hurrah my boys' to go faster – climbing the foremast to furl or release the square sails that lay across the line of the hull. The average crew was made up of hard-drinking, illiterate, quarrelsome men but they prided themselves on their teamwork. They depended on one another to stay safe and no one would make allowances for George's age or his size. His life depended on his ability to keep his balance. At the command 'Lay aloft and furl', the men scampered up into the rigging and hung from the yards, bare feet gripping the wire toe rope while they grappled with the folds of wet canvas. In rough seas they swung high above the deck, up and down with each roll of the ship like overgrown children on a giant seesaw, one that dunked them into the water with every downward arc. George soon learned that he would never, ever, be completely dry, but perhaps took comfort in the old sailor's dictum, 'You can't catch a cold from salt water'.

His mate's certificate shows that he spent a year on the Bristol-registered *Esther* and then there is a gap of twelve months for which he provides no testimonial. But in 1856 he shipped out on the barquentine *Eling* from Bristol to the West Indies, returning with a cargo of sugar and rum. With each

voyage George was travelling further from home. His brother
Sharrock, seven years his senior, was recently back from
Australia, no doubt full of the excitement of the new world.
After a year on the Atlantic run, George, not to be outdone,
signed on for the long passage to the Antipodes. He was not
at home to see his sister Kate married because in November
1859 he was on his way back from New Zealand.

Wellington Independent 16th July 1859
The barque Queen of the Avon, Captain Gilbert, from
London, arrived on Wednesday last after a passage of 110
days. She sailed from Gravesend on the 23rd March, and
experienced rough weather and contrary winds until she
passed Madeira, when she had fine weather and light winds
until rounding the Cape, when she encountered a severe gale,
which carried away her mainsail yard, and she shipped some
heavy seas, which washed away part of the port bulwarks,
poop ladder, hencoops, &c. Shortly after crossing the Line, a
seaman of the name of Painter fell off the foretopsail yard and
was unfortunately drowned, although the lifebuoy was thrown
overboard, a boat lowered, and every exertion made to save
him. The Queen of the Avon brings 131 passengers, 70 being
for Wellington, and the remainder for Nelson. There were four
births and two deaths during the passage. She proceeds to
Nelson as soon as the passengers for here are landed, all her
cargo being for that port.

The Bristol-registered *Queen of the Avon* was a dumpy,
round-hulled sailing barque of 538 tons, with a square stern
and a blunt snout that butted through the waves with the
dogged determination of a terrier. She was around 120 feet
long (which is longer than my back garden but not by much),
and 25 feet wide (which is nearly twice as wide as my narrow
Victorian town house). It is only by using these everyday
comparisons that I can get a true sense of scale. She had three
masts, a square-rigged main mast and foremast, and behind
them the mizzen, which was rigged fore and aft with
triangular lateen sails in line with the hull. Sheathed in the
mixture of copper and zinc known as yellow metal to protect

her wooden hull against the dreaded teredo worm, that termite of the seas, which could rapidly reduce solid planks to lacework and sawdust, she was leaky, fire-prone, and bobbed about like a cork in rough seas. But she was twice the size of George's previous ship and she was to take him safely around the world.

The *Queen of the Avon* was carrying two dozen passengers in the first and second cabins, and in steerage more than a hundred immigrants, under the system of guaranteed payments by friends. As well as her human cargo the barque was transporting tea, coffee, cheese, whisky, cases of saws and other tools, as well as a much-needed supply of books for the colony's public schools. Her captain, Charles Gilbart (this seems to be the spelling he used), was a Hayle man and inclined, no doubt, to look favourably on a youngster from his home port. Back in the 1830s when Gilbart was skippering the small coastal vessel *Amelia* and George's father had first joined the *Herald*, the two had quite possibly drunk together in the Royal Standard. Since then Captain Gilbart had sailed to the west coast of Africa, South America, and Australia; George could have confidence that the master of the *Queen of the Avon* knew what he was about.

The seventeen-year-old sailor would by then have become accustomed to the discipline of the bells, which sounded every half hour as the sand drained from the glass and it was turned once more in the endless sequence of time-keeping essential to safe navigation. He would have learned the routine of a life lived in watches, four hours on and four hours off, punctuated by the two-hour dog watches that allowed the hours worked to shift across the day and everyone to eat an evening meal. A surviving crew list for a voyage to Sydney in 1858 shows a small complement of eight Able Seamen, two Ordinary Seamen, and two apprentices. They would have been divided into two watches of six men each, headed by the first and second mates. The only other specialist crew members listed were a carpenter (essential for

keeping the ship in a good state of repair), a steward to take
care of the passengers, and a cook.

Prayers were confined to Sundays, and then only if the
weather permitted, but George used a 'bible' and a
'prayerbook' every day: they were the nicknames of the blocks
of soft sandstone used to scrub the deck clean each morning
before breakfast, when the whole ship was washed down and
made ready for the day. A sailor's work was constant,
overhauling and replacing the rigging, spinning new rope
from old, as well as making and mending his own shirts and
wide-bottomed trousers. Stitching was not despised as
women's work by men who spent their lives at sea; amongst
their meagre possessions they would always have a hussif, a
neat housewife's roll containing needle, thread, and thimble.
At home, there had generally been a kind sister to mend a
rent in your breeches or a hole in your stockings but now
George had to rely on his own skill to patch and repair his
torn and worn out clothing. At night he slept, exhausted, in a
hammock slung in the dark, damp, fetid space beneath the
forecastle, his sea chest stowed beneath him. The close-
packed conditions were nothing new. He can never have had
a sleeping space of his own; there had always been at least one
of his brothers, sometimes two, fighting for their share of the
bed and bedding. But the smell was unspeakable, of foul
water that swirled in the bilges, the rancid remains of old
cargo, and the inevitable stench of human excrement and
vomit that could never be completely washed away.

If George was tired enough to sleep soundly for the hours
he was off duty, hardly noticing the cockroaches and rats that
scampered beneath and over him, nibbling at the hard skin on
his feet, he would have been permanently hungry. This was
before the Board of Trade regulations of 1869, which laid
down minimum rations for each man. The basic diet was
ship's biscuit, the rock-hard squares of twice-baked bread that
were kept for months if not years, until they were full of
weevils that scurried from the holes when you knocked your

biscuit against the wooden tub that served as a table, or floated to the surface if you dunked it in your tea. Not that you could see what you were eating half the time. The crew's quarters were lit by a single, smoky oil lamp, or sometimes just a piece of rag stuffed into a cork and set afloat in a shallow dish of fat. With the biscuit they had salted beef or pork, which was mostly bone and gristle by the time the officers had had their pick, and watery pea soup three days a week, with boiled rice on Saturday and plum pudding on Sunday. The chickens that were kept on deck to provide eggs and meat were for the passengers not the crew, so when the hen coops were swept overboard in a gale it was no great loss to George and his fellow sailors. To supplement their diet they fished for turtles, sharks, and dolphins, or trailed a baited wooden triangle behind the ship in an attempt to catch one of the great albatrosses that glided by on wings half as wide as the deck.

The *Queen of the Avon* was far too small to carry a condensing engine to make fresh water, so except when they could catch rainwater in a sail, crew and passengers alike relied on the stagnant liquid that was carried in barrels and grew steadily more noxious as the voyage went on. Everyone was supposed to take a regular dose of lime juice to prevent scurvy but supplies were frequently adulterated or insufficient and the disease was still prevalent in the merchant marine long after it had been eradicated from the Royal Navy. Even if George escaped scurvy, he undoubtedly had lice, rotten teeth, and chilblains. Life expectancy for the average sailor was just 45 years.

Their route took them south past Madeira and the Azores, then far out into the Atlantic, passing through the windless doldrums off the coast of South America. If they were lucky they would not have spent too many days becalmed in the stifling airless heat, waiting for a breeze to spin them southwards. To pass the time, a boat was perhaps lowered for the crew to row the passengers around for a while. George may have taken the opportunity to jump into the sea to cool off. Unlike many sailors of his generation, I expect he was a strong swimmer – his brother Ernest wrote in his logbook of how much he enjoyed bathing and I imagine this was true of all the Dupen boys.

The *Queen of the Avon* was sailing the newly established great circle route, following the curvature of the earth. While a pure circle was impossible because it would have taken ships straight into the Antarctic ice, a series of arcs shortened the journey by many days, although it made it infinitely more uncomfortable and dangerous. A Captain Godfrey was the first to test the theory, making a stunningly swift 77 day voyage to Adelaide in 1850, but the route was not adopted as standard until 1857, when miners making a dash for the Australian goldfields clamoured for a faster passage than the leisurely cruise via Rio and Cape Town.

Once over the equator they swooped on ever further south. If Captain Gilbart was a confident navigator, they may have gone as far as the fiftieth parallel and almost to the edge of the pack ice. In those latitudes the waves that broke over the snow-covered deck were at times forty feet high, and the helmsman was lashed to the wheel as, fifty feet above him, the crew clung like black spiders to the frosted white rigging, slipping on the ice-covered yards as they searched with numb feet for a toehold and clutched at the iron jackstay with fingers that burned with cold. Perhaps when passing the remote Kerguelen Islands a shout came from the lookout, 'Iceberg on the port bow', and a great slab of dark Prussian blue, its edges fading away to clear crystal, loomed out of the grey mist ahead of them, rearing higher than the main mast.

Leaving the ice behind them they were buffeted through the Roaring Forties along the south coast of Australia and beyond Tasmania to Wellington on the southern tip of the North Island of New Zealand, and then across the narrow strait to Nelson on the South Island. As they approached their final destination the emigrants must have wondered what kind of place they were coming to, for no houses were visible, just densely forested, uncultivated slopes and in the distance, mountains. But after they nosed their way into the harbour, a collection of modest wooden dwellings with tin roofs appeared, nestling beside the bay and cut off from the rest of the island by a range of low hills. They moored at the new deep water wharf and were welcomed with enthusiasm, since by this time the residents and shopkeepers of this raw, new town on the edge of the known world were getting desperate for the supplies that had been expected daily, especially the tea and tobacco.

On their arrival in Nelson the grateful passengers issued public testimonials to the steward, Mr Hartshorn, who also received a gold ring in thanks for his 'kind, obliging and impartial manner'; to the surgeon, Mr Thorpe, who was praised for his courtesy and gentlemanly deportment and assured that, 'By [his] self-denial and attention the hearts of the sick and the faint have been made to rejoice'; and to the chief officer, Mr John Jones:

Nelson Examiner 6th August 1859
Care, industry and attention have characterized your proceedings throughout the voyage, combined with that devotion to your profession, which commands our admiration and esteem. And we pray that as you have been faithful in things temporal, you may prove faithful to the grace of God which bringeth salvation, so that ultimately you may receive an inheritance incorruptible and undefiled and which fadeth not away.

One of the cabin passengers, a Reverend Shaw, who was surely the author of this text, was welcomed enthusiastically by the Methodist congregation of Nelson, only to be instructed shortly after his arrival to proceed on the mission brig *John Wesley* straight to the Friendly Islands (the present day kingdom of Tonga).

The crew of the *Queen of the Avon* spent some days in the small town, which had for a year been entitled to call itself a city after an Anglican cathedral (the size of a modest parish church) was built and a bishop installed. The ship then departed 'in ballast for Guam', a subterfuge much used by wily ship owners who wished to keep their trading intentions to themselves. She may or may not have sailed north into the islands of the Pacific before making her way back to England, either via the west coast of America and around Cape Horn as she had done in 1858, or possibly, as she was to do the following year, via Ceylon, where there were ample quantities of tea, coffee and spices to collect and carry to London for sale at a solid profit. Whatever the route, I like to think that when George reached home at the end of this, his longest voyage so far, he was no longer a carefree boy but a man, with a man's awareness of his own mortality.

Atlantic Ocean, April 1859

They are just over a month into the voyage and the *Queen of the Avon* is sailing like a stout and determined water fowl through a great sunlit emptiness of green water under a cloudless blue sky. The islands of Cape Verde are long behind them and although they are as close as they will get to the coast of Brazil, no land is in sight. After an initial lengthy confinement below, since Madeira the passengers have been able to sit on deck, reading, sewing, playing cards or chatting, while their children run around and get under the feet of the crew. Even so, they are bored. It has been a long and tedious month and they are barely a third of the way into their journey. But their desire for entertainment is about to be met in a most unexpected fashion. They are approaching the equator and George realises he is in for it now. His shipmates know that he is a polliwog, one of those unfortunates who have never before crossed the line of the equator, and thanks to his older brother he knows exactly what to expect.

He watches as, shortly after four bells in the forenoon, a sail is stretched out on the main deck to create a makeshift

bath and filled with seawater to a depth of some four feet.
Despite the fact that they are in the middle of the ocean, the
call comes from the bow as if they are entering shallow
waters:

'By the mark five, and a half four, by the deep four.'

All hands are piped on deck to shorten sail and the ship's
progress is slowed until she is drifting in a leisurely fashion
with the current. A bearded gentleman suddenly appears
from behind one of the boats, having apparently clambered
up over the side. He is dressed in a long robe and wears a
gilded crown on his shaggy locks. In one hand he carries a
rough wooden pole with pieces of iron lashed to the top to
create the three points of a trident. Beneath this disguise it is
not difficult for George to recognise the ship's steward, a
jovial character who gives every appearance of enjoying
himself tremendously.

'Pipe to grog and bring out the greenhorns,' comes the
shout.

The cabin passengers assemble on the poop deck as King
Neptune climbs up to meet the captain, who receives him
with great ceremony. In a booming voice the royal visitor
makes a grandiloquent speech.

'How does your great Queen Victoria?' he enquires
finally, 'and her illustrious consort and many fine children?'

On being reassured of the good health of the royal family
he picks up a tankard and proposes a toast to the queen, God
bless her. The men on the poop deck raise their mugs of grog
and the toast is echoed by the whole audience, including the
steerage passengers and the crew, who are crowding around
the foot of the ladder to watch the spectacle. Neptune makes
his way down to the main deck, where he takes his seat,
regarding the assembled throng with an air of regal
benevolence. The chief officer, Mr Jones, walks forward
holding an impressive-looking scroll. Next to the 'bath' a
powerfully built sailor called Amos, the acknowledged leader
in the forecastle, is standing by with a foot-long 'razor' made
from an old iron hoop, a tin bucket of suds, and a large

paintbrush, while another sailor dressed in the long black robes of a doctor brandishes a bottle labelled 'PILLS'.

Mr Jones proceeds to read out, one by one, the names of those who are to be initiated.

'Dupen,' he calls and George walks forward. The 'doctor' feels his pulse and jabs him painfully under the nose with his 'smelling salts' – a cork stuck with pins. George then takes his seat in front of the barber, who starts to lather his chin with the greasy, tar-coated brush.

'This will smarten you up for the ladies,' he says. 'Got a girl back home have you? Where do you call home, young feller-me-lad?' he enquires innocently.

George considers keeping mum but fears that it will go harder for him if he refuses to play the game, so he replies,

'Cornwall, sir.'

His words are stifled by the filthy, soapy brush that is stuffed into his mouth. Choking and spluttering, George grins to show no hard feelings and pretends to struggle as two brawny seamen grab him and tip him backwards into the water-filled sail. As he comes up for air he is cheered by his audience and allowed to move away to make room for the next victim. It is Painter, a quiet young man a year or two older than George. Having seen what happened to his shipmate he clamps his mouth firmly shut at the barber's questions. It is not a wise move; a bucket is emptied over his head and the brush forced between his teeth. He is tipped into the bath and George notices a look of terror on his face as the water closes over his head.

Once the crew have been dealt with, Mr Jones calls out to the passengers and a few of the hardier young men come forward to take their turn, while others slip him a coin to be let off. 'What a lark!' chuckles young Mr Hackett, one of the first class travellers, while his sisters squeal in dismay as he is dunked unceremoniously into the makeshift bath. In the heat of the afternoon sun he will soon dry off. That evening an extra ration of grog is dispensed to the crew, they bring out a fiddle, fife and drum, and sing shanties and dance as the passengers look on.

It is only a few days after the jollity of the Crossing the Line ceremony that the first death of the voyage occurs. It is a young child, the daughter of one of the steerage passengers, who had been ailing for some time. George watches with his head bowed respectfully as the body is stitched into a shroud made from an old sail and weighted with lead to ensure it sinks. The child's mother is distraught, cradling the pale face in her hands and kissing it as if she cannot bear to let it go.

'Not even to have a grave, my poor sweet darling. What sin have I committed to be punished thus?'

She is drawn away by Mrs Shaw, who puts her arms around her.

'Don't watch, my dear,' says the minister's wife, as two grave-faced sailors pick up the child and move towards the rail.

'Your cup is indeed full but God's will be done. His ways are not our ways. Remember that His angels will surely welcome your little one into His mansion and she will wait faithfully for you there.'

The mother buries her face in Mrs Shaw's shoulder, weeping hysterically as the Reverend Shaw reads from the burial service.

'We therefore commit her body to the deep, to be turned into corruption, looking for the resurrection of the body when the sea shall give up her dead, and the life of the world to come, through our Lord Jesus Christ.'

George observes the body as it is tipped over the side and sinks rapidly from sight. What was she called? Eliza, was it, or Clara? She must have been just a year or two younger than Hester, but so thin and wasted compared with his bright, lively little sister. He wonders when he will see his family again. It is not that he misses them particularly, but he likes to think of the house in Penpol Terrace carrying on without him, his sisters practising the piano, or sewing as their mother reads from the New Testament, a safe and unchanging

harbour. It is sad, he thinks with vague sympathy, that a
mother has lost her child. At home they rarely speak of the
missing babies: Charles, who he is too young to remember,
and Rhoda, dead before he himself was born. He knows his
mother still prays for them, but it is not something that he has
ever paid much attention to.

The next day George is aloft, sitting on the foreyard with
his back to the foremast, scanning the empty sea for a passing
sail, or the fin of a whale; it is one of his favourite places. He
learned to climb when he was still too young to know fear,
clinging to the rigging of the ships in Hayle harbour. He
would slither back down, pursued by angry shouts from the
mate or boatswain, and skip quickly away to avoid a
thrashing. After years at sea he has developed powerful arm
and shoulder muscles that do much to compensate for the
short stature he has inherited from his father. His hands have
grown horny and cracked. He can hold his own in a fight
and defend himself against insults with language that would
have horrified his older sisters, although he generally finds
ways to sidestep a confrontation. His shipmates mock his
facility with the art of reading and writing, calling him 'the
schoolmaster' on the rare occasions when he can find a quiet
perch on deck and take out his bible or a small volume of
poetry. They eye him with respect, mingled with mild
suspicion, as they sit mending their clothes, knitting, or
smoking their foul-smelling pipes. But the teasing is good-
natured and they are not above asking for his assistance
when they want to write a letter to send by a passing home-
bound ship. George knows that he has proved himself to be a
competent deckhand so he is forgiven the peculiarity of his
education.

Perched high above the waves, moving easily with the
pitch and roll of the ship, smelling the clean salt air, George
reflects that he would be happy to stay up here all day, away
from the noise and hubbub of the deck. He doesn't
understand his brothers. The role of steward has never
interested him; on this voyage he has observed the servile

manner of Mr Hartshorn, at the beck and call of the first class passengers, and wonders how Sharrock can stand it. But then, thinks George scornfully, he is only interested in making money and chasing after girls. He'll get himself in trouble one of these days. And as for John and his beastly engines. George finds it incomprehensible that anyone would prefer the noisy, filthy vibration of a steam ship to the soaring grace of a barque under sail, but there is John, serving out his apprenticeship in the foundry just so that he can go to sea as an engineer when he's older.

A stiff breeze gets up and the order is given to get aloft and furl. He shins neatly up to the foretopsail yard with Painter and third man from his watch, while another team of three do the same on the main mast.

'Watch what you're at,' George calls as, out on the yard, Painter fumbles with the heavy folds of canvas. He will never afterwards be sure but he thinks Painter glances down at the deck just as the sail billows under his hands, and that is when he loses his balance and falls with a terrible cry into the sea.

'Man overboard,' shouts George and his call is echoed from below, 'All hands ahoy! Man overboard!' He watches horror-struck as a lifebuoy is thrown towards the place where Painter fell, but there is no sign of him. Of course, the man can't swim, he realises. George slides at top speed down the mast, careless of the burning sensation as the skin of his palms is torn, and pushes towards the group of men who are preparing to lower one of the ship's boats.

'Let me go after him,' he says, preparing to climb onto the bulwarks and jump.

'Nay lad,' says Amos, 'we don't want to lose you too. You'll do more good coming with us.' So George climbs in as the boat is lowered into the water and takes an oar. They begin to row towards the spot where Painter disappeared but it is already far astern. The task is surely hopeless. George is suddenly aware of the unimaginable depths beneath him. He remembers the child in her shroud and wonders in surprise why he never thought about how long it would take her to reach the floor of the ocean, miles below. Painter's bloated, unweighted body won't sink, though. He will rise to the surface and drift with sightless eyes turned to the sky until the circling sharks turn and devour him.

They row and row until the ship is hidden by the towering waves and their boat starts to ship water.

'That's it lads. Time to turn back,' says Amos. 'Here,' addressing the one man wearing seaboots, 'give us your boots.'

He hands one to George and one to another man and they start to bail. When they finally sight the *Queen of the Avon* again it has been two hours since they set out but George, grimly bailing and rowing, thinking only of the task at hand, is unaware of time passing. A rope ladder is lowered for the men to come on board and the boat is hauled back up on deck. Grave-faced, Captain Gilbart thanks them for their efforts.

'Thank God you are safe, men. We were beginning to fear we had lost you too. Painter's gone. You did your best. His cruise is done. Let us pray for his soul.'

George turns to the Reverend Shaw with a set expression.

'Why, Mr Shaw? Why? If I had been just a couple of feet closer I might have caught him.'

'It is not for us to question the mysteries of the Lord,' replies the minister quietly. 'Painter knew his work and did his duty and now he is with his maker. Remember this, my boy: without God we cannot live, but without God we dare not die.'

He begins to murmur the familiar words of Psalm 107: 'They that go down to the sea in ships, that do business in great waters; These see the works of the Lord, and his wonders in the deep.'

The loss of Painter from their small, tight-knit crew is like the loss of a limb; his absence leaves a painful, phantom ache that George resolutely ignores as he continues to climb and jump with the same confident agility. A few days later when Captain Gilbart auctions off Painter's kit, George watches with a face as impassive as that of old Amos.

The Blackwall Frigates

George missed his sister Kate's wedding but he seems to have been ashore and quite possibly at home in Hayle when his father died. Three months after the funeral, in December 1860, he signed on as an Ordinary Seaman again, but this time on the *Dover Castle*, one of the crack Blackwall frigates that competed for business between London and Australia.

In the seventeenth century the king's ships were built in the Blackwall Yard on the north bank of the Thames and a century later it was where the vessels of the East India Company, the backbone of England's merchant marine, were constructed. A young apprentice called George Green, the son of a Chelsea brewer, by a judicious combination of hard work and marrying his employer's daughter, became a partner in the business. On the death of his father-in-law he went into partnership with a Robert Wigram, but when this arrangement expired in 1843 the yard was divided, with Green taking the east side and Wigram's sons the west. The two companies traded side-by-side, building ships to high standards of comfort and efficiency and with a superb safety record. George Green's son Richard, the owner of the *Dover Castle*, was also a noted philanthropist in Poplar, funding the construction of a sailors' home, schools, a chapel, and almshouses.

Even after the ending of the East India Company's stranglehold on India in 1858, the Blackwall ships still sailed to Indian ports, but the Australian gold rush of the 1850s brought a surge in demand for superior passenger accommodation on the Melbourne route. The two firms of Green and the aptly named Money Wigram were well placed to offer suitable first and second class cabins. They recruited masters who were not only known as some of the best

navigators afloat, with a rare ability to sail by the stars, but
often also keen amateur naturalists, who made observations
and collected specimens that advanced scientific knowledge.
A Blackwall captain was entitled to call himself 'esquire', and
could be paid up to £5,000 a year at a time when it was
possible to live like a gentleman on £150. He ruled as 'master
under God', and under him a typical Blackwaller carried a
crew of sixty or more: four mates, a surgeon, a dozen
midshipmen (trainee officers whose fathers paid £60 for the
privilege of sending their sons to sea), a boatswain (who was
effectively the foreman of the crew), a carpenter, a sail-maker,
a donkeyman to operate the winch, and three quartermasters
to steer the ship. There were two cooks, a butcher, a baker,
and eight or nine stewards to attend to the needs of the cabin
passengers.

With three square-rigged masts, twenty Able Seamen were
required to keep the sails trimmed in immediate response to
every change in the wind. And at the bottom of the heap were
the four Ordinary Seamen, who were responsible for all the
general maintenance while having a chance to quite literally
learn the ropes, and four ship's boys. George had gone from
being a junior but essential member of a small team where
everybody needed to turn their hand to everything, to a lowly
member of a large hierarchy, where tasks and status were
much more sharply delineated, but where at the same time he
had the chance to learn from the very best in the business. He
would return from this voyage equipped with all the necessary
skills in mending sails and rigging, wielding a marlin spike,
and helmsmanship.

The *Dover Castle*, was, at 1,000 tons, twice the size of the
Queen of the Avon, and built for speed, with sleeker, sharper
lines. With her deck guns, painted gun ports, and immense
topsails, she could easily be mistaken for a man of war. Along
with her five sister ships belonging to Greens of Blackwall,
she made the run from London to Melbourne once a year,
transporting cargo and passengers to the colony of Victoria

and bringing back Australian wool and gold. She was officially a 'ship' (the name used for the biggest type of sailing vessel), but was referred to in advertising as a 'splendid A1 clipper', with very superior accommodation and an experienced surgeon. Fares ranged from £65 to £90 in the first cabin, £35 to £40 in the second, £25 in the third, and £19 5s in the open berths of steerage.

The outward voyage seems to have passed without incident. They would have celebrated Christmas soon after their departure, with amateur theatricals or a concert, and then, a month into the voyage, when the crew had worked out the advance on their pay (which they mostly spent as soon as they were given it), it was time to 'bury the dead horse'. On a smart ship with plenty of cabin passengers this was an opportunity for the men to put on a show in the hope of receiving a few generous tips to supplement their drinks kitty.

During the second dog watch, while the older members of the crew sat around smoking and spinning yarns, the younger ones were singing or dancing hornpipes when a sailor appeared on deck straddling a rather lumpy stuffed sack, its mane and tail made of oakum.

'Gee up, old feller,' the jockey cried, but the crudely fashioned horse quickly collapsed onto the deck in a lifeless heap of canvas and straw.

'What's wrong with the old nag, doctor?' the rider asked another sailor.

'You rode him too hard and wore him out,' pronounced the 'doctor', prodding at the sorry carcase lying at his feet. 'Nothing to be done, I'm afraid. Now where's the auctioneer?'

A crewman stepped forward and called for silence.

'What am I bid for this fine horse?' he cried.

The cabin passengers threw coins to the men, who attached a rope to the sack and pulled it the full length of the ship. They hoisted nag and jockey up so that they hung from the yardarm and then, as the rider dropped neatly to the deck,

the dead horse fell into the sea to the sound of loud cheers.
The crew then sang the traditional shanty:

> *They say my horse is dead and gone*
> *And they say so and they hope so*
> *They say my horse is dead and gone*
> *Oh poor old man.*

The crew of the *Dover Castle* undoubtedly also celebrated
Crossing the Line in the usual fashion but this time George
would have been spared a shaving. On a ship with a bigger
crew perhaps he had more time to watch the schools of
porpoises and flying fish that leapt across the bow, and to
wonder at the silvery, phosphorescent glow of the waves at
night as they neared the equator.

At last, after successfully navigating the treacherous waters
of the Australian Bight, they arrived in Hobson's Bay in
March 1861. George's first impression of the wealthy city of
Melbourne, home to half a million people, would have been
of an unprepossessing, flat, muddy swamp, with a haze of
mountains away in the distance, but when a steam tug took
the *Dover Castle* in tow for the nine miles up the Yarra Yarra
river, the landscape changed to one of lush greenery, where
tall greenish-grey eucalyptus shaded ferny undergrowth and
reddish-brown cattle grazed in open fields, while in the
distance rose an imposing skyline the equal of anything in
Europe. It was the height of the gold fever that attacked so
many otherwise reasonable men in the 1850s. The population
of the state of Victoria trebled in just twenty years after gold
was discovered at Ballarat, and on arrival in Australia some
shipping companies had their crews arrested on trumped up
charges to prevent them deserting to go and join the diggers.
After docking in Melbourne, where George experienced for
the first time the Blackwall tradition of discharging cargo to
the tune of a fiddle, he would have been paid his wages of
around £3 or £4 (minus the month's advance received and
spent in London) and been at liberty to visit the city.

In April 1861 the *Dover Castle* was cleared for departure to London, carrying in the first class cabin eight families and their unnamed servants. There were in addition five gentlemen travelling alone, perhaps successful prospectors who could afford to spend the equivalent of a year's earnings on the fare home. One of them may have purchased his cabin furniture at auction the previous month, when the complete fittings of a Gentleman's Cabin from the incoming voyage were sold, comprising, 'a double sofa bed, cushions and pillows, a mahogany table, washstand and furniture, chest drawers, baths, swing lamp, chairs, carpeting, sodawater machine etc.' It was an acknowledged difficulty that rough characters, who were clearly not true gentlemen, could afford the trappings of wealth and expected to sit at the captain's table with their well-born fellow passengers. Diplomatic incidents threatened and were not always averted.

A further 197 anonymous passengers travelled in the second and third cabins, and in the hold were 22,156 ounces of gold, 653 bales of wool, 161 casks of hide, 37 bales of sheepskins, 125 casks of tallow, 61 bales of leather, 1,037 bags of bark, 4 bales of glue pieces, 3,157 bags of copper ore, and 1,119 cakes of copper. The newspaper editor commented admiringly that: 'The strict punctuality with which these vessels are despatched prevents a great deal of inconvenience to passengers, and reflects the greatest credit on all concerned.'

Soon after his arrival back in London, and without even enough time to visit his mother and sisters in Hayle, in July 1861 George transferred to another Blackwall frigate, the *Yorkshire* owned by Money Wigram, to return to Melbourne. Gruesome stories have attached themselves to this fine ship like barnacles. There was the Irish Italian driven mad by pain in his head, who appeared one day on the poop brandishing a knife and a bible. He proceeded to preach a lengthy sermon to the terrified passengers and dance a jig before he was lassoed by the mate and taken safely into custody. Then there

was the sad case of the lady passenger so weakened by
constant seasickness that, on arriving in Hobson's Bay, she
disembarked into the arms of her waiting husband and
expired. Most tragic of all was the tale of a child who was
buried not in the usual weighted canvas shroud but in a
wooden coffin, a flimsy box that was broken open by a shark
and the body devoured under the very eyes of the grieving
mother.

There is nothing to say if George was present at any of
these events but he must surely have witnessed many less
melodramatic but equally sad instances of sickness, madness,
and death. The long voyage has been compared to a
nauseating prison sentence for passengers and crew alike, but
despite the many hardships, it offered adventurous, ambitious
young men the chance to work their way up to the exalted
rank of master, some of them commanding their own ship by
the time they were thirty. After serving the obligatory four
years as an Ordinary Seaman George had qualified as an Able
Seaman, capable of taking a bearing, carrying out all the work
associated with the rigging, and sometimes entrusted with the
helm. I like to think he became one of the fabled topmen,
spending most of his time aloft and ready at a moment's
notice to race up the ratlines to furl the topgallant that hung
above the mainsail.

Like the *Dover Castle*, the *Yorkshire* was advertised as a
'favourite' passenger ship. On 27th November 1861 she
arrived in Melbourne after a swift passage in weather so fine
that, 'not once have the topgallant sails been in for twelve
consecutive hours'. Her cargo ranged from 3,333 railway
chairs (not seating but the cast iron fastenings used to attach
the rails to the sleepers) to butts of wine, cases of butter and
cheese, currants and raisins, tobacco, seeds, boots and shoes,
and a piano. She also brought some three dozen cabin
passengers and a hundred more in steerage. Among the new
arrivals was a Mr George Wells, who was to umpire the first
test match between England and Australia at the Melbourne

ground on New Year's Day 1862, a tour arranged as a substitute for a lecture series by Charles Dickens, who was the organisers' first choice of entertainment. The newspapers reported his arrival:

> Among the passengers by the Yorkshire [...] was Mr George Wells, the well-known English cricketer, who is, we believe, going to take up his residence permanently with us. He is one of the chosen Eleven to play against our Twenty-two. Mr Wells paid a visit to the Melbourne ground, and expressed himself highly satisfied at its appearance and good order.

The whole city came out to enjoy the warm sunshine and festivities. A quarter of the total population went to watch the cricket, marking the start of a national obsession, while others took trips along the river or used the new railway to travel to the seaside, where they strolled along the shore and admired the ships in the bay. The *Yorkshire* rode at anchor dressed with flags of all nations, dwarfed by Brunel's massive iron steamship the *Great Britain*, which lay alongside her. Sharrock Dupen may well have seen Prince Albert launch the *Great Britain* into Bristol's Floating Harbour in 1843, just two years after George was born, and now George himself could admire the famous vessel. She had by this time been converted, for reasons of economy, from her original ground-breaking design as the first screw-driven passenger liner to a four-masted sailing ship that used her engine as back up. The 'Eleven of all England' had travelled out on her as first class passengers from Liverpool, practising their skills by playing deck quoits and Aunt Sally on deck. It is puzzling that Mr Wells was reported as arriving on the *Yorkshire*, but unlike his team mates he was believed to be coming out with the intention of settling in Australia so perhaps he arranged his own passage. Even if George was not given shore leave to attend the match, he may have had an opportunity to play quoits with the illustrious sportsman, whose first act was apparently to present his hosts with a cricket ball 'appropriately inscribed in gold letters'.

After the excitement of the cricket match, the *Yorkshire*
made ready to sail once more for London and prospective
passengers were invited to visit the ship, which was lying
alongside the railway pier at Sandridge, to inspect the
accommodations:

Messrs Money Wigram and SONS (of Blackwall Yard,
London), LINE of PACKETS, comprising the Kent,
Lincolnshire, Yorkshire, Norfolk, Suffolk, Sussex, and other
well-known clipper ships, which have been built expressly for
the Australian passenger trade.
FOR LONDON DIRECT
To Sail with the Strictest Punctuality.
On Saturday, the 11th January,
The celebrated clipper ship
YORKSHIRE, 1200 tons, A1 at Lloyds, E. A. Reynell,
Commander.

The advertisement went on to describe the
accommodation in the saloon as lofty, spacious and well-
ventilated, with the added benefit of a 'milch cow', while in
second and third class the berths were comfortable and the
'dietary scales' most liberal, with a weekly allowance of wine
for those travelling in second class.

They undoubtedly sailed via Cape Horn, for the following
year, with the experience of eight such passages behind him,
Captain Reynell put up a spirited defence of the route in a
letter to the editor of the Melbourne *Argus.* He argued that if
a ship kept within the 48th parallel until near Cape Horn, the
risk of meeting ice was very slight, and, 'Even when ice is
encountered at night, provided the ship is placed under such
canvas as will allow of her being manoeuvred in any way that
may be necessary, and a good look-out kept, there is no
difficulty in avoiding danger.' He went on to point out that
the alternative of returning via the Cape of Good Hope also
meant encountering gale force winds, but they were
westerlies, driving the ship in the wrong direction, so the
storms of Cape Horn were to be preferred to those off

southern Africa. In conclusion he stated, and this is borne out by the records of the time, that there were fewer casualties on the passage to Australia than to India or North America.

The *Eastern Empire*

At the end of April 1862 George Dupen travelled to Bristol to take the examination to qualify as a second mate (a requirement that had been introduced in 1845), and then started the hunt for a suitable berth. This meant leaving the Blackwall frigates, where competition was fierce and most mates were selected from former midshipmen. He had to be satisfied with being taken on as third mate on a government-chartered emigrant ship bound for Sydney. Under Captain George Jury were three mates, a carpenter, a sailmaker, a steward and assistant steward, a cook, a baker and two assistants, nineteen able seamen, two apprentices, four ordinary seamen, and an engineer to run the water-distilling engine. At 1,014 tons the *Eastern Empire* was around the same size as the *Yorkshire* but carried no cabin passengers. Instead, crowded into the steerage accommodation were 35 married men, 41 married women, 157 single men, 81 single women, 33 boys, 26 girls and 14 infants. They were mostly Irish farm labourers, housemaids, dairymaids, washerwomen, and dressmakers. There were a few miners from Durham, Scotland, and Cornwall, a silk weaver from Warwickshire and another from Nottingham, a blacksmith or two, a couple of policemen, and a cluster of Scottish wives coming out to join their husbands. To look after them all a surgeon superintendent was employed, a Dr Newbold, who was assisted by a matron. He was apparently both competent and lucky, since they arrived in Sydney on 29th November 1862 after a passage of 99 days from Plymouth with an unblemished record: no sickness, no deaths, and no births. He would have earned his gratuity, a bounty of up to £1 for each live passenger landed.

The government ships were on the whole better regulated
than those belonging to private companies, where
unscrupulous cabin passengers sold liquor to the men in
steerage and tried to seduce the women. They led the way in
enforcing rules for sanitation and hygiene that were not yet
widespread on shore, and on the whole death rates were no
higher than on land, unless an outbreak of measles, scarlet
fever or whooping cough carried off the infants on board.
Double tiers of bunks on each side of the hull, just over six
feet wide and separated by low wooden partitions, held two
people each, with designated sections for families, single men,
and single women, and hospital bays at each end. (The *Eastern
Empire* was praised for enforcing a proper segregation of
single females from the male passengers and crew.) Long
tables extended down the centre with storage space
underneath. There was no privacy and it was impossible for
the women in particular to wash. Most of the passengers were
quickly prostrated with sea sickness and the conditions below
became quite disgusting. With the hatches sometimes
battened down for days against the Atlantic storms the stench
was overpowering, and it was not just the vomit; many of the
emigrants had no idea how to use a WC even if they had the
strength to stagger as far as the two overflowing privies
allocated to each sex. In the heat of the tropics flies,
cockroaches and other vermin multiplied and many of the
male passengers chose to sleep under the stars, begging to be
hosed down with seawater when the decks were washed in
the morning.

The emigrants were organised into 'messes' of up to a
dozen people, with single women allocated places with
families. Each mess elected a captain, whose job it was in the
morning to fetch the day's allowance of water in the lidded tin
hookpot, and at dinnertime to take the piece of meat or
pudding to the galley to be boiled in the huge communal pot.
For reasons of respectability the job was never given to a
woman, in case she came into unsupervised contact with the

crew. A sailor caught talking to a female passenger could be mast-headed, sent up to stand on the yard for hours in all weathers. As third mate George was probably appointed as purser with responsibility for handing out the food rations. He would have been glad of his berth in the cabin beneath the poop, where for the first time he slept in a bunk not a hammock, as befitted his new status. I imagine that he adapted well to his new responsibilities and gained the respect of the crew for his agility aloft, but he would have watched them with a wary eye, knowing they could turn in a moment over some perceived slight or injustice. He was no longer one of them.

There was little for the emigrants to do except chores, a strictly enforced routine of sweeping, cleaning, washing of dishes, airing of mattresses, and laundry twice a week. (Mothers were advised, somewhat unrealistically, to bring a large stock of cloth nappies to throw overboard after use. The problem of menstrual napkins was not addressed.) They rose at seven and by ten at night they were in their berths with the lamps extinguished. Once they reached warmer waters they could sit on the main deck amidst the clutter and noise of the cookhouse, farmyard, wheelhouse machinery, distilling apparatus, and the long boat. There was always mending to do, reading from the ship's library or journal writing for the literate. The *Eastern Empire* carried a schoolmaster, who would have taught scripture and the three Rs to the children, with an evening class where the younger adults could also learn to read and write.

Most emigrants were travelling under the remittance scheme, meaning that friends or relatives in Australia had paid a deposit and nominated them for the passage. On board was another George, a lad of thirteen who was travelling with his older brother John to join their brother and sister in Goulburn, New South Wales. Young George Fife was the son of a devout Wesleyan farmer from Fermanagh. The family farm of twelve acres was completely inadequate to sustain a total of eighteen children and over a period of five years all five children by William Fife's first marriage departed for Australia. Their father grieved for them deeply and sincerely, writing to Nixon, the oldest boy: 'when I think and think again am I never to see either of yous [*sic*] in this Life this is what wounds my heart'.

Even the thought of being reunited in the afterlife was no consolation. But the family had no other choice, and as soon as Nixon could afford it he paid £10 each towards the fare for his siblings to come out and join him. The youngest boy appears to have been something of a scapegrace, described by his father thus: 'George will be a young traveller wherever it may be his lot to Go. Good sometimes comes out of Evil.' It is a description that reminds me of George Dupen. Although the crew were strictly forbidden to speak to the passengers, surely the children roaming the deck came into contact with the sailors and if they did, the young third mate would perhaps have recognised in the lively, underfed, youngster a kindred spirit. I can't help hoping that my George, as I have come to think of him, took the Fife boy under his wing. My research has convinced me that any life story is full of unexpected connections and coincidences.

Once they reached Sydney, Captain Jury paid for the inmates of the Female Refuge in Sydney to be supplied with roast beef and plum pudding on Christmas Day in return for getting the ship's laundry done. He seems to have been of a benevolent disposition, or perhaps just filled with seasonal cheer. His chief mate, on the other hand, was a pugnacious character who appeared before the Water Court charged with common assault on the young assistant steward, a man more than twenty years his junior. The *Eastern Empire* was possibly not an entirely happy ship. And now the question of the return voyage had to be addressed. Unlike the masters of the Blackwall frigates, Captain Jury could not count on attracting cabin passengers who would pay handsomely to travel back to England. Instead he set about finding new cargo, advertising

the ship as 'capacious and well-ventilated' and well suited for
carrying horses to India or sheep to New Zealand. The
steerage accommodation would need little adjustment to
prepare it for the transport of livestock. When no such
business was forthcoming, he accepted a commission to
collect a less troublesome but surely also less appealing cargo:
in January 1863 the *Eastern Empire* was cleared to depart in
ballast for the island of Ichaboe, off the coast of Namibia, an
important source of guano. Or was that, like Guam, a ruse
designed to conceal their true destination?

It was not until late in my research that, by a roundabout
route originating with a distant cousin in the Blue Mountains
of New South Wales, I acquired the story of how George left
the sea. Vivian Cecil Dupen, grandson of George's brother
Sharrock, was 73 in 1977 when he wrote a set of notes about
the family history, believing it to be his responsibility as the
last of the Cornish Dupens left in England.

```
DUPENS IN INDIA
About 1860 George Semmens, the son of
Sharrock Semmens the elder, sailed as
mate of a windjammer around the Cape on
a voyage to Chittagong. He quarrelled
with his Captain and prosecuted him
when the ship reached Madras.
He won his case and jumped ship,
knowing that his life on board was not
worth much purchase. While stranded in
Madras he met a Tom Stanes, who offered
him a job on the coffee plantations in
the Nelliampatty [sic] hills in Cochin
State.
```

This typescript somehow ended up in Australia and was
sent to me when I had already written most of my account of
George's life. Vivian Cecil lived another twelve years; I could
have heard his reminiscences at first hand. He was living in
Hampshire, a mere hour's drive away, and yet I never knew of

his existence. This is how living history slips from our grasp, unnoticed until it is too late.

I decided that this particular story bore all the hallmarks of a family myth, undoubtedly true in part, but confused in the detail. Ships' masters were of course acknowledged in those days as being 'next after God'. One of them vividly described his power in his autobiography: 'A captain, when he's at sea, he's judge, jury, and everything else; he has the law in his own hands. If a mutiny starts he can shoot every man of them down to save the ship.' His crew might protest that the ship was overladen, or being pushed too hard in heavy seas and strong winds, but there was little they could do about it. The captain's main concern was to satisfy the owners' desire for profit. But the Merchant Shipping acts of 1850 and 1854 made ship's masters rather more accountable for the health and safety of their crew, and by the middle of the nineteenth century it was not unheard of for one of them to be prosecuted back on land. Most recorded cases seem to have been for particularly vicious cases of assault, sometimes resulting in death. The incident described by Vivian Cecil was possibly true, but to my frustration I realised I had little chance of uncovering the full story without the name of either the 'windjammer' or its captain.

I acted on a hunch that George was still serving on the *Eastern Empire*. I knew that she had sailed to Madras in August 1864, after transporting another cargo of 388 emigrants from Plymouth to Melbourne. On that voyage, controversy surrounded the surgeon, a Dr Baker Brown, and the religious instructor, a Mr Lionel Stanton. Dr Brown had laughed at one of the Reverend Stanton's sermons and in return, Stanton charged him with inappropriate behaviour towards the female immigrants. The captain seems to have been unable to resolve the dispute, suggesting some lack of authority. The last that is known of Captain Jury is that he washed up in Port Adelaide in 1871, a shadow of his former self and unfit to take charge of a vessel. He was said to have suffered 'a sunstroke' in

India. He seemed an unlikely candidate for the role of villain. I recalled that his chief officer, on the other hand, had been prosecuted for assault in Sydney.

George was not listed as a member of the crew in 1864 but it seemed worth paying to get hold of a copy of the *Eastern Empire*'s logbook for her previous voyage, the one that ended in London in the January. I sent off a request to have it scanned and emailed to me from Memorial University in Newfoundland, where so many maritime records have been sent for safe-keeping. If I worked in an archive I would like to know why people ask to see apparently random documents, so I included a brief explanation of my interest. Then I settled down to wait. Shortly afterwards a reply popped into my inbox with payment instructions and a note. The logbook, said the archivist laconically, will not disappoint. He was right.

George was recorded as joining the ship in London in May 1862, and being discharged in Madras on 21st September 1863. The columns for grading his conduct and ability were blank. In Sydney on Christmas Day the log read as follows,

> George Dupen 3rd officer asked for liberty and was refused as the ship was laying at single anchor and laying in the roads. At about 12 o'clock he left the ship and went on shore and on his return being asked the reason for leaving when the captain had refused him he said if he could not get liberty he would take it.

It sounds like the behaviour of a rebellious teenager (he was by now 21 years old) but there is nothing to say that he was punished for it. The same spirit of seasonal goodwill that led Captain Jury to provide dinner for the orphan laundresses may have persuaded him to be merciful.

From Sydney, where several of the crew deserted, the *Eastern Empire* proceeded not to Ichaboe but to Calcutta and Mauritius, arriving in Madras in August 1863, which is where an incident unfolded that matched the story inherited by my distant Australian cousin. It was, as I suspected, with the chief officer, a 39-year-old Irishman, that George fell out. In the log (which was customarily kept by the chief officer) the story was recorded as follows:

> August 12th: J. J. B. Travers chief officer ordered George Dupen to return to duty. This he refused. I then ordered him to go and see the captain. He again refused saying my life has been threatened twice and I wish to go on shore. He was again ordered aft for the captain to decide what should be done. He still refused to go aft and on the chief officer pushing him he used the most insulting language. I have got you now I will make you pay dearly for this.

> August 13th: George Dupen 3rd officer went on shore with a constable and returned again to the ship at 3 pm.

> August 14th: At 6 am George Dupen being at duty was ordered to the post to receive cargo and after receiving a few bales of cotton he threw the slings overboard. On the chief officer then remonstrating with him for his negligence and want of attention he turned round in a most impertinent manner and commenced humming a tune beating time to the same with his foot. On this being reported to me I ordered G. Dupen to do no more duty until the case was decided by the magistrate.

This vivid description of a mutinous youth is one that every parent and teacher will recognise but there was surely more to his behaviour than the logbook recorded. The *Eastern Empire* seems to have haemorrhaged crew at every port, including a dozen men who refused duty in Calcutta on Good Friday, even though the ship was loaded and ready to depart. If the assault case brought in Sydney was recorded in the newspaper, perhaps the Madras papers covered what happened there. The British Library India Office catalogue listed just one source for 1863, the *Madras Times*, so fragile that it could only be consulted on microfiche. I set off for London with no great hope of finding anything – a couple of lines at best – and arranged to meet a friend for lunch so that it would not be an entirely wasted journey. But lunchtime came and I was still sitting in front of the microfiche reader scribbling urgently in my notebook. The scene that I found was so full of dramatic potential that I wanted to bring it to life in a way that just reproducing the newspaper report never could. I have simply added a few extra bloodstains and adapted some of the dialogue from the court report to make it less formal (but kept the obsolete term 'commit' as a way of saying compromise oneself, or expose oneself to risk). Here then is George's version of the truth.

Madras, August 1863

It is seven o'clock on a morning that promises to be as hot and humid as the ones that have gone before. The *Eastern Empire* is lying at anchor in the roads off Madras and George is in his berth, turning over the events of the previous day and contemplating his future. He has finally made up his mind to take his chances in this foreign port rather than stay on a vessel where he has been constantly harassed and insulted, but every time he asks the captain for his discharge he has been refused or put off, as he was again yesterday, with a vague promise to consider his request. He knows why. The captain depends on his bookkeeping skills to keep track of the cargo and the stores.

With a sudden bang the door is flung open and Mr Travers looms over him.

'Let's see what you're going to do now,' he jeers.

George pushes past him and makes his way to the galley, where the captain is waiting impatiently as a pot of fresh coffee is brewed on the stove.

'I must ask you once more, sir,' says George, 'to grant me my discharge.'

'Oh, don't bother me now,' the captain replies, turning away.

'Then I respectfully request your permission to take my case to the authorities. Mr Travers has threatened my life twice now and you will not let me remove myself from danger by quitting the ship. I regret, sir, but I can no longer do my work without a guarantee of proper treatment.'

'Insolent puppy. If you refuse to work then you shall have no more rations,' the captain says, and walks off to the back of the galley to inspect the distilling apparatus.

'Right then!' says Travers. 'Aft you go.'

He grabs George's shoulder and gives him a violent push towards the main hatchway. Even as George stumbles to right himself, Travers throws a vicious punch that fells him to the ground. He lies there winded but the chief officer grabs him by the hair and hauls him to his feet.

'You damned little hound,' he growls.

George is yelling in pain and struggling to be free but the Irishman is too strong for him. The second officer and the ship's carpenter are watching aghast but unwilling to intervene. It is no light matter to get on the wrong side of Mr Travers.

'Mr Travers,' calls Captain Jury from the back of the galley, 'mind you do not commit yourself.'

Kicking and squirming, George is pushed towards the capstan.

'I will make you pay for this,' he gasps.

'Pay be damned. I've had my money's worth out of you,' says Travers, pushing him into a side cabin.

The chief officer's hands are round George's throat and he wonders if this is finally the end as he gasps for breath and claws in vain at his attacker. Suddenly Travers releases him and he falls to the floor. The chief officer administers a few savage kicks and hauls him to his feet again.

'Stand here,' he says, pushing him outside the cabin. 'If you move from this spot I swear I will give you a beating you won't forget.'

He strides off but a few minutes later he is back, swishing a rope end in his hand.

'I know damned well that I'll have to pay for this,' he says, a vein pulsing at his temple, 'but just give me a chance and I'll beat you again.'

George remains standing, dizzy with pain, the taste of blood in his mouth, until past eight o'clock, when the captain sends for him to make up the day's books. He has had no breakfast but he knows better than to complain. He quickly enters the figures and tots them up, and then taking a fresh sheet of paper he composes a letter:

> *Ship "Eastern Empire" Thursday*
> *Sir, — I am third officer of this vessel now off duty on account of the abusive and threatening conduct of the Chief Officer. He has twice threatened my life and has this morning brutally assaulted me. The captain has refused to let me come ashore so I write this with the hope that you will be good enough to enquire into this matter. With the assurance that you will give this affair your kind attention*
> *I am Sir*
> *Your obedient servant*
> *GEORGE DUPEN*

He goes to find the captain on the poop deck and requests permission to go ashore.

'No, you had much better go to your duty,' is the brusque reply.

So George finds a man who is leaving the ship that morning and entrusts the letter to him.

'See that it reaches the Magistrate,' he says. 'My very life depends upon it.'

Then he goes to his berth and curls up with his arms around his aching belly.

The next morning he is still in so much pain that all he can do is lie across a chest without moving. He almost succumbs to tears of relief when, that afternoon, a policeman arrives to take him to lay his complaint before the magistrate in person. He had hardly dared hope that his letter would be delivered, let alone attended to. George clambers down into the open *masula* boat crewed by a dozen native rowers in white loin cloths. As they get close to the shore the men ship their oars, waiting for the next big wave. The boat flies through the surf and grounds on the beach, tipping onto its side as the crew leap out to secure it before it can be washed back out to sea. Bruised and sore, George crawls onto the sand and gets unsteadily to his feet. The policeman escorts him towards the line of fine white buildings that line the promenade.

Mr Campbell, the magistrate, is stern-faced but not unsympathetic.

'You must return to the ship and to your duty,' he says firmly, adding, 'Have no fear, I will send a police boat tomorrow to summon the parties to court.'

True to his word, at noon the next day a summons and subpoena are delivered to the captain, chief officer, and the two witnesses, and a date is set for the hearing of the following Tuesday, 18th August.

It is hot and close in the courtroom, the air stirred but not cooled by the big ceiling fans pulled by the squatting punkah wallah. George is sweating; he has taken care to dress neatly in a clean shirt but he can feel the wet patches spread from under his arms across his back and chest. The big, red-faced Irishman who sits across from him looks even more uncomfortable, dabbing at his neck with his handkerchief. George is sure that if he were to come closer, he would smell whiskey fumes.

James Butters, the ship's carpenter, is the first to take the stand. He testifies that he witnessed the assault but cannot swear that the captain did so, and he is in any case, he declares, 'perfectly satisfied that the captain would not allow any man to be ill-used on board'. The second officer John Lamarquand is the next witness to be called.

'On Thursday morning about seven o'clock or so,' he says, 'I heard the chief officer order the prosecutor out of his berth and immediately afterwards my attention was drawn to an exciting scene on the aft part of the vessel. The chief officer had hold of the prosecutor by the hair and the latter was making a violent effort to get free. I saw no more.'

'But you've heard the chief officer abuse me on many occasions, haven't you?' asks George.

'Yes indeed, I've heard the chief officer abuse you often.'

'Would you say that was every day?' the magistrate enquires.

'Not daily but about two or three times a week. I've heard the defendant call him a damned hound and useless wretch. But I can't say that I ever heard him threaten his life.'

The captain then intervenes to ask a question of his own.

'Mr Lamarquand, have I ever neglected to address any complaints made by members of the ship's company?'

'No sir. To my knowledge you have always attended to complaints made on board.'

The captain is then asked to give his own evidence and states that he knows very little of the case. He did not see the assault committed but hearing the prosecutor cry out he merely told the chief officer not to commit himself. Finally Travers is called and with an air of bravado admits having committed the assault, but under what he claims was very severe provocation.

George watches anxiously while the magistrate considers his verdict. Throughout the proceedings Mr Campbell's face has given little away. He seemed to be a fair man when George first went to speak to him, but his inclination will be to side with authority. There is not long to wait. The charge against the captain is dismissed. No surprise there, thinks George.

'But with regard to the chief officer,' continues the magistrate, 'no circumstances whatever can have justified him in treating the prosecutor in the manner he has done. The defendant is certainly liable to be fined to the utmost

extent. The prosecutor has given his evidence in a very
straightforward manner and his witnesses have borne him out
in the main points. The defendant is ordered to pay a fine of
seventy rupees, out of which fifty rupees are to be given the
prosecutor as compensation.'

He pauses and looks severely at George before adding,
'And also with a view to putting a stop to any further
litigation.'

'Do you wish to return to your vessel?' he enquires.

'I would rather go to jail,' replies George with some heat.

'Then, Captain, you must give this man his discharge.'

On the Indian Hills

That, then, was the truth behind the family myth. The story
had proved more accurate than I ever imagined I could prove.
Travers was a bully and Captain Jury weak and ineffectual.
George had stood his ground and won his case but what was
he to do now? If he went looking for another ship, hoping to
make his way home, he would undoubtedly be rejected
because of his reputation as a trouble maker. Even allowing
for the optimism of youth, it must have been an anxious time
until he met the man called Stanes who, according to Vivian
Cecil Dupen, offered him a job on a coffee plantation.

Before I knew anything of this story, because Dupen is an
unusual name I had tried typing it into Google from time to
time to see what was thrown up. One such idle search
produced an entry from the *Madras Revenue Register* of 1868. It
told of an Agricultural and Industrial exhibition held in the
southern town of Palghaut in November, where George
Dupen of the Varlavchar estate in the Cochin hills had taken
second prize for his coffee. According to other records
available through the Families in British India website, in the
August he had married Jane Tomlinson, oldest daughter of
Mr J. J. Tomlinson of Palghaut, a member of the organising

committee for the show. The 1881 census was starting to make sense.

Armed with this information I searched for anything that had been written on the plantations of southern India. An illustrated book about the early pioneers led me to a memoir published in 1881 entitled *On the Indian Hills*. I kept it unread on my Kindle for the best part of a year, mentally filed as possible background information. When I finally sat down to skim through it, I found it an unexpectedly good read. The author, Edwin Lester Linden Arnold, went on to write Jules Verne style science fiction with jolly schoolboy titles like *Gulliver on Mars*. Volume 1 of his travelogue took me on a voyage out to Ceylon and on to Calicut in South India, then up into the Nelliampathy hills, where just five minutes from the end of the book, young Arnold arrived at 'Polyampara, the oldest coffee estate on these hills, under the management of an energetic Cornishman, Mr Gr D., who has been out here for some fifteen years, and may be considered the founder of the district'. Only those who share my obsession with uncovering forgotten lives will understand why at this point I shrieked. My friends and family were polite but baffled as I attempted to explain the thrill of finding evidence of a real person behind the official records. I had no idea then that I was simply resurrecting a fact that had been common knowledge in the family within my own lifetime.

The first coffee plants had been imported from Mysore to the Western Ghats of southern India, where the jungle-clad mountains, rising to an altitude of 2,500 metres and more, offered an ideal opportunity to open up land for crops. From the Nilgiri district around Ootacamund (familiarly known as Ooty), in what is now Tamil Nadu, south to the Wynaad, and the Nelliampathy Hills of Kerala, European and Indian planters proceeded to chop down trees and slaughter wildlife with indiscriminate enthusiasm, making way for regimented lines of coffee bushes that would eventually generate handsome profits for both individual owners and shareholders back in Britain. By the time George arrived, more than twelve million kilos of coffee were being exported from British India each year, five times the amount recorded in 1856. There was clearly an opportunity for an ambitious man to make money.

Tom Stanes was one of four brothers, sons of a London glass merchant, who founded a dynasty that is still remembered with pride in their adopted country. The first brother to sail for Madras was James, who was so taken with the charms of the Nilgiris that he purchased a coffee estate in Coonoor and set to work to bring it into production. Tragically, he drowned two years later while bathing under a waterfall and was buried in the churchyard at Ooty. He was just 22 years old. The next brother to arrive was William, who took over James's estate and opened up another one, and then in 1855 came Tom, who took on one of William's properties. The final arrival was Robert, who together with Tom started a coffee curing plant, and independently set up one of the first textile mills. The family were non-conformists with a strong commitment to public service, founding schools in both Coimbatore and Coonoor. Robert was eventually knighted for his services, while a photograph of Tom Stanes in later life shows an impressive patriarch with a long white beard, the picture of authority and respectability. (Although in 1877 he was sued for divorce by his wife, an unusual and scandalous course of action just twenty years after the passage of the Matrimonial Causes Act that made such a course of action possible.)

I imagine that the brothers, based in Tamil Nadu, also bought up land in the Nelliampathies. In late 1863, Tom, recently returned from a visit to London, must have been looking for a man who could open up a new plantation for him. It was possibly in a Madras hotel or club that he met George, just a year or two his junior. I imagine them dining together and after a game of billiards, settling themselves on the veranda in long rattan chairs, calling for iced brandy and soda, and lighting their cheroots. Stanes would have listened to George's story of how he challenged the bullying Mr Travers and decided that this was a man who could be trusted to tackle the dangers of the jungle with a similar display of courage and the energetic support of his Christian faith.

Edwin Arnold's book places George at an estate named Polyampara, but the *Madras Revenue Register* has him first at Varlavchar (or Varlavachen – the spelling varies). This was the earliest estate to be carved out from the virgin forest of the Nelliampathies. It also happens to be the only one where the estate records have been preserved in the India Office archives, and so it was that I found myself sitting at a desk in the British Library under the mistrustful eye of the library staff ('no photography, handle with care'), gingerly unfolding a large piece of white tissue paper. The boundaries of the 250 acre estate were marked with careful pink lines and the features labelled: grass hills to the north, Manalora river to the south, bungalow in the centre. I doubt if I will ever know the exact details of the ownership or the deal struck with George, but even by the 1870s there were only a dozen estates in the Nelliampathies and the same cluster of names recur as owners and managers. It was a very small cohort of men who opened up the land, mainly British but a few Indian, and they must all have moved around as they became more experienced and saved up money to purchase additional acreage for themselves.

Like ships' mates, the managers and supervisors worked alongside their labourers in all weathers, returning to the shelter of a tent or basic thatched hut to sleep at night. They felled and burned the trees, laid out a network of tracks, and established plant nurseries where the fragile young seedlings would spend their first year to eighteen months. The area to be planted was marked out into precisely measured rows some six feet apart, pits were dug at least three feet deep and the same across, and refilled with a mixture of topsoil, leaf mould and manure. Then, at the start of the monsoon rains, the young plants were transplanted in light wicker baskets into their final growing positions, where they would require constant weeding and guarding against attacks by the hungry deer known as *sambar*. It was a long wait for the fruit; the new coffee plants took anything from three to five years to reach maturity but once they were producing, the yield could be as much as 450 kilos per acre. Holdings ranged in size from just a handful of acres to several hundred, and new land was constantly being opened up. The planters paid with their health. Alternately burning and shivering with malarial fever they took refuge in Ooty until they regained enough strength to return to work, where there was always a chance that a snake lurking unseen on the path or a panther springing from a tree might bring a premature end to their discomfort. This was another side to Indian life, far removed from the class-ridden pomp and ceremony of the Raj.

When I visited Kerala more than 150 years later, I found a state with a Communist government, high levels of literacy, and a decent standard of healthcare. But many Keralans work overseas, like the Cornish before them, sending much-needed remittances to their families. I spoke to one young man who was on his way to his first job in the Arabian Gulf. He seemed heartbreakingly young, showing me photographs of people he called 'Mummy' and 'Daddy', but he was probably around the same age as George was when he arrived in Madras. I doubt if George packed family photographs in his seaman's chest at that early date, but perhaps his mother embroidered him a pincushion, a good luck mascot to keep with his sewing kit.

Like every other tourist, I enjoyed a cruise in a converted rice barge along tranquil waterways lined with coconut palms, before setting out for the mountain resort of Munnar. The road wound ever upwards past hillsides smothered in glossy, neatly trimmed tea bushes. Today coffee is a much less important crop, grown in smaller quantities alongside cocoa, cardamom and other spices. From the tea plantations our route took us higher still, to the grassy uplands of the Periyar national park, where a rare breed of amber-eyed goats posed smugly for photographs on outcrops of grey stone. It could almost have been the north of England, if it were not for the red roofed bungalows dotted here and there amongst the green folds of the hills and a sign in my hotel room that warned me to keep the window closed against marauding monkeys. George's plantation was to the north of Periyar, but set in a similar landscape. On my visit to the British Library I was allowed to view a folder of watercolour sketches from the 1830s in delicate shades of green and burnt orange. One showed a broad track shaded by tall trees leading to a wide, shallow river. In my mind's eye I saw a bullock cart preparing to cross, carrying an Englishman to his new home.

Although Edwin Arnold started out from the opposite coast, I have relied on his descriptions to visualise George's journey. With much bustle and confusion, his bags, tent, and the precious tin box of coffee seeds would have been handed over to a collection of porters as George himself set out in a *palki*, a rattan-roofed litter, for Madras station, which lay just north of the city walls, close to the beach. The new railway line was pushing further and further west every year and would soon reach Palghaut, the nearest town to the Nelliampathy district, eventually terminating at Beypore on the coast near the port of Calicut. But for now, it had only been completed as far as Coimbatore, where Robert Stanes had established himself.

I imagine a long day of jolting and swaying, punctuated by the occasional sudden stop to clear a slow-moving, supercilious buffalo from the track. George would have descended from the train as night was falling, to be greeted by an agent for the Stanes company. The streets were no doubt still lively with crowds going about their business: scrawny men in loin cloths and women in saris carrying heavy loads on their heads, children and dogs scuffling in the dirt, chickens scratching and squawking, and cows ambling confidently past.

George may have dined with Robert Stanes in his bungalow, before taking gratefully to his bed, the last time he would sleep on a mattress for many months.

The following morning perhaps he was woken by a white-clad servant bearing a steaming cup of spice-scented tea and enjoyed, also for the last time, the luxury of a cool morning tub. He would have made the next part of his journey by *bandy*, a brightly painted wooden box with open sides shaded by bamboo matting. This primitive cart was perched on top of two high wheels and drawn by a pair of white, humped oxen with sharp, curved horns. After his luggage was piled onto the roof and the essential tiffin basket produced from the kitchen, George would have clambered into the cramped interior and settled himself on the bed of straw. His short stature enabled him to sit in comparative comfort whereas Edwin Arnold, a taller man, had his head wedged against the roof. Time passed slowly in a *bandy*, as the bullocks made their leisurely way along narrow lanes lined with banana and fig trees, passing bright green paddy fields surrounded by low mud banks and stands of gently waving bamboo. Even if the driver employed the usual tactic of cursing and twisting their tails, they would not be hurried. Passengers were glad of their placidity, however, when the time came to ford a river and the great beasts ambled calmly through the water, which soon rose to the very floor of the cart.

George must have endured several long days of cramped discomfort, in limbo between his old life and the new one that awaited him, occasionally getting out to walk beside the cart and stretch his stiff legs while he kept a wary eye open for snakes. Eventually he would have arrived in the town of Palghaut. This was the nearest outpost of civilisation to his new home in the jungle, and the closest place of worship. Pictures of St Stephen's church with its square tower show it to have been the equal of St Felicitas back home in Hayle, but Palghaut hardly deserved the designation of town, since there was just a single shop that catered for Europeans. Like

Arnold, George perhaps ordered supplies of tinned food, wine, brandy, and boxes of Peek Freans biscuits to be sent up to the clearing in the jungle that was to be his home.

The final stage of the journey would have been undertaken not by cart, but in a hammock known as a *munchiel*. George was very familiar with hammocks but not ones that moved down the road. Arnold describes how a team of ten wiry, bare-chested, turbaned men hoisted up a long bamboo pole, from which was suspended a length of heavy-weight blue cotton cloth piled with pillows. The passenger clambered in and pulled on the ropes to adjust the awning of leaves that sheltered him from sun and rain alike. It was significantly more comfortable than the *bandy* and afforded better views of the countryside, while the men jogged along at a much greater speed than the dawdling oxen. As they zigzagged up a narrow stony path that wound its way in ever tighter curves into the mountains, the air grew cooler, a damp white mist descended, and the trees, with their tall grey trunks rising hundreds of feet towards the sky, closed in around them. The only creatures to be seen were birds, flocks of vivid green parakeets, squawking black mynah birds, pheasants, and the ever-present kites keening high overhead. Eventually the bearers had to turn back, so that they could reach their village again before nightfall.

I visualise George watching his team gallop off down the mountain carrying the rolled-up hammock and poles, leaving him alone with his native guide and porter, who probably spoke little or no English, on a trail so shrouded in mist that it was hard to see more than a few feet ahead. He would have made his way cautiously over wet, slippery leaves and sharp stones. It wouldn't do to turn an ankle. George may have been used to swarming up rigging without a second thought but there is nowhere to walk on board ship once you have taken a turn around the deck so he had much greater strength in his arms and shoulders than in his legs. It was going to be a long, miserable trek to his final destination. Romantically, I

like to think that it was just as the sun was starting to set that
the clouds lifted sufficiently for George to see a clearing in
the trees ahead: Varlavachen, the place where he hoped to
make his fortune.

At this point I expect that he was still buoyed up by the
excitement of a new adventure. It would have taken some
months for him to become conscious of the enormity of his
decision and for its long-term consequences to sink in. Edwin
Arnold paints a vivid picture of life in a planter's hut and I
have used this to imagine the discomfort and anxiety of a
young man who has started to worry that he may never go
home.

Nelliampathy Hills, 1864

It is an evening like any other when George strikes a brass
gong suspended from a nearby tree to signal the evening
muster. The first six months have passed in a blur. He has
replaced his canvas tent with a small hut, its walls made from
the woven mats known after their place of origin as *palghaut*
and sheaves of long grass for a roof. Word spread that he was
recruiting and soon fifty or more workers arrived, building
themselves rough shacks where they live with their families.
Under his direction the men have felled trees, cleared away
undergrowth and laid out tracks across his land. He has
opened up a nursery area and planted his first batch of
precious seeds, which have begun to germinate. George's
coolies, men, women and children, wrapped in thin shawls
or *cumblies* against the damp chill of the evening, congregate
in front of him. He calls out a long string of names, struggling
with the pronunciation. He has learned enough of the
language to issue commands but he is hardly fluent yet. As
the workers answer, they deposit their tools on the ground,
George checks off their names in his register, and they are
free to go. Once the last man has been dismissed, George
counts off the tools and locks them safely away in the shed
he has had built to serve as a store. Returning to his hut, he

sees several people crouched in front of it. These are the workers who need medicine. Their maladies range from pus-filled leg sores to rashes, fever, and infected wounds. George hands out ointments and bandages and doses of quinine, for which basic remedies the patients seem embarrassingly grateful. George is not used to so much deference. His mother would have something to say on the subject. 'We are all God's creatures,' he hears her voice in his head.

The cook boy produces dinner prepared over the kerosene stove: curry, made from some unidentified meat, washed down with brandy. George thinks he should take his gun out to shoot a few birds again soon, or perhaps he'll try for one of the wild deer. Venison, that would be a welcome treat. He is glad he has turned out with practice to be a good shot. Alone, with no companion but his own thoughts, he finds himself repeating the same arguments that have occupied his mind for months. There has been no word as yet from Penpol Terrace in reply to his letter telling them of his change in circumstances but he hopes the family believe his confident statement that he is safer up in the hills than on the high seas. And it is a financial opportunity not to be missed. With their usual quiet determination, his mother and Annie have carried on with their lives since his father's death, making no complaint and asking for no help, but if his coffee venture does well, he will be able to send a little money to make their lives easier. 'I'm used to hard work,' he thinks, 'and I must put my trust in God.' But he longs for news from home. On board ship, when he contemplated the future of the emigrant families, he was grateful that he was not destined for a life of exile in an alien land. But here he is, facing an even more uncertain future. On board ship he used to crave solitude, but now he would give anything to hear another European voice.

Rain has begun to lash at the roof of the hut and George hears the distinct sound of dripping next to his right ear. He thinks with longing of the swinging hammocks of the Blackwall frigates, or even his cramped berth on the *Eastern*

Empire. Not for the first time, it occurs to him that he is going
to spend years away from the sound and smell of the sea. For
a man accustomed since his earliest days to the constant
accompaniment of breaking waves, it is a sobering thought.
But this chance has been given to him for a reason, even if it
is as yet an obscure one. In the fullness of time God's plan
will be revealed and for now all he can do is set his hand to
the task in front of him without complaint. He is so tired that
it would take a stampeding herd of wild elephants to keep
him awake and, although that has occasionally been known
to happen, the night passes free from disturbance. If rats
scamper over the bed and snakes slither under it, if
mosquitos whine menacingly overhead and spiders spin their
webs under his nose, George remains unaware. The next
thing he knows, it is five in the morning and time to sound
the gong again to rouse the workers.

The cook boy brings him coffee sweetened with sugar
from his rapidly dwindling supply, and then it is time for
morning roll call. George divides up the tasks: tree felling,
weeding, digging, clearing away sticks and stones, all require
the right tools to be collected from the store. George decides
to escort a group of women and children to weed the nursery
of young coffee plants. It is a job requiring the greatest care
and attention and he hopes the women will be gentler than
their menfolk. He has no idea how to deal with these strange,
chattering creatures. He has learned to command men but he
retains a chivalrous impulse to protect females, not chastise
them. And yet they clearly require discipline. Progress is
slow; the smallest children keep darting off into the
undergrowth, pursued by their mothers, while some of the
older women seem to want to stop and pray at particular
trees that must have some significance for them. Once they
reach the nursery, George counts his charges and realises he
has lost at least half a dozen along the way. He feels himself
getting hot and agitated as he turns to search for the missing
members of his flock. He is not afraid of hard work but this
job demands new skills, and not just in agriculture. What

would his sister Annie do? Just remember how she manages her schoolroom and be firm, he thinks.

11 Other People's Children

Those of us who belong to the tribe of readers understand that to know our books is to know us. As a child I spent long hours sitting on the floor behind the sofa exploring the contents of my parents' bookcases, where orange and white Penguins sat alongside classic novels in faded bindings, Virginia Woolf's *Orlando* next to that other story of transformation, Charles Kingsley's *Water Babies*. The results were sometimes unpredictable. After I discovered *Animal Farm* at the age of eleven, the livestock that lived peacefully on my brother's toy farm were sent to war with the plastic dinosaurs we collected from cereal packets. A few years later I dipped into *Lady Chatterley* but it was, deplorably, *Gone with the Wind* that shaped my ideas of romance.

With the tokens that arrived every birthday and Christmas I bought school stories (that are now, bizarrely, collectors' items), historical novels, and classics that sometimes disappointed. *Jane Eyre* kept me enthralled so I moved on to *Villette*, but that turned out to be a mistake. I did not deal well with unhappy endings – see also *The Mill on the Floss* and most of Thomas Hardy. I grew up in a world inhabited by the girls of the Chalet School, Jo March and her sisters, Elizabeth Bennett, and the spirited heroines of Georgette Heyer. All these characters existed in the same amorphous, pre-war period called 'the past' that was often more real than the present – a place where I was not always particularly happy.

I wish I had inherited more clues about the literature that shaped Annie Dupen and her sisters, but apart from a gory *Foxe's Book of Martyrs*, there is virtually nothing that survives from those early years. I will never know if they preferred Charlotte Yonge to Maria Edgeworth, or if they read Jane Austen and Walter Scott aloud in the evenings as they worked. My grandfather Harold is forever defined for me by his collection of the works of H. G. Wells. The small red volumes, *Mr Polly*, *Kipps*, *Tono Bungay* and their companions, went to my brother, but most of the other books that I grew up with are now stacked on the shelves that line every room of my house. I did not keep the crumbling, leather-bound works of Dickens that were too heavy and fragile to read, replacing them with modern paperbacks. The volumes of *Cornhill* magazine went too; I regret that decision now. More recently I have also reluctantly disposed of my father's science titles. I didn't understand them and they were out of date anyway. But a book with stained brown board covers and roughly cut pages coming away from a cracked spine, entitled *Conversations on Chemistry*, survived the cull – out of respect for its great age and the astonished realisation that it was intended for girls.

Printed in 1822 for Longman, Hurst, Rees, Orme, and Brown, of Paternoster Row, the content takes the form of a series of illustrated questions and answers exchanged by the ever-patient Mrs B. and her pupils, studious Emily and irreverent Caroline:

> EMILY
> But if an atom was broken into two, an intermediate combination would be obtained?
> MRS B.
> Yes; but the nature of the atom is incompatible with the idea of any farther division; since the chemical atom is the smallest quantity which chemistry can obtain, and such as no mechanical means can possibly subdivide.
> CAROLINE
> And pray, what is the use of all this doctrine of definite proportions?
> MRS B.
> It is very considerable; for it enables chemists to form tables…

There is no name inside and whoever owned it has not even finished cutting the pages but I am sure that Johanna Woolcock Dupen and her daughters were the only women in my family tree to have had serious schooling at that time. This fragile book has survived to hint at an education that went beyond the traditional needlework and scripture. Johanna's cousin Frederick, the one who gave her a copy of the New Testament to mark her marriage, tells us in his autobiography that he was extremely keen on chemistry. Perhaps he tried to share his enthusiasm for science as well as the word of God by giving her this volume too.

No author is credited on the title page but it was later identified as the work of Mrs Jane Marcet (1769–1858), a half-Swiss Londoner married to an exiled Swiss physician. Mrs Marcet was an early beneficiary of the popular Royal Institution Lectures, most probably Humphrey Davey's series on chemistry that began in 1802. Her husband helped her to gain a better understanding of the concepts and she decided to write her book in order to share what she had learned with other women who did not have the good fortune to be married to a man of science. It went into sixteen editions and sold some 20,000 copies in Britain with many tens of thousands more pirated in America, where it became a set text in seminaries for young ladies. Although it was written for women, it was equally appreciated by men, including the young Michael Faraday and Thomas Jefferson. Mrs Marcet was not a radical, although she became a close friend of the abolitionist writer Harriet Martineau, but her book sheds a new light on girls' education in the nineteenth century.

The girls who had access to *Conversations on Chemistry* would of course have been from the middle classes. Elementary education for five to ten-year-olds was not widely available until 1870 and those working class children who attended school often did so erratically. They were needed at home to mind younger siblings or help in the fields, or they might not have the penny fee that week. When they did go to

school, whether it was a National (Church of England) or
British (Nonconformist) one, they would have found
themselves in a class of seventy to eighty or more, tracing
letters in trays of sand until they were allowed a slate. A single
master kept everyone occupied by using older pupils as
monitors to cascade the lesson to the younger ones. In these
conditions it was often Sunday school that offered the best
opportunity of acquiring basic reading skills. But parents who
could afford to pay had an increasing choice of where to send
their sons and daughters. It is possible that the Dupen sisters
were sent to some sort of girls' seminary; their father may
have considered the expenditure a worthwhile investment.
But it is equally possible, given what I think I know about
Johanna Woolcock, that their mother taught them herself.
The distinction between home schoolroom and school was
deliberately blurred in order to reconcile the ideal of feminine
domesticity with the reality of women's working lives, as this
typical advertisement shows.

> *Bristol Mercury 8ʰ September 1860*
> TO PARENTS AND GUARDIANS
> A first-class PRIVATE EDUCATION may be secured for
> One or Two little Girls in a Family of the highest
> respectability, where unremitting care and attention will be
> paid to the health and happiness, as well as the religious and
> moral training of pupils; they will in every respect be
> qualified to fill good positions in society. Accomplishments
> efficiently taught without the aid of masters and the French
> language spoken during each day. This will be found a
> valuable home to children deprived of maternal care. Terms
> moderate.

The absence of masters may have been intended to
underline the moral character of the school – visiting male
teachers were known to pose a risk to susceptible older pupils
and impressionable young governesses. An emphasis on an
aristocratic fluency in French is common to all such
establishments, although it can hardly have been of much

practical use to the average middle class girl. It was this requirement that led Charlotte Brontë to beg her aunt for the money to travel to the continent for six months. She believed that in order to have any chance of competing in the crowded school marketplace she must improve her command of languages: certainly French and possibly also Italian and German.

By the time of the 1851 census there was an exaggerated perception of a huge pool of surplus women, who were unlikely ever to marry. (In fact 30% of women aged 20-40 were unmarried and of these, 2% or around 25,000 women were working as governesses.) Professional men were delaying marriage or even choosing not to marry at all – they were said to be having far too much fun at their clubs – and more men than women were emigrating to the colonies. By 1861 the number of governesses was recorded as 21,567, with another 6,791 'general teachers'. While the daughters of the gentry and wealthy businessmen could be kept at home, and working class women went into factories or domestic service, there was effectively only one solution for impecunious ladies of the middle class, to 'turn out' as a governess or teacher. The two terms were pretty much interchangeable, serving to distinguish 'lady' teachers from the schoolmistresses who worked in elementary schools. While most were employed in private homes, where they occupied an uneasy place between the servants and the family and were often very lonely, some taught in schools like the one at Roe Head where Charlotte Brontë went as an assistant at the age of nineteen. Such posts were often less financially secure but offered a degree of companionship and independence, as well as basic training for those who joined as pupil teachers.

Governesses often moved between a resident position with a family, a visiting role as a 'daily governess' (like Mary Shelley's half-sister Claire Clairmont), and a post in a private school. The subjects studied were the same and the number of pupils often not very different. While Hayle Academy offered boys instruction in bookkeeping, mensuration, algebra, geometry, trigonometry, Euclid, and Natural Philosophy (science), the curriculum for middle class girls throughout the first half of the nineteenth century resembled that of the Clergy Daughters' school at Cowan Bridge, the Lowood of *Jane Eyre*, with its heavy emphasis on domestic arts. Pupils were instructed in history, geography, use of the globes, grammar, writing and arithmetic, as well as needlework and the 'nicer kinds of household work', such as getting up fine linen and ironing.

The most popular textbook of the day was structured as a series of questions and answers. Its author, Miss Richmal Mangnall, was born in the same year as Jane Marcet but lacked her talent for lively dialogue; she invented no Emily or Caroline to engage the interest of her young readers – although she shares her unusual first name with the creator of that antidote to serious scholarship, Just William. In her *Historical and Miscellaneous Questions*, the schoolmistress took her readers at a steady gallop through history ancient and modern, scripture, mythology, the elements of astronomy, and such useful general knowledge as 'Whence have we the best Olives?' 'What are sponges?' and 'How are candles made?' She ensured that pupils would be able to recognise the features of Gothic architecture and name the symbols of heraldry, and posed such brain-teasers as: 'Which four of our British queens have given the greatest proofs of courage and intrepidity?' (Boadicea; Philippa, wife to Edward III; Margaret of Anjou; and Elizabeth, as I'm sure you already knew.) It was material that would have been familiar to the Brontë sisters. The two oldest girls, Maria and Elizabeth, briefly attended Crofton Old Hall, where Miss Mangnall was headmistress, and Charlotte's copy of the book is preserved in the museum at Haworth. The rote learning of questions and answers was a format well-suited to the model of education where children studied their lessons individually and took turns to come up to the teacher's desk and recite them. This was seen as the only practical method of dealing with a class that contained a range of ages and abilities and it remained common to elementary schools and boys' public schools as well as private seminaries for girls up to the 1860s.

Annie Dupen was listed as a 'school governess' in the 1851 census and a 'governess' in 1861 but I am fairly sure she was working as what we would recognise as a schoolteacher each time. She probably started like Charlotte Brontë as an assistant to a lady running a local private school but by 1856 she was listed in the Post Office Directory as running a seminary of her own in Penpol Terrace. There was another seminary in Hayle Terrace and a girls' boarding school on Foundry Hill, as well as two 'daily' schools, but the market was a volatile one with rapid turnover of establishments. It was all too easy to fail, but with careful management, a school was a business opportunity that could do well. Perhaps, alongside the standard curriculum Annie offered her pupils an introduction to the rudiments of chemistry as set out by Mrs Marcet.

Sharrock Dupen's death in 1860 must have thrown the family into a state of confusion. They would be almost entirely dependent on the income from Annie's school. The two oldest boys were on the other side of the world while Salome, as a teacher of infants, probably earned very little. Ellen was working as a governess in Wiltshire but could ill afford to send money home. Estimates of a resident governess's wage vary from £20 to £35 a year, out of which it has been suggested that she would need to spend £27 to keep herself clothed and pay for such items as toiletries and postage and stationery for her letters home. John was as yet only an apprentice at the foundry and the others too young to go out to work. The loss of the main breadwinner meant their home was at risk, whether it was rented or if by that time Sharrock had purchased it – another question that I have been unable to answer.

I turned once more to fiction to help me imagine the
scene. If George's maritime story is a Conradian one, his
sisters are to be found in the pages of the Brontës and
Elizabeth Gaskell. Anne, the youngest Brontë sister, is the
most down to earth of the three, and despite my early
allegiance to *Jane Eyre*, in later life she has become my
preferred reading. In *Agnes Grey*, the eponymous heroine sits
down with her mother to discuss their future after her father
dies. The strong-minded Mrs Grey refuses to become
dependent on her older, married daughter and declares her
intention of looking for a house, 'commodiously situated in
some populous but healthy district, where we will take a few
young ladies to board and educate'. It was a scene Anne
Brontë may have drawn from life, remembering the time
when she and her sisters thought of taking a small number of
girls to board at the parsonage in Haworth, although their
home town was neither particularly populous nor healthy.
Hayle on the other hand was. Why should the Dupens not
start to take what were known as parlour boarders? In
addition to the shopkeepers, ship's captains, and mine agents
who resided in the town and sent their daughters as day
pupils to the school in Penpol Terrace, there were all the
families living on remote farms who wished their girls to be
educated, while the mild, health-giving sea air of west
Cornwall might attract those from even further afield. They
could start in a small way, reorganising the house to make
space for one or two girls and giving up the luxury of live-in
servants. No significant capital investment would be required
and Annie, at the age of 28 and with at least ten years'
teaching experience, was well known in the town, so they had
that other business essential, goodwill. By the time of the
census in the following spring they already had at least one
boarder, a thirteen-year-old miner's daughter from St Day,
near Gwennap Pit.

Annie's sister Ellen was one of a growing number of
teachers from relatively humble backgrounds who in the

1850s and 1860s found employment in equally modest households. Fifty years earlier these families would never have thought of educating their girls in anything other than domestic skills but now the daughters of farmers and shopkeepers were being sent away to school or taught at home by governesses. Farmers in particular found it easier and cheaper to employ a young woman to take care of their children and perform other domestic duties than to pay boarding school fees for two or three girls. Ellen travelled to Box to take up a position at Cheney Court farm, the home farm attached to the big house. It was rented by a Mr Octavius Player and at 300 acres was just large enough for him to squeeze into the upper end of the middle class. But his position was more precarious than I initially realised. Out of curiosity I traced Mr Player through the rest of the century and found that by 1881 he had moved to Bath and was dealing in hay, but he seems not to have made a success of the business because ten years later he was a sub-postmaster and by the time of his death in 1900 he was the manager of a public house, with only £60 to leave to his widow.

Twenty-one-year-old Ellen was the Players' only servant, apart from one maid of all work, who was only fifteen. There were five small children: three boys, Henry, William and Fitzroy, and two girls, nine-year-old Mary and her sister Alice, aged four. I imagine Ellen was employed to be a nursemaid quite as much as a governess and probably lived as part of the family, helping with all the household chores and working at least twelve hours a day. It would have been a way of life not very different from the one she was used to at home and I imagine that she coped better than gentle Agnes Grey, whose experiences ring horribly true to anyone who, like me, has spent time as an *au pair* to arrogant French teenagers or cocky little Italian boys. If the Player children, like Agnes's pupils the Bloomfields, pulled the legs and wings off sparrows, rolled around on the floor, or spat and bellowed like a bull when crossed, Ellen would surely have known what to do. In the 1861 census, which was taken just before Easter, her thirteen-year-old sister Hester is listed as staying with her, a visit that must have provided a valuable insight into what awaited her when she in turn left home to earn her living.

Hester would have set out from Hayle on the *Cornubia* late one afternoon, in the charge of her sister Salome, who spent the night of the census at the Bristol home of Captain Rosewarne and his wife, former neighbours from Penpol Terrace. I have always imagined Salome as a gentler character than her older sisters, a good person to escort a nervous child on her first trip away from home. I don't suppose Hester ever thought she would travel on the Bristol packet without her father but I'm sure Captain Gill and his stewardess took good care of Sharrock's daughters. Dressed in mourning black, with their belongings packed neatly into covered baskets, they would have stood by the rail as the paddles started to churn, watching Penpol Terrace recede into the distance until it was time to go below. I expect they were impressed by the magnificence of the saloon, which even on a grey day was full of light from the large plate glass windows. Beneath an ornate ceiling of white and gold, the walls were panelled in polished wood with gold mouldings. A dozen mahogany sofas upholstered in red velvet were set along the sides with velvet-covered armchairs scattered around the centre of the room. But it cost an extra ten shillings to travel in such style and the sisters probably made their way through to the less expensive berths in the forecabin.

Arriving at the Cumberland dock the next morning, Hester was perhaps met by her sister Kate, who took her to stay overnight above the grocer's shop she kept with her husband in the working class district of St Mary Redcliffe, behind the wharfs and the tobacco factory. Or it may have been her brother Sharrock who came to collect her. He was living next to the water in a small terraced house beyond the swing bridge. Victoria Place has long been demolished to make way for a busy flyover but there is an addictive website where you can call up layer after layer of old maps. I discovered that his address was one of a row of half a dozen houses on the opposite corner from the big (and probably noisy) Cumberland hotel. How Sharrock's wife Julia adjusted to this environment after living in her grandfather's Gloucestershire manor house, I can only guess. The couple had to take in a pair of lady lodgers to help pay the rent but Julia seems to have insisted on employing a nursemaid for her baby son, named (perhaps with an eye to a future inheritance) after his illustrious uncle, General Sir John Lysaght Pennefather.

From Bristol Hester would have travelled on to Box by train, alighting just before the famous tunnel constructed by Brunel twenty years earlier. There is no longer a station there but the two-mile long tunnel is still a feature of the main line from Bristol to Paddington. The massive archway with its stone balustrade and carved lintel looks quite out of place, as if it belongs in an elegant city like Bath not a country village. According to popular myth, at dawn on Brunel's birthday, 9th April, the sun can be seen to shine through it in a modern Stonehenge effect. To imagine Hester's visit to Ellen, I turned to Anne Brontë, whose vivid descriptions of a governess's life reassured me that small children in Victorian times were the same then as they are now, and just as difficult to manage.

Box, Wiltshire, March 1861

Hester scrambles down onto the platform clutching her basket. There is Ellen waiting for her. She gives her sister a warm hug. It is six months since they last saw each other, when Ellen came home for her father's funeral.

'Tell me,' asks Ellen, 'how is everybody? And what about Sharrock and Julia? Did she look after you well?'

Hester explains about the nursemaid and the lady lodgers and how Julia was really very kind and not a bad cook, considering.

'I felt quite sorry for her,' she says, 'which is strange, isn't it?'

'I'd feel sorry for anyone married to Sharrock,' says Ellen briskly. 'Come along, I'm needed back at the house. Mrs Player can't manage the children on her own. You needn't think you're here for a holiday. There'll be plenty of work for you to do.'

The two sisters walk along a muddy track between green hedgerows for a mile or so until they reach the stone farmhouse where the Players live. Cheney Court farm is a sizeable one, Ellen explains and Mr Player employs eight men and four boys. But there is only one maid so Ellen has a lot to do in the house as well as looking after the children. Hester soon finds herself feeding the chickens and hunting for eggs while her sister helps to prepare the dinner.

The next morning she wakes early in the small truckle bed that has been placed in Ellen's room at the top of the house. In the grey light she lies quietly observing the plain, whitewashed walls, the pine washstand with its chipped white china, and the single hard chair where Ellen has placed her candlestick. It is smaller than the bedroom she shares at home with her sisters, and very bare, but there is something to be said for having a room of one's own. She wonders how it feels to be alone at night. Her thoughts are interrupted by a voice calling from the night nursery next door. Little Fitzroy is awake. Hester slips out of bed and opens the connecting door.

'Shsh,' she says to the sturdy two-year-old, who is staring at her in dismay.

'Where Nellie?' he demands loudly. His brothers Henry and William have also woken up and soon all three boys are chasing each other round the room and jumping on their bed. 'We're pirates,' they shout, waving imaginary cutlasses above their heads. Their sister Mary sits up, rubbing her eyes.

'Oh do make them stop,' she says, just as Ellen comes in and grasps the two older boys firmly by their arms.

'Enough,' she says. 'Now let's get you dressed and you can have a run in the garden before breakfast. Hester, go and get yourself ready and then you can help me with the girls.'

She marches her charges to the washstand, pours water into the basin, and hands Henry a cloth. 'Neck and ears too, remember,' she says, as she turns to pick up their small brother and hold him over the chamberpot.

Hester dabs at her face and armpits with a damp flannel, scrambles into her chemise and petticoats and puts on her black dress, a faded hand-me-down like all her clothes. When she returns to the nursery, Fitzroy is galloping a small wooden horse over the floor and Ellen is helping his brothers with their buttons. Seven-year-old Henry is managing well but William, two years his junior, is struggling.

'Yes I know you want to do it yourself,' says Ellen, 'but we don't want to be late for breakfast, do we?'

Once they are dressed she sends the two older boys downstairs.

'You can go onto the lawn, but no further,' she tells them. 'You won't be allowed in the dining room with muddy boots.'

She moves on to the girls.

'Can you help Mary with her hair while I do Alice?'

Hester rubs pomade through Mary's unruly curls and swiftly plaits them into neat pigtails while Ellen does the same for her younger sister.

'At least we don't have to be ready in time for morning prayers,' she says. 'The Players are Quakers, you know, and they don't believe in public ritual.'

Hester finds this very strange. At home they come together to pray every morning.

'Should I say my own prayers, then?' she asks in confusion.

'If you like,' says her sister. 'I usually leave it until I go to bed at night, when I can be sure of five minutes' peace. Now, can you watch Fitzroy while I dress myself?'

After breakfast, which the family takes together, the children go up to the schoolroom. Mary sits quietly in a corner to learn a poem while Ellen settles Henry and William at the table with a page of sums to complete. They kick their legs, chew the ends of their pens, and gaze into space while Ellen takes Alice onto her lap to spell out the letters in her reading primer. Hester sits down on the floor with Fitzroy and a box of wooden blocks. She helps him build a tower, which he immediately knocks down.

'Again!' he shouts gleefully.

Do you remember,' says Hester, 'when Ernest was a baby and kept interrupting our lessons?'

Lunch is brought up to the schoolroom and in the afternoon Fitzroy is settled for a nap while Ellen and Hester take the other children into the garden. The boys head straight for a muddy stream and start poking around with sticks, looking for fish. William kneels on the bank and stretches down into the water.

'He's going to fall in,' says Hester, alarmed.

'Let him,' says Ellen. 'Then I can take his breeches away to be dried and he'll have to stay in bed for the rest of the afternoon and miss tea with his mother. I am lucky that Mrs Player doesn't interfere with my punishments, otherwise I'd never be able to keep them in order.'

Hester is filled with admiration for her sister. She had no idea that being a governess was so difficult. And it's not just that the children are so demanding. She has seen the piles of mending waiting for their attention in the evening. It's no wonder that the letters Ellen sends home are so short. When does she have any time to herself? It is a woman's lot to be always sewing, she reflects. At home her mother's hands are never idle, and here is Ellen, who is supposed to be employed to educate the children, spending her time turning collars and cuffs, replacing torn ruffles and darning stockings.

But on Easter Sunday Ellen is given a whole free day after breakfast and the sisters attend the service in the Methodist chapel in the village. As they sing the familiar hymns Hester

marvels as always at Ellen's soaring soprano. With a voice
like that, their brother Sharrock once said, she should have
gone on the stage. But he couldn't have meant it seriously –
no respectable woman would dream of performing in a
concert unless it was for charity.

On the way back to the farm Ellen takes her sister to peep
at the big house. Cheney Court is a great square stone
building, four storeys high, with a gabled roof and a wide
terrace looking out onto the extensive grounds. There are
plenty of servants there, Ellen says, not like the farm. But on
the other hand the Players treat her like one of the family; she
is not sure she would like to live separately as she has heard
governesses do in big houses, not allowed in the drawing
room but unwelcome in the servants' hall too. Hester should
think carefully about what sort of position she will look for
when it is her turn to leave home. In any case, Ellen adds,
she will soon have saved enough to start her own school.
Hester could come as her assistant. She is thinking, she says,
of St Ives. Near enough to visit mother but not so close that it
will put Annie's nose out of joint – and Annie's nose, as
Hester is aware, is rather easily put out, particularly by her
energetic and musical sister Ellen.

12 'A most useful class of men'

Guarding the Queen

When Sharrock Dupen died in 1860, his third son John was only part-way through his apprenticeship and unable to contribute much beyond his keep to the family budget. But there would have been no question of him leaving the foundry; it was his passport to a career with better prospects than either of his older brothers. He was perhaps already thinking of the navy and the chance to serve his country in a fleet that was acknowledged to be the greatest in the world. The conflict in the Crimea had been over for four years but by 1861 the editor of the *Royal Cornwall Gazette* was amongst those much exercised by the question of the 'internecine' war that had broken out in America. It was possible that it could spread to the other side of the Atlantic in the fallout from the *Trent* affair. The *Trent,* a British mail packet carrying two Confederate commissioners, was intercepted by a US warship in November and the men seized and imprisoned. The British government, outraged by this violation of the laws of the sea, threatened to recognise the Confederate government and declare war on the North if the men were not released immediately. Prince Albert was the voice of reason in this major diplomatic incident, helping to avert an outbreak of hostilities.

It was with a sense of disbelief, therefore, that the country learned of the sudden death of Prince Consort. In black bordered columns, the newspaper announced:

Royal Cornwall Gazette 20th December 1861
DEATH OF HIS ROYAL HIGHNESS THE PRINCE
CONSORT

> The country has been overwhelmed by the most unexpected death of the Prince Consort, in the prime and full vigour of his life.
>
> He was 42 years old and had been married to the queen for twenty years. In the opinion of the editor the country had experienced no such stunning shock since the death of Princess Charlotte in childbirth in 1817.
>
> The domestic virtues of the deceased Prince, his exemplary conduct as a husband and father, which, with the admirable example of the Queen, made the Royal family a pattern for every household in her dominions, were most certainly the most extensive cause of the popularity which he enjoyed.

Any fear of republicanism in Britain had receded by this date; people had become attached to Victoria and her hardworking consort, with their visible respectability and solid family values. With generous hyperbole, the newspaper editor went on to declare that the queen had 'the prayers and blessings of all her subjects, who love her as probably no Sovereign was ever loved before', and expressed the hope (that we know with hindsight to have been sadly misplaced) that the Prince of Wales would step up to his responsibilities and learn to take his father's place.

The American war was to have desperate consequences for the manufacturing towns of northern England. The blockade of the Southern States by the US navy led to a shortage of imported cotton and by 1862 hundreds of mills lay idle, leaving their workers destitute. Sympathy for the South was particularly strong in Liverpool, the main port for the Lancashire cotton trade. A fleet of fast steamers was built there and on the Clyde to run the blockade via the Bahamas or Bermuda, carrying arms and ammunition to the beleaguered Confederate forces and returning with much-needed supplies of raw cotton. The profits from this illegal and dangerous trade were so great that two return journeys were said to be sufficient to fund the investment in a ship, even if the vessel was subsequently lost – and many were.

Hayle was, if only for the time being, protected from the worst of the depression. Although the Cornish mines were in decline, there was still a market overseas for pumping machinery, and the shipyard had turned to the manufacture of iron ships. At the second Great Exhibition of 1862, Harveys won the prize medal 'For excellence and practical success of engines', for a model of the engine they had made for the East London waterworks. But the packet boat service was finding it increasingly difficult to compete with the expanding network of the Great Western Railway, which had reached Truro in 1859, and the *Cornubia* was sold in November 1861 after just three years on the Bristol run. By 1862 she had arrived in Bermuda and was being used as a blockade runner. A year later she was bought by the Confederate government and by the time she was captured by the Federal navy six months later, she had run in and out of North Carolina 22 times.

Britain was split in its view of the war. There was strong support for the right of the Southern States to self-determination, especially amongst the Tories, but *Uncle Tom's Cabin* had been in circulation for the past ten years and a powerful antipathy towards slavery led many others to support the Union. The editor of the *Royal Cornwall Gazette* knew what to think. The young upstart nation of America had been getting too big for its boots and like the bully in the playground, should be dealt with severely. It was clear that the two sides could never more be brought together as a single nation and the war should be ended now, if necessary by outside forces. In an uncanny echo of the argument that was to be made for intervention in so many later conflicts, the editor declared:

Royal Cornwall Gazette 20th December 1861
This state of things cannot be allowed to continue; and if the Federals should not decide on war with England, it must soon become necessary, in the general interests of humanity, for

those powers who, like France and England, have a right to interfere, to stop these horrors and crimes.

Britain did not, however, declare war on the United States, and a naval officer was more likely to spend his time patrolling the coasts of Africa and China on the lookout for pirates and slavers than find himself in the midst of a pitched sea battle. But John Dupen must still have thought that a naval career offered more opportunity, or perhaps more excitement, than a job in Hayle, because after completing his apprenticeship, in February 1863 he moved to Sheerness in Kent to work as a fitter in the naval steam factory.

At Sheerness the old dockyard had been extended and refitted earlier in the century, but on the outbreak of the Crimean War in 1854 a steam factory was hastily added – a belated response to the navy's need to maintain its growing fleet of steam vessels. Together with the yards in Chatham, Portsmouth, and Keyham (Plymouth Devonport), Sheerness became where future naval engineers were trained, serving their time on land before having the opportunity – if they wished – to go to sea. The normal length of an apprenticeship was five years but for skilled workmen like John, who were, as his service record stated, 'brought up in the private trade', this requirement was waived or reduced. Two years after his arrival in the dockyard, on 5th January 1865, 21-year-old John Dupen qualified as an Assistant Engineer 2nd class. Later that year he was posted to the training frigate *Bristol* in lieu of a chief stoker, a supervisory role that was a common way of inducting a new young engineer into life at sea. Three years later John passed for Assistant Engineer 1st class, with the encouraging assessment: 'A good mechanic & draughtsman and promises to be a valuable officer'.

In May 1868 John was sent to the *Hector*, one of two armoured frigates designed as smaller and cheaper versions of the *Warrior*, that extraordinary battleship built for the Royal Navy eight years earlier. This historic vessel has now been restored and lies like a great, captive whale in the dockyard at

Portsmouth. The *Warrior* was the first British iron-hulled,
armoured ship. Her revolutionary design consisted of a huge,
floating box protected by a two-foot thick armour of teak and
wrought iron. The boilers, engines and guns were housed in
this central citadel and as a further safety measure, a series of
watertight compartments were incorporated for the first time
in a warship. It was a chilly, grey spring day when I visited her
to see for myself what life was like on board, the ghost of
John Dupen hovering at my elbow. Clambering up and down
the steep ladders that connect the four levels, I was struck by
the immense open space of the gun deck where the 700-
strong crew of sailors and marines, stokers and coal trimmers
lived and worked. At night, hammocks would be brought
down from the storage compartments on the upper deck and
strung above and between the rows of tables and benches that
alternated with the gun ports. The seamen's belongings were
stowed in kitbags stuffed into long lines of shelving on the
lower deck; all they could keep with them was a small wooden
box containing essentials like a sewing kit, a few family
photographs, and a small bible. Also on the lower deck were
three baths and a couple of washing tubs with mangles, where
the coal-blackened stokers could attempt to get themselves
and their clothing clean. In contrast the officers had
individual cabins, each with a comfortable single berth, a
writing desk, a washstand and mirror, and even a small
Persian rug on the floor, while the captain and commander
had their own spacious quarters on the half deck at the stern,
with armchairs and a cosy stove. They dined separately at a
table draped in spotless white linen and set with fine china
and crystal.

Engineers occupied an uncomfortable position in this
sharply divided world, not dissimilar to the awkward status of
the governess in a large household. Described by one
correspondent to the *Times* as 'a most useful class of men, but
not gentlemen', their oily overalls had no place in the
wardroom, or even the more relaxed gunroom, where the

young midshipmen were brought up by the rough and ready
methods of the chief gunner. Engineers had their own shared
cabin, pantry and wash place on the lower deck next to the
warrant officers – the carpenter, the paymaster, and the
boatswain – and close to the hatches to the engine room. The
engines themselves were at the very bottom of the ship
alongside the boilers, which were fed by a set of furnaces that
required vast quantities of coal to be shovelled constantly. To
be a stoker you needed even more stamina than a sailor
whose life was spent hauling on ropes and chains, together
with the additional ability to endure extreme heat and noise.
The engineers may not have had to shovel coal, but they too
worked in this dark and smoky environment in temperatures
that reached well over 40 degrees centigrade, breathing in the
black coal dust, developing a system of signs to communicate,
and invariably damaging both their hearing and their lungs.

The squat, blunt-ended *Hector* was 280 feet in length and
56 feet wide. Barque-rigged with three masts, she had six
boilers to drive her single engine and her funnel was semi-
retractable for the occasions when she was under sail. She
carried a total of eighteen guns but John Dupen would not
have seen these in action because when he joined her in 1868
she was part of the reserve fleet. The dozen or so ships that
made up the country's second line of defence were normally
stationed as guard and training vessels at the various home
ports, rather than cruising the oceans of the world. The *Hector*
was about to take up a very special role as Queen Victoria's
guard ship while she summered at her palace of Osborne on
the Isle of Wight.

In her journal Victoria complained of the oppressive heat
as she took breakfast on the terrace and tea under the trees.
She walked and drove out in the cool of the evening and in
mid-July made a visit to the naval vessel commanded by her
second son, Alfred, affectionately known as Affie. She
recorded that everything was most beautifully kept and it was
a most interesting visit, particularly because it was her son's

ship, but it was dreadfully hot in his cabin where they took
tea. Since the death of her husband the queen had become all
but invisible to her subjects and was losing popular support.
Prime Minister Benjamin Disraeli, who was to overcome his
sovereign's initial hostility and become a cherished friend,
would be instrumental in reversing this process, but he had
only formed his first government earlier that year. I imagine
John Dupen would have been intrigued at the possibility of
catching even a brief glimpse of the reclusive monarch.

Cowes, Isle of Wight, 13th July 1868

John stands rigidly to attention on the deck of the *Hector*,
looking across the water towards Cowes and the Trinity Pier
where the royal yacht *Alberta* is getting up steam. The band
of his round, peaked cap feels tight against his forehead and
he can feel the sweat trickling down his neck under his
collar. It is another hot summer's day and he wishes the sun
had not chosen to shine quite so auspiciously on Her Majesty
as she makes her official visit to the *Galatea*, riding at anchor
next to them. The frigate has recently returned from a voyage
to Australia under the command of young Prince Alfred, the
Duke of Edinburgh, and the queen has expressed a desire to
see her son's ship. Shortly after eight bells sounded for the
end of the afternoon watch, John was relieved of his duty in
the engine room and ordered to join the men mustered on
deck to cheer the queen as she passed. He quickly scrambled
out of his overalls and into his dark blue trousers and
woollen frock coat with its double row of brass buttons and
purple engineer's band nestling between the gold on the
sleeves. When they had escorted the *Alberta* across the
Solent a few days earlier, carefully shepherding her to the
pier at Osborne like a mother duck with her last remaining
duckling, John had caught only a brief glimpse of a group of
tiny, black-clad figures disembarking in the dusk. Now
perhaps he was going to have a chance to see the queen.

There is a flurry of activity on shore and soon the smart little black-hulled paddle steamer with her twin cream-painted funnels bustles out into the bay, ignoring the pleasure yachts scudding jauntily across her wake and the fishermen in their small boats piled high with nets and creels, who have shipped their oars to watch. John can see the crew of the *Galatea* assembled on deck, seamen in blue and white, stokers in all-white duck, and officers smart in gold braid and lace. Which one is the duke, he wonders? He has heard that His Royal Highness is a proficient sailor, and at least he has buckled down to a real job, unlike his older brother. John's mother, he knows, disapproves of the rackety behaviour of the Prince of Wales. It occurs to him that she must have had similar worries about her own oldest son, but if so, she keeps her own counsel, and Sharrock certainly seems more settled since his marriage. John knows it is wrong to be envious of the material good fortune of others, but he could not help but be impressed by his brother's fine house in Clifton last time he passed through Bristol. He wishes he could afford a similar residence for his own dear Julia when they marry. But he must be grateful that he is able to support a wife at all. Many men have to wait much longer before they can enter into the blessed state of matrimony. Only three more months, he thinks, and then she will be his.

The wheels of the *Alberta* stop turning, there is a rattle of chains as the anchor is lowered, and a small woman veiled in deepest black is helped into the ship's barge along with a number of other ladies and gentlemen. John strains to see while remaining completely motionless. His sisters will want a full account. The widowed queen lives in a seclusion that would be impossible for his own mother, even if she wished it. Prince Leopold, her youngest son, is a constant anxiety to her, so they say. Again, his mother would sympathise. Poor old Sam finally lost his long battle with ill health a year ago, while John was away at sea. It felt strange, when he finally went home on leave, not to hear his brother's soft, wheezing breath at night. Sam was the quietest of them all, but always there, an eager audience for the stories the others brought home. God's will be done, thinks John. At least he has been spared any more suffering. But how Sam would have loved to hear about the queen.

John sees the *Alberta's* barge being lowered into the choppy water. The oarsmen pull away in perfect unison, covering the short distance to the *Galatea* in a few minutes. 'Hurrah!' comes the cry from the crew of the Duke's frigate, and 'Hurrah!' the men of the *Hector* roar in reply as they raise their caps and circle them in the air in the traditional sailor's salute to the monarch, for all the world, thinks John, as if they were polishing a window. The small black figure disappears below and John must hurry to change out of his uniform and snatch a mug of tea and a hunk of biscuit on his way back down to the engine room. It is nearly six o'clock and time for the next dog watch. As John makes his careful inspection of the boilers, his heart swells with patriotic fervour at the thought that the safety of the royal family is entrusted to his ship.

Two hours later he is again free to make his way on deck, where as night falls he sees the *Galatea* twinkling from stem to stern with strings of green and white lights. As he watches, colourful rockets shoot up into the night sky, a display of fireworks to entertain Her Majesty. John drifts into a delightful daydream where some unexpected danger allows him to show his courage and loyalty: a sudden squall that capsizes the barge transporting the queen, or an attack by a Fenian gunman like the one who shot the Duke of Edinburgh in Sydney just a few months before. How delighted Julia would be if he earned a medal, even a small one.

But no dramatic events disturb the peace of the summer and the long, hot July days drift by in a monotonous blur. Occasionally the *Hector* steams out into the Solent to test the engines and once or twice the crew are given leave to go ashore and bathe, or hire a rowing boat. But mostly they sit at anchor looking over towards the twin ivory towers of the great Italianate palace, just visible in the distance above the tree tops, knowing that Her Majesty is breakfasting in the shade, strolling in the gardens, driving out in the afternoon or dining on the terrace. Mr Disraeli arrives and spends a day with the queen but there is no sign of any Irish rebels attempting to land on the beach where the royal bathing machine lies unused. By the time the queen leaves on 5th August John is thoroughly bored. He is glad of the chance of a short cruise across to Cherbourg as escort to the larger of the two royal yachts, the *Victoria and Albert*, which is transporting the queen on the first stage of her journey to Switzerland, but after that the *Hector* is back on regular coastguard duty in the Solent.

The time drags as John waits for his wedding day. The date has been set for 21st October and Julia's letters are full of her preparations, what the dressmaker has said, the menu for the breakfast, the embroidered linens she is working on for their first home. It is more than a year since she lost her mother and it seems to be a comfort to her that she can put off her mourning and order a new gown for her marriage. She is such a dear, sweet creature, he thinks. She deserves to have a pretty dress. He finds her girlish chatter restful, so unlike the conversation of his sharp-tongued sisters, who have no patience with a girl who has never had to earn her own living. He is a lucky man. He was just an apprentice engine fitter when he and Julia started walking out together but now he is set to have a steady career in the navy, and in the face of Julia's stubborn loyalty to her first and only suitor, her father could not withhold his consent. John wants her to be proud of him, but there is not much chance of distinguishing himself in the Solent.

Southampton Water, September 1868

It is a Saturday afternoon and four bells have just struck when John becomes aware of a commotion as he leaves the clammy heat of the engine room to come up on deck. Wiping his hands on an oily piece of rag, he looks across

towards the northern shore where a black cloud of smoke is
rising into the evening sky. Mr Plumbly, the boatswain, calls
to him,

'We're off to fight a fire again, Dupen. Want to come with
us?'

With a surge of excitement John remembers how just a
couple of weeks earlier, they were called to a major incident
in the docks. Despite their efforts to bring the blaze under
control, a quantity of valuable equipment was destroyed, but
John had felt a sense of satisfaction that when a real crisis
came he demonstrated initiative and a cool head. There are
few enough opportunities in the routine of shipboard life to
show what he is made of. This time he does not hesitate.

'Yes, of course. I'm with you.'

Mr Plumbly musters a party of some forty sailors and
marines and a collection of equipment including tomahawks
and grappling irons. They are joined by Mr Lyne and Mr
Salmon, the assistant paymasters, and set off to row to shore,
crammed into two boats.

'Put your backs into it, my boys,' shouts the boatswain.
'There's no time to lose.'

After landing at the hard they cover the mile or so to the
fire at a quick double pace. They can hear the crackling of
the fire and the air is thick with smoke. Terrified horses are
whinnying from a field where a herd of cows huddles
together in a corner. Some fifteen hayricks and corn stacks
are ablaze and the flames have already spread to a collection
of sheds and outbuildings, but a fire engine is in place and a
brigade of soldiers is tackling the conflagration, pumping
water from the horse pond.

'Must be the men from the military hospital,' Mr Lyne says
knowledgeably.

An officer who appears to be in charge calls out to them,

'Hey, you chaps, get us some more water, and see what
you can save from the yard, will you.'

Plumbly and Lyne do not hesitate. They direct their men
to chop at a wire fence with tomahawks and plunge through

the gap into the stifling smoke and sparks to rescue a number
of carts and waggons standing in the farmyard. The heat is
almost unbearable. John's eyes are smarting and he has
started to cough uncontrollably, but he runs towards the
house, where labourers and maidservants are milling around
in confusion and a distracted-looking lady is kneading her
apron with anxious fingers and wailing,

'Oh, what am I to do? What am I to do?'

'Calm yourself, madam,' says John gently. 'Help is a
hand. We are come from Her Majesty's ship *Hector* to render
what assistance we can. May I avail myself of the services of
your people?'

'Yes, yes, whatever you need.'

John turns to the servants.

'Come on, you men, where are the buckets? Bring them
here. Look sharp.'

A dozen or so pails and containers are brought out and
John organises the dazed-looking crowd into a line from the
scullery to the yard. He fills a bucket and passes it to the first
person in the chain.

'Send it back when it's empty,' he instructs.

Turning to a sensible looking woman in a smut-covered
apron with the well-muscled arms of a laundress or a
dairywoman, he asks,

'Can you take charge of the filling? Just keep pumping,
and shout for someone to take over when you need to stop.'

He runs off to the head of the line to make sure the water
has arrived at its destination. The blue jackets are pulling
down the burning sheds using their grappling irons while the
marines have been sent to chop at a dried hedge. John sees
that it leads to a nearby copse that must not be allowed to
catch. A seaman is lying on the ground groaning, his clothing
singed. Mr Salmon is beside him.

'You'll be fine, Ned,' he says. 'Here, Dupen, can you get
us a pail of water over here?'

Soon after, Lieutenant Coddington and the *Hector*'s
surgeon, Dr Ward, arrive and the injured sailor is bandaged

and settled at a safe distance from the fire. John is kept busy chivvying the chain of water carriers and directing the water to where it is most needed, while his shipmates make a valiant but ultimately unsuccessful attempt to pull down the piggery. They can hear the dreadful squealing of the sow and her litter. With grim humour Mr Plumbly sniffs the air and says,

'Roast pork for dinner tonight, me lads.'

At around ten o'clock the fire engine from Southampton finally arrives. It is dark by then but the fire is still glowing red. The horse pond is reduced to a puddle of mud, so a length of hose is pulled and pulled until it reaches the fishpond at Netley Abbey, some 500 feet distant, and gallons more water are pumped onto the flames. An hour later the crew of the *Hector* are dismissed, to trudge wearily back to their boats and row out to the ship, where a double ration of grog is issued along with the inevitable biscuit and, despite the grumbling of the cook, a fresh brew of hot tea. John reflects, as he rubs at his sore, reddened eyes, that although he has of course no intention of boasting, at last he has something to tell Julia that will impress her.

The China Station

A month after the fire in the Solent, John returned home to Hayle to marry his childhood sweetheart:

Royal Cornwall Gazette 29th October 1868
Marriages
At Phillack Church Oct. 21st by the Rev. F. Hockin John
Dupen RN of HMS Hector to Julia Spray, second daughter of
Capt. P. B. Spray Hayle.

Julia and John had known each other all their lives. She was a year younger than him and the daughter of Phillips Bigglestone Spray, a sailor who began his career as an apprentice on Harvey's brig *Phoebe* back in the 1830s when the Dupens first moved to Hayle. Captain Spray had rapidly earned his promotion to mate and then master of a series of coastal trading vessels, but at the time of his daughter's marriage he was the harbourmaster, with a house just round the corner from the Dupen home. Julia had grown up in Hayle Terrace in a cluster of Spray uncles and other master mariners and their families. She knew what to expect as a sailor's wife, but perhaps not quite what it would be like to be married to the navy.

Three years later John and Julia were living in Plymouth, in a neat, white-painted end of terrace house close to the Royal Dockyard, with their daughter Mary and newborn son Arthur. While France and Prussia were embroiled in a bloody conflict that changed the face of continental Europe, Britain had been nominally at peace since the end of the Crimean War. When Gladstone first came to power in 1868 he not only withdrew almost half of all British troops stationed across the empire but also cut naval forces overseas from 17,000 to 11,000 men. This did not however mean an end to any chance of action. In the view of Gladstone's administration, Britain's role was that of policeman to the world, hunting down pirates and slavers and seeking to impose Liberal values of free trade and Christian civilisation. The mid-nineteenth century, a period that I had naively classified to myself as peaceful, was in fact riddled with minor skirmishes across the globe.

In June 1871, after receiving his promotion to Engineer, John was posted to the frigate *Topaze*, one of the detached squadron that cruised the world flying the flag and generally making the British presence felt in foreign ports. A newspaper report summarised the voyage of the four frigates and one screw corvette, which, for reasons of economy and a lack of coaling stations on much of their route, was undertaken mostly under sail. What the *Times* failed to note was that, in one of those coincidences that give walk-on parts to famous names in a cast of largely unknown characters, Charles Dickens' fifth son Sydney was one of the sub-lieutenants on board the *Topaze*. He fell ill in April 1872 on the return voyage from India and died at sea, two years after the death of his father. If John Dupen and Sydney Dickens ever spoke to each other (and given the social gulf that separated officers and engineers they may not have done), it is unlikely to have been a significant moment for John. He was not to know that ten years later his youngest sister would marry a master tailor who, as a young journeyman, had made suits for the Dickens boys.

The Times 28th September 1872
The squadron, under command of Rear-Admiral Beauchamp Seymour, C.B., left Portland on Nov. 19, 1871, and arrived at and sailed from the following ports on the dates specified:-
Vigo, Nov. 24, 29; Lisbon, Dec. 2, 7; Madeira, 10, 11; Rio Janeiro, Jan. 8, 18, 1872; Cape of Good Hope, Feb. 14, 27; Bombay, April 22 and May 6; Mauritius, June 5, 20; Cape of Good Hope, July 7, 27; St. Helena, Aug. 8, 13; Ascension, Aug. 17, 20; the Azores, Sept. 13, 16. The total distance traversed by the ships is 29,414 miles, accomplished almost entirely under sail. The general health of the crews has been good. The cruise from the Cape to Bombay was very tedious, owing to the prevalence of light winds and calms the whole way. The squadron steamed from the equator to Bombay, the ships towing each other alternately, the Inconstant and Volage doing most of the work. Steam was used for one day in crossing the equator, going out and coming home, and advantage was taken of it to exercise the squadron in steam tactics.

John too fell ill on board the *Topaze* and when he returned to Devonport in October 1872 he was hospitalised for two months with fever, but unlike Sydney Dickens he recovered and spent some months at home again in a guard ship of the reserve. In the spring of 1873 came the news that he was to be deployed to the China station. Julia would have to go home to Hayle. A house was found in Commercial Road, near her recently married brother Bigglestone, the proprietor of a chandlery business. She was sadly lacking in female relatives of her own, but would not be far from her mother-in-law in

Penpol Terrace. Although John would be absent for the next
four years, and unable to provide the steady guidance of a
loving father, his children would benefit from the moral
influence of their grandmother and aunts.

John's health was still uncertain and upon his arrival in
China on the flagship *Iron Duke* in August 1873, he found
himself once more hospitalised, but by November he had
recovered sufficiently to be posted to the gun vessel *Ringdove,*
one of the Plover class, the last all-wooden gunboats built for
the Royal Navy. After their success in the Crimean War,
gunboats and the larger gun vessels (generically referred to as
gunboats) became the workhorses of the navy despite their
lack of durability – the early models had been built in haste
when seasoned oak was in short supply and the green timber
soon started to rot. Britain was looking for financial savings in
defence and it was cheaper to operate unsuitable ships than to
build new ones. The gunboat fleet was deployed to the
Mediterranean, along the west coast of Africa, to North
America and the West Indies, Zanzibar and the East Indies.
But the largest concentration was on the China station, with
one in each consular port to keep the peace, protect life and
property, and clear the waters of pirates.

It must have been a strange experience to join a small
vessel like the *Ringdove* after years spent in big frigates. The 51
gun *Topaze* was four times the size of a gunboat, with
nineteen naval and marine officers and eight midshipmen, as
well as five engineers, three surgeons, and a total complement
of 500 men. The *Ringdove,* by contrast, had just three officers
besides the commander, one surgeon, and three engineers.
They would all have shared the tiny, dark, stuffy wardroom
next to the commander's cabin in the stern and used the same
tiny washbasin and cabinet toilet in the stern. There was so
little headroom below in these vessels that it was rumoured an
officer had once been observed shaving with his head sticking
out of the skylight and the mirror propped up on the deck in
front of him. But there was none of the starchy formality of a

big ship, and if young Lieutenant Kenyon-Slaney came from a home where he enjoyed the services of a butler, a coachman, and a footman, he put on no airs and graces when expected to dine with the engineer in charge, Mr Harrison, whose sister was a Manchester steam loom weaver.

The rest of the crew of eighty sailors and stokers were crammed into the forecastle or slept on deck to escape the stifling heat, taking their chances with the sudden rainstorms that could drench them in minutes. The *Ringdove* carried three guns, a seven inch muzzle loader midships and two breech-loading Armstrongs fore and aft. (The men must have hoped that they would not have cause to use the latter, which had a terrible reputation for blowing up in the face of the crew.) She had a narrow, telescopic funnel, three masts, and two engines driving twin screws. With a draught of just ten and a half feet these did not lift out of the water, making her sluggish in the extreme when under sail. On deck she also carried two gigs, a steam skiff, a cutter, and a whaler.

After some time spent cruising Chinese waters, in 1874 the *Ringdove* was sent to Japan, that mysterious society that had been forced open to western vessels in 1853 by the American Commander Perry. It was here that John received a letter that must have brought home the reality of being separated from his family for four long years, when any news, whether joyful or sad, was several months old by the time he received it.

Yokohama, April–May 1874

The *Ringdove* lies at anchor with her sister ship *Thistle* off the port of Yokohama, which serves the ancient capital city of Edo. Around them, dozens of fishing boats with single, square sails dart backwards and forwards across the metallic grey water. The steeply pitched roofs of the wooden cottages that line the bay have weathered to a dull pewter to match the sea. John has been ashore to wander through the bustling streets lined with saloons and brothels that have sprung up to serve the hundreds of foreign seamen who are stationed in the port. Unreadable banners in the mysterious script of the country hang from the low, two-storey buildings. He is surprised to see that there appear to be no beggars or vagrants, just dozens of bare-legged workmen in wide conical hats, trotting about their business, carrying baskets on yokes across their shoulders or pushing heavy two-wheeled carts. For once, he feels tall in comparison with this strange race of wiry, concave-chested men. At open-air eating places customers squat by miniature charcoal stoves, eating from doll-sized bowls. Vendors of strangely shaped fruit and vegetables display their wares next to tin tubs of glittering silver fish. Ladies with ink-black hair swept up in smooth chignons teeter by on high wooden clogs or sit with straight backs in carriages pulled by running men. There appear to be almost no donkeys or horses. Everything is transported by the power of human muscle.

John stores up all the sights and sounds to describe to Julia when he writes. He looks forward eagerly to her replies, bringing news of the children: the new baby he has never seen, Arthur, who is learning to be the man of the house, and his clever, curious Mary. She is learning her alphabet, Julia says, and soon will be able to read his letters for herself. Imagine, he will tell her, the ladies wear robes like dressing gowns, with no crinoline, and great fat sashes wound round their waists. I don't think you would like to dress like that, would you?

The latest package of mail from home arrives from Southampton on the P & O steamer *Behar*, with the *Ringdove*'s new commander, Mr Corbett Uvedale Singleton. The crew watch with curiosity and a little trepidation as he is rowed out to the *Ringdove* on one of the flat native boats known as *sampans*, propelled by two men in blue cotton jackets and straw sandals. A new commander is always an unknown quantity. Mr Singleton turns out to be an aristocratic Irishman in his late thirties, a few years older than John. With his case of guns and his gundog he seems more interested in getting some good shooting than anything else,

but when he visits the engine room his questions show that
he has a good understanding of steam power.

'He'll do,' says Mr Harrison gruffly to his colleagues.

The time passes in routine maintenance and testing of the
boilers. Towards the end of April they dress the ship in
honour of the Emperor of Russia's birthday and the next day
sail out into the gulf for firing practice. On their return
another package of mail is delivered to the ship. John
wonders why he has a letter addressed in Annie's
unmistakable hand but nothing from his wife. Anxiously he
breaks the seal and reads:

> *My dear brother I write with grave news. Your sweet
> child Mary has been taken from us and is at rest in the
> arms of the Lord. She was stricken with the croup and
> fought for her life for four long days and nights but
> despite the efforts of faithful Dr Mudge, who did
> everything in his power to ease her suffering, she
> breathed her last on 28th February. Julia is too
> distressed to lift her pen and write, but rest assured,
> dear brother, that we are doing all we can to comfort
> and sustain her in her grievous loss. Little Arthur is well
> and your new daughter, who we have taken to calling
> Lissie, is thriving. I am sure that in the fullness of time
> Julia will come to see that she has been blessed with
> the gift of a baby girl at the very moment when she has
> had to bid farewell to her firstborn. The ways of the
> Lord are mysterious indeed, but we all pray for you to
> be strong and resolute in the face of this letter, which
> gives me as much pain to write as it does you to
> receive. We all loved Mary dearly and will miss her
> bright face and affectionate ways.*

It is as if he has been punched in the chest and all the air
knocked out of him. He blinks fiercely and bites his lips
firmly together.

'Bad news, Dupen?' asks Commander Singleton. Blindly
John thrusts the letter into the hands of his captain.

'Read it, sir,' he mutters, his voice cracking.

'Oh my dear chap, I'm so sorry. It's dashed hard being away from home at times like this. But it's what we signed up for and we must do our duty. You won't want the men to see you like this. Come with me.'

In the commander's cabin Singleton unlocks his liquor case and pours John a large glass of brandy.

'Here. Get that down you man. We'll soon have you feeling more the thing.'

Commander Singleton's voice sounds muffled and distant and John's vision is blurred, but he gulps the brandy and realises that he is not after all going to suffer the embarrassment of a public collapse.

'Thank you, sir,' he says. 'I'll do now.'

In the days that follow John goes about his duties in a daze but he is glad to keep busy. Then on 19th May the *Ringdove* is sent to the dry dock at Yokoska for repairs and he has far too much time on his hands. One day he walks up through the woods to the tomb of William Adams, the English navigator who came to Japan in 1600 and never returned home to his family. Imagine, John thinks, never to hold Julia in his arms again, never to see Arthur grow up or meet baby Lissie. When he finally sees her she will be almost the same age as Mary was when he left. How will he bear it, he wonders? Another three long years before he can kneel at the little grave in the churchyard at Phillack and bid farewell to his darling.

He hires a *jinrikisha* to take him across the peninsula to Kamakura, where there is said to be a fine specimen of a Japanese temple (if, as Commander Singleton says, you should happen to care about such things). The route takes him up a rough, stony track to a viewpoint where the rickshawman stops and points to the perfect, white tipped cone of Mount Fuji away in the distance. The elusive volcano emerges from the pale sky as if conjured from the mist by a magician, and evaporates once more into the clouds. The words of the psalm echo in John's head:

'I will lift up mine eyes unto the hills from whence cometh my help.'

Then they are off again, descending through the woods to the small town.

Beside a red-painted archway John climbs down from the carriage and signals to the man to wait. He enters the temple complex over the high arch of a wooden drum bridge, and finds himself beside a tree-lined lake where ducks splash energetically and fat, lazy fish bask just beneath the surface. To one side of the path a stone tank sits under a wooden roof, long-handled brass dippers resting along its edge. John, hot from the long ride, scoops up a mug of cool water. Looking around, he notices massed banks of hydrangeas, blue as the Cornish sky, blue as a little girl's dress. His tears start to fall, mingling like raindrops with the water that trickles from the bamboo spout into the basin.

Send a Gunboat!

Long tours of duty meant that sailors and officers alike were absent from the deathbeds of parents, wives, and children. But it did not do to dwell on such things; bereavement was something to be borne in silence, like a true man. Births too, like that of baby Lissie, were missed, and on their return home fathers had to become acquainted with toddlers who eyed them suspiciously. Who was this stranger they were told to call papa? Seamen channelled their emotions into the crafting of gifts and mementoes for their families, while their wives depended on a wider circle of relatives for support. John's older sisters may not have had children of their own but they must have played an important role in the upbringing of their nephews and nieces.

Once the *Ringdove* was back at sea, John would have closed the door on his memories of his daughter and busied himself with the never-ending tasks required to maintain the engines in top condition. From Yokohama they cruised to Vladivostok, where Commander Singleton again went ashore to shoot. Returning to Japan in November, they were disappointed that clouds over Nagasaki prevented them from observing the transit of Venus, but soon they were on the move again, this time to Shanghai. By early 1875 they were patrolling the Yangtze Kiang river, surrounded by flooded paddy fields that promised a generous supply of snipe and woodcock. A year earlier John's brother Ernest, visiting the same river in search of a cargo of tea, had remarked with fraternal pride:

> The river "Yangtze" was opened up by the English in the war of 1860, the remains of some of the "Chinese" posts are now to be seen. All the towns are walled in, but the walls would be like so much paper before the guns even in our smallest gunboats.*

*(*In extracts from his logbook I have retained Ernest's original spelling and punctuation.)*

Ernest also enjoyed the cheap food, commenting that:

> Fowls, ducks, and geese can be had for a few cents each. Ducks are to be seen in immense flocks, being taken down the river, the old Chinaman coming along behind them in a boat, steering them with a long pole.

But Commander Singleton was more interested in game than domestic fowl. In his logbook he carefully recorded in tabular form his 'bag' and that of his two companions, the paymaster of the *Ringdove* and a Mr Martin, on one of their shooting trips in January 1875: one deer, four quail, 35 pheasants, and a single pigeon, most of them shot by Singleton himself. During the eight-day trip they consumed (again noted in a neat table) 23lb mutton, 24lb beef, two oxtails, 3lb cheese, two dozen eggs, 20lb rice, 25lb of vegetables, a tin of marmalade and another of sardines, four bottles of brandy, three of whisky, seven of sherry and two of claret, as well as four dozen of small ale, and 2lb each of tea and coffee.

In late March the *Ringdove* put into the dockyard in Hong Kong, where ships on the China station were maintained, just missing Ernest, whose ship had also put in for repairs that spring. She spent the next few months cruising the Canton river, and in November 1875 arrived back in Hong Kong for a refit. Far away in the Malay States trouble was brewing. Malaya had assumed a new importance earlier in the century with the discovery of tin. The British claimed that they had no interest in turning the collection of states that made up the peninsula into a colony, but their role as world policeman committed them to keeping order in a society riven with dynastic disputes. The Straits of Malacca between Singapore and Penang were a vital section of the trade route between India and China and needed to be kept clear of the *prahus* manned by 'pirates' who regarded raids on merchant vessels as a legitimate form of subsistence.

In one of the native states, Perak, a land of impenetrable jungle traversed only by elephant tracks, where all communication followed the course of the river, the succession was disputed. In 1874 the various parties had signed an agreement known as the Pangkor engagement, by which the elderly Raja Ismail conceded the Sultanate to another Raja called Abdullah, accepted a pension and retreated upstream to plot against his rival. Raja Abdullah, whose home territory was downstream, did a deal with the Mantri or chief of the tin mining district of Larut – which was in reality under the control of the Chinese secret societies, who supplied labour and management to the mines and regularly fought amongst themselves. But the Mantri, who was out to maximise his own influence and tax revenues, quite unscrupulously played one side off against the other. Everyone chose to ignore the claim of a third Raja, Yusuf, who had his headquarters even further upstream and was universally loathed. Trouble rumbled on, coming to a head in the following year.

There has been almost too much written about the 'small war' in Perak. Not only was it widely reported in the press at the time, including the *Illustrated London News*, but the naval dispatches were published as an appendix in the *London Gazette*; the young assistant commissioner Frank Swettenham published both his diaries and a later, tidied up version, in his autobiography; and the traveller Isabella Bird wrote her own account after visiting Perak some ten years later. So it was with no particular expectation of finding anything new that I ordered up Commander Singleton's logbook from the archives of the Caird library in Greenwich. This must be one of the most atmospheric places for a maritime researcher to visit. Leaving the DLR station I made my way past the *Cutty Sark* before entering the great park that surrounds the National Maritime Museum. I was walking with the great names of the past: Christopher Wren, Samuel Pepys, and clockmaker John Harrison. Despite the temptation to linger in the museum itself, I climbed the back stairs to the library, where my order was waiting for me.

I was expecting a simple log of dates, ports, wind direction, and coal consumption. What I found was a seam of pure gold (or more appropriately, tin). Commander Singleton had written a day-by-day account of leading the naval brigade up the Perak river against a force of hostile Malays. Poring over his handwriting, following the route taken by the troops with the help of his sketch map, I was able to experience the expedition as it unfolded. The only disappointment was that nowhere did he mention the name of his engineer, John Dupen. I have had to imagine John's role. But if I have placed him closer to the action than he really was, I believe my account is a true picture of how it felt to travel up that distant river in search of the enemy. John's perspective is naturally of his time. It would not have occurred to him that the British resident was at least partially responsible for his own fate, nor that the British reprisals were unnecessarily punitive. Writing about colonial aggression is an uncomfortable but illuminating exercise.

Malay States, November 1875

Commander Singleton has unexpectedly called all hands on deck. Wondering what could be afoot, John joins his shipmates.

'Men,' says the Commander, 'a telegram has arrived with news of a crisis in the Malay States. The British Resident in Perak had been foully murdered and thirteen British officers and men slain in an attempt to avenge his death. We have orders to proceed immediately to Singapore and from there to Penang and up the coast to Perak. Look lively. We need to be under weigh before nightfall.'

John feels his stomach cramp in anticipation. At last he is going to see some real action. All repair work is hastily put aside, by 5 p.m. the boilers are alight, and the *Ringdove* steams out of the harbour on the evening of 9th November. The rigging that they had not expected to use for some weeks is hastily fixed and soon the sails are hoisted, they catch the south-west current, and in the engine room the order is received to reduce coal consumption to seven hundredweight an hour. It is always a tricky calculation to balance economy of fuel with speed but John has confidence that the commander knows his business.

A week later they put into the coal wharf at Singapore, where they rendezvous with the P & O steamer *Kashgar* carrying 300 men of the 80th regiment. Major General Colbourne and 83 officers and men board the *Ringdove* for passage to the Perak river. The rest are taken on board the sloop *HMS Egeria*. The men and their kit are packed tightly in on deck. They will be lucky if it does not rain; unlike some other vessels of her class the *Ringdove* has no poop to provide shelter. On 20th November they are close to the mouth of the river when they spot the gunboat *HMS Fly* coming towards them. Commander Singleton orders a gun to be fired and the recall hoisted so that *Fly*, with her shallow draught, can take the troops from the *Egeria* up the river. The two gunboats are steaming cautiously into the estuary when there is a grinding thud and John realises they are aground.

'Dashed pilot got the tide wrong!' fumes Valentine Hughes, the young Scottish navigating lieutenant. Not yet 25, he already has his master's certificate and prides himself on his skill in the shallowest of waters.

'We need to lighten the load,' says Commander Singleton. 'Blow the two foremost boilers.'

John opens the valves and water gushes out. It is still not enough so they proceed to roll the ship, the men running from one side to the other to tilt her at an angle, until finally she shifts and two hours later they cross the bar, closely followed by the *Fly*. They steam slowly through the murky water, between banks where thick-set, black-haired men in dugouts are hunting for shellfish amongst the tangled mangrove roots. Birds on thin, stilt-like legs turn their snaking necks to observe them thoughtfully. The river must be at least 200 yards wide and the banks are lined with coconut palms, their leaves dipping down as if to admire their own reflection. The air is filled with the stench of fish drying on racks next to the clusters of thatched houses that are built out on piles over the shallows.

At sunset they drop anchor just past the first point and at 9 p.m. the colonial steam vessel *Pluto* comes up the river carrying Governor Jervois from Singapore. Commander Singleton goes on board. When he returns he gives the order to get under weigh once more and they proceed up river until by 2 a.m. the night is too dark for them to continue. The next morning the troops are transferred to *Pluto* from *Fly*, which then leaves for Singapore, while the *Ringdove* follows *Pluto* up the river as far as Durien Sabatang, where they find *HMS Thistle*. This is the furthest point that the gunboats can reach.

In the evening Commander Singleton again goes on board *Pluto*, this time to consult with Major Dunlop, the Acting

Commissioner, and Mr Swettenham his deputy, who have
arrived from the residency at Bandar Bharu. The remainder of
the 80th regiment arrives the next day in the steamship *Pyah
Pekhet* and the decision is taken to send all the troops up to
the front. John is starting to wonder if he will have the
chance to go any further up the river himself or if he will be
obliged to remain with the *Ringdove*. While there is plenty of
work to be done organising the transport of stores and
provisions up to Bandar Bharu, it is unlikely to offer the
opportunity to engage with the enemy. But on the morning of
26th November Commander Singleton calls him over and
says,

'I'm going to need you to man the steam skiff, Dupen.
Fetch one of the stokers and prepare to get under weigh just
as soon as you can.'

John oversees the loading of a supply of coal into the
small wooden craft, the fire is lit in the single boiler that
drives the engine, and they get up steam. Mr Singleton and
Commander Stirling from the *Thistle* come on board and they
nose out cautiously into the shallow waters of the winding
river. The two cutters belonging to the gun vessels follow,
each with a complement of fifteen sailors and stokers,
catching the light breeze and tacking painstakingly
backwards and forwards behind the skiff, which forges
ahead, smoke puffing energetically from her tall funnel. Later
that day they arrive at the residency in Bandar Bharu, a basic
thatched bungalow on an island in the middle of the stream,
where small crabs scuttle amongst the tree roots and clouds
of mosquitos hover aggressively at head height. All is
peaceful. The troops are already camped on the shore beside
clumps of banana trees heavy with fruit, and a few villagers
peer cautiously from the undergrowth, reluctant to show
themselves. Mr Swettenham hails them in fluent Malay and
whatever he says seems to reassure them because shortly
afterwards they reappear with fresh coconuts, which they
offer to the party. The men pitch their tents and brew tea to
accompany their dinner of tinned meat and biscuit.

John finds himself invited to dine with the two commanders, Major Dunlop, and Mr Swettenham. The latter is a slim young man with smooth dark hair, a thin moustache, and strongly marked brows that almost meet in the middle. He must be, thinks John, around the same age as his young brother Ernest, no more than about twenty-five. But of them all, he is the one who has the best understanding of the local people and their customs. When he offers his perspective on the various claimants to the Sultanate, they all listen attentively.

Ismael he writes off as 'alien, old and stubborn'. Yusuf, he says, while having probably the best claim by birth, 'is disliked and distrusted by almost everyone in Perak.' He is an inveterate gambler, a determined robber who steals elephants and buffalo whenever he is pressed for money, while his ill fame as an abductor of the wives and daughters of the peasants is the talk of the district. The Bandahara Usman, another of the many petty chiefs, is quite simply a lunatic, 'sometimes for weeks together imagining himself a dog or cat'. And as for the Mantri, concludes Swettenham, 'his double-dealing – his barefaced falsehoods, his cruelty and vacillation render him totally unfit to manage the smallest territory'. Abdullah, he tells them, who was installed as Governor Clarke's puppet the previous year, has proved himself to be just as unsuitable.

'He has not only embraced the vices of opium smoking and cock fighting, but also encourages the iniquitous custom of debt slavery in its worst forms. When Mr Birch was installed as Resident he attempted to introduce a centralised system of taxation, as well as a new police force and judiciary. Abdullah, despite having requested the support of a representative of our great Queen Victoria, refused to follow Birch's advice when he realised that the new system threatened to undermine the authority and income of the Malay chiefs. Jervais, the new Governor, was forbidden by his political masters in London to annex the territory, but in October he felt obliged to declare that in future the British government would rule Perak in the name of the Sultan. It was this threat that led to the death of poor Birch.'

'Can you explain to us this custom of debt slavery?' asks Commander Singleton. 'We know, of course, of the disgraceful trade that continues along the coast of Africa, but I understand this is something quite different?'

'Yes, indeed,' replies Swettenham, drawing on his pipe. 'It is a most iniquitous practice that permits a chief to seize a man and his wife as slaves in settlement of a debt, a debt that is often invented. Or he may allege that they have failed to pay a fine for an offence that they never committed. Over time the unhappy creatures accumulate so-called living expenses that add to the imaginary debt, meaning that it can never be paid off. This goes on for generations. Debt slaves can be inherited or bought and sold like any other possession and if the unfortunate devils attempt to flee, they can quite legitimately be killed. Here in Perak it is one of the pillars of the state, as you might say, and is jealously guarded by the Rajahs and chiefs.'

'By jove,' exclaims Commander Singleton. 'What a truly shocking practice. Not something that would be tolerated in a decent Christian society. No wonder the government wanted to bring these chaps to heel.'

'Indeed,' says Swettenham. 'And it's what did for Birch, poor chap. You know he was originally one of yours, a midshipman?'

'No, I was not aware.'

'Yes. It was later that he joined the government service in Ceylon. When he was appointed as the first British Resident here in Perak he lacked, of course, any knowledge of the local language and customs, but he installed himself here in this primitive hut and proceeded with the energy and moral courage of a true crusader to oppose debt slavery and redress injustice. He hoped that the ordinary Malays would come to view the British government as a firm but fair father, providing for their needs and punishing wrong-doing, and there is no doubt that he saved lives. But he made himself heartily disliked by all those who benefited from the traditional state of lawlessness. He was a good man who did not deserve to die like a dog.'

The men fall silent as they contemplate the fate of the brave Resident.

The next morning the steam skiff sets off for Pasir Sala, five miles up river, carrying Commander Singleton and Commander Stirling. Major Dunlop and Mr Swettenham follow in the *Ringdove's* cutter, which is transporting a gun. Mr Swettenham has also commandeered two native boats, broad shallow-draught vessels, each one topped with a kind of open-ended thatched hut and propelled by men at either side of the stern, who push long, heavy poles into the muddy riverbed. One boat carries the thirty men who have come up in the cutters and a rocket tube, the other a detachment of artillery with a gun and another rocket. One hundred men of the 80th are to march up the bank of the river to check the stockades that were taken previously. When the boats reach Pasir Sala there is no sign of any hostile Malays so while they wait for the troops to arrive Mr Swettenham tells them the full story of how Birch was murdered.

'You see the bath house over there?' he begins, pointing at a floating structure made of two logs and a number of crosspieces of wood, covered by a small roof of mats, like a tent about five feet high with two open triangular ends. The mats are somewhat ripped now, but it was obvious that before they were damaged, a person in the hut would be unable to see what was happening outside.

'That is where it happened. It was the holy month of Ramadan, known here in Malaya as *bulan puasa*, when the upper classes spend their time sleeping during the daylight fasting hours and sitting up all night eating and talking. Tempers are easily inflamed.'

Swettenham explains that he and Birch agreed that Swettenham would proceed upstream to post the governor's proclamation and the resident, despite being on crutches with a badly sprained ankle, would make his way

downstream with a guard of fifty Sikhs and Pathans together
with his guest, Lieutenant Abbott of the Royal Navy, and
Abbott's escort of four bluejackets. They would rendezvous
at Pasir Sala, home to a chief known as the Maharajah Lela,
to deal with the central area together. The Maharajah refused
to acknowledge the authority of the British, and Birch in
particular, and had fortified his home with a ditch,
earthworks, and a palisade.

'We later learned,' continues Swettenham, 'that he had
instructed his men to kill Birch if he tried to post the hated
proclamation.'

When Birch reached the village on 1st November it was
dark and he moored in midstream until dawn, when he
moved to the shore and anchored next to the floating bath
house, which belonged to a Chinese goldsmith. Some sixty
or seventy men armed with spears and the daggers known as
kris ranged themselves near the resident's boats while his
interpreter pinned the notice on the wall of the goldsmith's
shop. The father-in-law of the Maharajah, the Pandak Indut,
tore down the paper and Birch calmly handed over new
copies. Then he went to take a bath.

'I can't make up my mind,' says Swettenham, 'if he was
exceedingly courageous or had simply underestimated the
lengths to which the Malays were prepared to go.'

At ten o'clock the Pandak Indut stabbed the interpreter
and then rushed into the bath house with three or four of his
men, brandishing spears and crying *amok, amok*. They
stabbed Birch to death. His Sikh orderly made no attempt to
save him but swam away to save himself. Recognising that
they were outnumbered, the rest of the party made their
escape to Bandar Bharu, including Lieutenant Abbott, who
was away hunting snipe on the opposite bank when the
drama unfolded and managed to depart unseen. This custom
of running *amok* in a frenzy of anger or revenge is, explains
Swettenham, unique to the Malays but is rarely political in its
motivation.

The young assistant commissioner describes how he arrived at the upstream settlement of Blanja on 4th November with his friend and ally from the neighbouring state of Selangor, Raja Mahmud, to be told of the murder.

'I was informed that if I continued downstream they were waiting at Pasir Sala for me, declaring that I was ten times worse than Mr Birch. The villagers tried to keep me at Blanja, but faithful old Mahmud and I were of one mind, to go down like the martyrs. Mahmud is a plucky fellow and I count myself fortunate in having him as my friend and ally. God willing, we said to ourselves, we shall get through to Singapore and tell the whole world of this cowardly murder. Eight of us set off downstream in the boat belonging to the Residency. It is, as you have seen, painted white and highly visible, so we determined that there was no point in attempting to disguise ourselves and we might as well fly the Union Jack. So off we went, not knowing what might befall us and commending ourselves to the Almighty. He was perhaps listening because most fortunately a dense fog descended as we passed Pasir Sala in the dark and we made it safely through to the mouth of the river, where a steam launch from Selangor awaited us.'

John feels there is a great deal that has been left unsaid in Swettenham's laconic account.

'What happened next?' he asks. 'I believe you attempted to avenge the murder but were driven back?'

'Yes,' says Swettenham. 'We poled our way back up to the Residency and reinforcements soon arrived from Penang. We had a total force of some 150 men when we set out to exact retribution and capture the perpetrators. We trekked in single file along the river bank towards Pasir Sala until we reached a field of Indian corn fully ten feet high. Ahead was a deep, wide ditch and a stockade built of trees and logs lying at right-angles to the river bank, with a thick plantation of bananas behind. We had not brought the two howitzers because of the difficulty of transporting them along the muddy bank, but it was a mistake that cost us dear. We were

unable to fire on the fortifications from a safe distance and so
Captain Innes attempted to storm the stockade and was
killed, while his two officers and some of his men were
wounded. We were forced to retreat to the Residency and
await further reinforcements. It was not until a week later
when Major Dunlop arrived with a small naval brigade that
we were able to take Pasir Sala and retrieve Birch's body for
burial. By that time the Maharaja and his men had fled to
Blanja, where we heard that they joined up with that old
fool, Raja Ismail.'

By the time Mr Swettenham has finished his story, the
troops have finally arrived, red-jacketed, red-faced, and
sweating, cursing the roots and branches that obstruct the
river bank and make progress so slow. They report that the
stockades are deserted and untouched and the decision is
taken to return to the residency in the afternoon and prepare
for a larger expedition further upstream in a week's time. The
following morning they are back at the *Ringdove*, where they
find both the *Fly* and the *Pyah Pekhet*, as well as the corvette
Modeste.

For the next week everyone is engaged in preparing for
the expedition to pursue the fugitives upstream to the
settlement of Blanja. A naval brigade comprising officers and
men from the *Modeste* and the *Ringdove* will accompany the
troops in four native boats which have been converted to
carry guns and rockets. A fleet of 27 further boats is
assembled, capable of transporting a force of around 250
men and guns, together with additional flats to carry
ammunition and stores. When they set out on the morning of
8th December there are one hundred men of the 10th regiment
and one hundred of the 80th with their officers; forty officers
and men of the Royal Artillery; and a naval brigade of ten
officers and 61 seamen and stokers, led by Captain Buller of
the *Modeste*.

General Colbourne himself and Captain Buller will travel
in the steam skiff along with Mr Swettenham. Commander
Singleton is to lead the way in his whaler, and Major Dunlop

will take the residency house boat, while Raja Mahmut and his seventy followers are to act as scouts along the river bank. John is gratified and nervous to be included in the party, having charge once more of the steam skiff, while Mr Harrison, the chief engineer, is left on board the *Ringdove* with Lieutenant Bayly, who is to take command of the remaining crew. Their job is to ensure that provisions and ammunition are sent up by boat to Bandar Bharu at regular intervals. Mr Hughes and the other lieutenant, young Harry Kenyon-Slaney, a jolly overgrown schoolboy who is well liked by everyone, are to join the naval brigade.

'What a lark!' he says to John. 'I've been hoping to see some action and this promises to be a terrific show.'

John is not so sure. He too is eager to show these heathen devils that they cannot escape justice, but he is 32, not 24, and better able to envisage the dangers they will face. Giving himself a mental shake he dismisses his over-active imagination and concentrates on the practical task of checking the skiff's engine.

The local boats have to be poled against a strong current in humid heat of 90 degrees or more and John is proud that the stokers were the first to volunteer. Their strength and stamina, acquired through long hours of shovelling heavy loads of coal in the gruelling temperatures of the boiler room, will stand them in good stead. At first it is tricky work since they are unfamiliar with this means of propulsion, and progress is slow. But the men remain cheerful and there is much good-natured ribbing when poles stick in the mud and men are nearly precipitated into the river. Sometimes, despite Commander Singleton's efforts to find a safe passage for his flotilla, they encounter deep water where they are unable to touch bottom and are carried backwards by the current. The Chinese men ferrying the troops have clearly never seen a pole before and make heavy weather of it, their boats swinging wildly from bank to bank, but by day two they are getting more into the way of it and pick up speed.

They make camp on an island half a mile from Pasir Sala on the first night and set off again at six the next morning. The river is becoming more intricate and sandbanks make navigation difficult. They find good camping that night but the following one they are obliged to cut away grass around their tents to discourage the snakes that are surely concealed there. John's bones ache from nights spent on the damp ground, the skin on his nose is peeling, and he has angry red insect bites on his hands and arms. At noon on the 11th they arrive at the village of Bora, where the general and the commissioner go ashore and order a bunch of local people to be captured and tied up. Despite being threatened with flogging the prisoners claim to have no information about the whereabouts of the fugitive Maharaja Lela. The troops proceed to make camp on a sand spit where they find a number of fresh coconuts piled around a staff bearing a white flag in a gesture of peace.

The next morning they have great difficulty navigating over the sandbanks and the men have to take off their boots and wade while the boats are floated off. When John gets back on board the skiff he finds the ugly, engorged bodies of leeches clinging to his feet and ankles. Raja Mahmud is sent ahead to discover if there are any stockades that will impede their progress but returns to say that the way is clear. Some two or three miles from Blanja the general sends a letter to Raja Ismail inviting him to confer, but the reply comes back that he has gone on to Kinta. On the morning of 13th December they arrive in Blanja to find it deserted, strewn with abandoned luggage, and covered in recent elephant tracks. Leaving some seventy or eighty men, with Mr Hughes in command, to occupy the village and guard the boats, the remainder of the naval brigade sets out to follow Ismail on foot to Kinta.

***

This is as far as my imagination allows me to take John. Much as I would love to send him upriver with the brigade, I cannot convince myself that he would have been chosen. My only

excuse for sending him even as far as Blanja is the steam skiff.
So he was not with the men who set off along a rough,
narrow elephant track, carrying the unwieldy rockets that had
been removed from their boxes to lighten the load.
Commander Singleton and Frank Swettenham tell the rest of
the story.

Shortly after leaving Blanja they came across a huge tree
trunk blocking their path. Swettenham hailed a group of
Malays that he could see partially hidden behind a thorny
thicket of creepers and immediately an answer came back: a
volley of musket fire. The chief medical officer, Dr Randall,
fell to the ground, blood soaking through the leg of his
trousers. The troops fired back, the rocket tubes were hauled
up to the front of the column and several rockets set off. Dr
Gorham from the *Ringdove* hastened to his colleague's aid,
binding his thigh tightly to staunch the bleeding. The firing
soon stopped as the Malays evaporated into the jungle. A
makeshift litter was put together, two men were directed to
carry the injured surgeon, and the troops resumed their
painful progress, dragging the heavy guns and rocket tubes
across the uneven muddy terrain as the temperature rose
towards its midday peak. But not a single voice was raised in
complaint. They passed a stockade on top of a hill, which had
very recently been deserted, leaving fires burning and pots of
rice on the boil, but there was no sign of any defenders.

The general called a halt at 6.20 p.m. and they made camp
for the night. They lit fires and watched eagerly as the
supplies of preserved meat were opened, but a foul stench
rose from the open tins. The meat had gone bad. For dinner
that night, Commander Singleton wrote, he had nothing but
dry biscuit and a generous measure of brandy and water. The
next morning Major Dunlop set out with all the Chinese
labourers to fetch more provisions. That day the troops
managed only about one mile an hour through the soft mud
but by mid-afternoon they reached an ideal camping ground
on a small hill with a stream running below it and to

everyone's relief Major Dunlop arrived in time for dinner. The men cheered him and his indispensable Chinese factotum, whose tactful management of the labourers ensured the smooth operation of the supply chain. It was a tin mining area and the officers requisitioned the filthy miners' houses to sleep in while the men rigged up shanties for themselves of branches and leaves.

Swettenham and Mahmud had gone ahead with Mahmud's men to scout out the terrain. They sent back word that they had reached a paddy field within a mile of Kinta but the road was so bad that at times they found themselves wading up to their waists in water. Very early the next morning the artillery set out carrying their gun, followed shortly after by the naval brigade with their rockets, who soon overtook them. By eleven o'clock they reached the outskirts of Kinta, where Swettenham and his party were barricaded into the ground floor of a number of small houses. Earlier in the morning they had been surrounded by Malays firing off muskets and shouting threats but no one was injured. Commander Singleton took personal charge of the rocket tube and successfully fired off several missiles towards the village. Finally one of the rockets misfired. It must have got wet because flames shot from the tube, horrible growling noises were heard, and instead of soaring away towards the village, it simply dropped from the tube and snaked off through the rice stalks like a dragon with a tail of fire. Turning back on itself it set off a panic amongst the men, who tripped over logs hidden in the paddy as they scrambled to get out of its path.

At noon the big gun arrived. After taking their direction from the scouts, the gunners opened fire on the village itself, concealed behind a stand of tall trees. There was no returning fire and when they entered the village they found it deserted apart from a few Chinese miners. Sultan Ismail, these men said, left two days ago with his wives riding on elephants, accompanied by the Maharajah Lela. They had no idea where he had gone, except that it was upriver. There was nothing to be done except set up camp while Major Dunlop returned for orders from Penang. It was all something of an anti-climax.

The brigade was still encamped at Kinta on Christmas Day. Champagne and beer were brought from Blanja and they organised athletic sports in the late afternoon when it was slightly cooler. Back at the *Ringdove*, in Durien Sabatang, there was no such jollity for John. After the steam cutter from the *Fly* came to grief on a sandbank Mr Harrison had the bright idea of removing its engine and mounting it in a flat-bottomed craft that would be at less risk of running aground. John was no doubt kept hard at work from Christmas Day until the new year, removing the engine from the cutter and installing it in the flat. He would have had no time to brood about his family, spending their first Christmas without Mary.

On 6th January the brigade arrived back from Kinta and on 10th March the *Ringdove* left for Penang. While they were there, news was received that the fugitive Ismail had given himself up to the Rajah of Queddah and on 20th March the two chiefs arrived at the port. Two days later ex-Sultan Ismail handed over the regalia of Perak to the Lieutenant Governor of Penang. It was a formal surrender. Commander Singleton received the regalia and the next morning Ismail and thirty followers came on board the *Ringdove* for passage to Singapore. They must have been a colourful sight in their turbans made of yards of muslin, short red jackets, and red sarongs over full white trousers. John would have had a chance to view at close quarters the obstinate old man who had caused so many deaths and yet still comported himself like a ruler. At 8.15 a.m. they left Penang with all boilers alight. The next day Singleton took Ismail down into the engine room and stoke hole, 'which he seemed highly delighted with, especially the Revolution counters'. On 27th March they landed the regalia at Singapore, where Ismail had an interview with the Governor. The *Ringdove* took him on to Johore and handed him and his followers over to the

Maharajah, who hospitably took Singleton and Mr Harrison to visit his personal railway station.

In June the *Ringdove* returned to the Perak river for the commission into the murder of Mr Birch but by the end of the month they were back in Hong Kong, where Lieutenant Kenyon-Slaney died of *delirium tremens*: 'his death cast quite a gloom over all – a young man thoroughly liked and a good officer,' wrote Commander Singleton. It was not until December 1876 that the Maharaja Lela and the other ringleaders were tried in Larut, with Swettenham and Dunlop prosecuting. Lela and his father-in-law were sentenced to death, Abdullah and the Mantri were exiled to the Seychelles, and the unpopular Raja Yusuf was made Regent and later Sultan.

By that time John had been paid off and returned to Devonport. In 1877 he passed for Chief Engineer and eventually, in 1881, he received the decoration awarded to all those who took part in the Perak campaign. The Queen Victoria India Service medal, a silver medallion with on one side an image of the winged goddess of Victory and on the other a profile of Queen Victoria, is attached to a striped red and blue ribbon by a silver clasp engraved with the name Perak. It was as far as I know John's only military honour and I would love to know where it is now.

CENSUS 1871

Widowed Johanna Woolcock Dupen was losing her children as, one by one, they made lives for themselves away from Hayle. By the time of the 1871 census Ernest is the only son still at home, apprenticed as an engine fitter at the foundry. George remains in India, with a wife no one in the family has met. He has not been home for the best part of a decade and it will be another three years before he can afford to come back for a visit. Kate and her husband are running a grocery shop in Bristol, where Sharrock is now trading in wine and spirits. This gave me pause for thought. He was a Methodist. What was he doing selling intoxicating liquor? Once again I found myself wrong-footed by history; it was not until late in the nineteenth century that abstinence became a tenet of Methodist belief. John is in Plymouth, and Sarah and Hester are both away governessing – the steam packet service and Great Western Railway, I have come to realise, opened up new horizons for women as well as men. Salome too is described as a governess, but on the night of the census she is once again visiting friends, this time the harbourmaster in her father's home village of Mylor.

Ellen is at home for an Easter visit. She and Annie are both described as Principal (Ladies School) but it was not the same school. On her return from Box, accustomed to her independence and unwilling to be under the thumb of her oldest sister, Ellen set up her own establishment in St Ives, where her musical talent made her a popular member of society:

> *Royal Cornwall Gazette 25th February 1871*
> THE CHURCH ORGAN FUND A successful concert was given on Tuesday evening, in aid of the church organ fund. The programme comprised vocal and instrumental music and recitations. Miss Dupen sustained a large share of the musical

part of the entertainment and her skilful rendering of "The
nightingale's trill" was particularly well received.

The song had been made famous by the delightfully
named operatic soprano Euphrosyne Parepa and out of
curiosity I downloaded the sheet music, which does indeed
require a high degree of skill and the ability to hit a high C.

The sisters, contrary to the popular view of the
downtrodden governess, were turning into successful
businesswomen whose schools went from strength to
strength. Under the Elementary Education Act of 1870,
schooling was provided for all children aged between five and
twelve through the establishment of school boards, which
were responsible for setting up new schools in areas where
there was inadequate provision. The existing Church schools
were left in place and both types of institution received
government grants, but parents still had to pay fees. Although
the boards had the authority to enforce attendance if they
wished, they were not obliged to do so and many working
class parents, who saw no particular benefit in literacy and
needed their children's wages, chose not to send their sons
and daughters to school, or not consistently. The middle
classes also ignored both voluntary (church-run) and board
schools in favour of private establishments like those of the
Dupen sisters.

An advertisement in a local business directory, illustrated
with a degree of artistic licence, shows a handsome detached
residence in its own gardens, rather than the quayside setting
of the real Cornubia Cottage. Parents of prospective pupils
were assured that the neighbourhood was a healthy one, being
by the seaside, and that domestic arrangements were 'under
the supervision of Mrs Dupen'. In her mid-sixties Johanna
was still working as hard as ever, keeping everyone clean, fed
and clothed (according to the census, there were still no live-
in servants). Day pupils were charged £3 a year, while those
under ten years old were offered a reduction of one pound.
Music, French, singing, and drawing were extras, as were

arithmetic and writing. The main curriculum, as described earlier, no doubt included reading, scripture, history, geography, and plenty of needlework. According to the advertisement, a very limited number of boarders were accepted, so that they might receive 'strict attention'. Given the size of the house, and the fact that Kate's two older daughters had been entrusted to the care of their aunts, it is probable that Annie Dupen was making a virtue of necessity. For £20 a year, a similar price to that charged by the Hayle Academy, pupils would benefit from an 'English education based on Christian principles' – but had to bring their own cutlery and towels. Unlike the Brontës' school at Cowan Bridge, however, with its plain straw bonnets, purple frocks and cloaks, there was no uniform specified.

Although money worries had receded for Annie and her mother, Hayle was succumbing to the effects of the mine closures and beginning its slow decline. In 1867 the firm of Sandys, Carne and Vivian, successors to the old Cornish Copper Company, sold off their waterfront premises to Harveys and in 1868 the Copperhouse foundry was closed, with the loss of several hundred jobs. That side of the town was essentially put up for sale. The whole of Bodriggy, where Johanna and Sharrock had begun their new life thirty years before, comprising 300 houses and gardens, was auctioned off at the Cornubia Hotel on 15th April. In the following June, Harveys sold most of Copperhouse: the engine works, shipbuilding yard, gasworks (leaving the local shops without lighting), and 140 houses. The estates of Trevassack and Ventonleague, including another 72 houses and the Great Wheal Alfred mine soon followed.

13 The Business of Schoolkeeping

The photographs that I have inherited are another random collection. Unique among objects, they are created as deliberate memories. I have displayed some of them on my staircase wall in a design that blends the different branches of my family tree. It is intended to be visually pleasing rather than historically informative; people who never met in life now find themselves sharing a frame. But at least I can put names to them. These are not anonymous ghosts to be sold on as generic Victoriana, alongside collections of old postcards and mismatched teacups. We are truly dead when there is no one left to remember who we were.

Sarah Wesley Dupen had no children and it may be that I have the only remaining portrait of her. It must date to around the 1890s, because she looks to be at least in her forties. She is wearing the sensible dark skirt and white pin-tucked blouse of a schoolmistress but, incongruously, her mass of dark hair is covered by a wide, frilled bonnet in the style of an earlier era and in one hand she holds a bunch of paper flowers. With these accessories she belongs in a cottage garden rather than a suburban schoolroom. It is an image constructed for theatrical effect and I feel this is a woman who would have enjoyed having her own Instagram account. While it saves the amateur genealogist a huge amount of time and effort to have access to the online census returns, a relatively minor error in transcription can lead to many wasted hours. Sarah proved particularly elusive. I felt sure that she became a teacher but despite numerous searches I could find no trace of her between 1861 and 1878. It can so easily become an obsession, typing variations into a search box, unable to accept that no plausible records exist. But in the end my persistence paid off; I found her in the 1871 census,

mis-transcribed as 'Duken' and working for an Anglo-Indian
military family in the spa town of Cheltenham.

When I was four we lived in Cheltenham for a year or so
and I was enrolled in a private nursery where I learned to
read, write, and do basic sums. Scraps of blue and white
checked gingham fabric survive as patches on the frayed paws
of an ancient teddy bear to remind me of my school uniform.
I thrived in this small, orderly community. But then we
moved to the new town of Harlow and I was sent to a state
primary school, where my forty classmates were mainly
children rehoused from north east London who viewed me as
an alien species, which I suppose I was. They were not
particularly unkind, but it was like being removed from a
warm bath and thrown into a deep, cold pool without having
been taught to swim. By the time we moved again and I was
returned to the security of a girls' high school, I had retreated
into a kind of self-conscious timidity that still surfaces
occasionally when I am least expecting it. In a parallel version
of reality, if we had stayed in Cheltenham I would perhaps
have gone on to the famous Ladies College and acquired the
kind of careless confidence that comes with privilege.

The most famous headmistress of the college, Dorothea
Beale, is usually bracketed with Frances Buss of the North
London Collegiate School as one of the most influential
figures in nineteenth-century women's education. The pair
were satirised in a well-known rhyme:

> *Miss Buss and Miss Beale*
> *Cupid's darts do not feel*
> *How different from us*
> *Miss Beale and Miss Buss*

In 1848 Miss Beale, a doctor's daughter, became one of
the first students of Queen's College in London, established
by the Governess's Benevolent Institution to train teachers.
Ten years later she moved to Cheltenham and proceeded to
transform a failing school into an academically rigorous

institution where middle class girls received an education comparable to that of their brothers. She spoke out against the popular belief that this was damaging to their health or morals and ensured high standards by bringing in external examiners. Her status grew along with the reputation of her college and she did much to support the growth in high-achieving girls' schools during the second half of the nineteenth century. Whether or not she was immune to romantic feelings as the rhyme suggests, she was a woman of strong religious faith and robust moral principles, who aimed to instil the same values in her girls. She wanted them to cultivate their minds, not in order to dedicate themselves to a life of scholarship, but so that they could fully realise their talents as wives and mothers and turn their backs on frivolous pursuits. It was a vision not dissimilar to that of Hannah More.

In some ways, the education of girls was more forward-thinking than that of boys. To be a master in a public school you just needed a degree, while women teachers often had some grounding in pedagogy and an interest in how learning could be tailored to individual needs and abilities. I am not sure how far this applied to the Dupen sisters. Although they received an education that extended beyond needlework and scripture, I can find no evidence that they received any formal teacher training, nor is there a newspaper record of their pupils passing any public examinations. They would probably not have been considered properly qualified by Miss Beale, but then their schools were catering for a lower stratum of society. The pupils at Cornubia Cottage were the daughters of farmers, shopkeepers, and master mariners, who would eventually have to earn their own living.

In 1871 my great-grandmother Hester appears in the census records for Dorset. The thriving town of Sherborne was of a similar size to Hayle, with a population of around 6,000, but very different in atmosphere. Its hinterland was deeply rural – fifteen years later, in *The Woodlanders*, Hardy was to rename it Sherton Abbas. The principal industries were silk throwing (a process equivalent to the carding and spinning of wool) and glove making. Tall, brick-built mills and terraces of workers' cottages surrounded the old farmhouses and fine town houses that dated back to the seventeenth and eighteenth centuries. Hester was employed in a school that was probably quite similar to the one run by her oldest sister. It belonged to a lady with the delightfully Hardyesque name of Miss Martha Puddicombe. She was ten years older than Hester and the daughter of a captain of marines. After his untimely death she had been despatched at the age of fourteen to the Regents Park Institution for Adult Orphans in London, to be trained as a teacher alongside other daughters of military officers and clergymen. Perhaps it was Hester's memory of her visit to Ellen in Box ten years earlier that persuaded her it was preferable to take a position in Miss Puddicombe's school rather than becoming a governess.

Much of the central area of the town was occupied by Sherborne School, one of the new public schools that had become increasingly popular with the upper classes and upwardly mobile businessmen, who wanted their sons to make the right sort of friends. Unlike the students at Hayle Academy, who were being prepared for a practical career in commerce or engineering, the boys learned Latin, Greek, and how to mix in polite society. The school facilities included cricket and rugby pitches, a ball court and a swimming pool, all helping to promote the kind of muscular Christianity made popular by Thomas Arnold at Rugby. Originally part of the old Abbey precinct, Sherborne had been transformed from a very ordinary grammar school to a successful boarding establishment by a charismatic headmaster who took charge in 1850. He used the arrival of the railway ten years later to attract the sons of gentlemen and professional families from further afield. After delivering their cherished offspring to the school, parents could stay overnight at the new Digby hotel beside the station, which, with its acres of ornamental gardens, resembled a country estate rather than an inn.

Miss Puddicombe's school would have been very different and one afternoon I set out on an online expedition to find it. This is where I admit to a weakness for property programmes on television. I can resist bake-offs and dance-offs and islands of marooned celebrities, but show me a house-hunting couple with ideas way beyond their budget and I am hooked. Exploring other people's homes allows you to try on alternative lives. For half an hour I can be a mother of four, living in a former rectory in the Cotswolds, where I cook big family meals on an Aga, prune my roses, and walk my elderly labrador. Or I can be an artist with a light, airy house by the sea, furnished with bleached wood, blue and white fabric, and quirky pieces of sea glass. Many people, including my own parents, make the decision to sell up and move hundreds of miles away when they retire, looking for an ideal life that was denied them when they were working. Sometimes they achieve their dream but too often it turns out to be an illusion. From time to time I imagine moving to a Docklands penthouse, a converted barn, or a dilapidated chateau in the south of France, but I am not going to do so. I have understood that no one place will satisfy my longing to see the world so I might as well stay where I am.

Television allows me to pretend that I am house hunting, and so do the websites of estate agents. They are also a great help to genealogists. Corn Hill, where Hester lived in 1871, is a short street with only three houses, all historically significant. According to the Historic Town Survey of Sherborne, they are Kitt Hill House (18th century), Cornhill House (19th century), and Newell House (17th century). The latter has been a school in recent times but when I clicked on the Google map and started my virtual walk down the road, it was Kitt Hill House that took hold of my imagination and would not let me go. It is an impeccably genteel, flat-fronted Georgian town house with a pillared portico and dormer windows, where the inhabitants of Cranford would be immediately at home: the ideal setting for a school run by and for ladies. When I found an estate agent's listing with 24 photographs, I hoped to be able to experience Hester's life.

Instead, rather like the Liverpool house featured in the first series of David Olusoga's *A House through Time*, I found a modern family home with, I assume, teenage children. The interior was light and spacious, with big sash windows and dark wooden beams overhead, but in the bedrooms were fluffy rugs in acid shades of lime green and turquoise and in one of the attics I spotted a drum kit. The house was crying out for a makeover with Farrow and Ball paint and bargains uncovered at a French *brocante*. Or maybe not. That is not how Hester would have lived. In her day, the big, light drawing room would have been full of dark furniture, flock wallpaper, and floral carpets. A typical mid-Victorian parlour had button back chairs, embroidered firescreens, and a mantelpiece cluttered with china ornaments. Every curtain, cushion cover, and tablecloth was fringed and adorned with tassels. There would have been a mahogany piano and a small herd of occasional tables. I abandoned the estate agent's website and decided to re-read my well-worn copy of *A Little Princess* to help me visualise a Victorian schoolroom.

Sherborne, Dorset, December 1873

'Enfin! We have our letters,' says Mademoiselle Bouchard, holding out a couple of envelopes to Hester.

From Annie, she thinks, seeing the firm black handwriting on the first one. Mademoiselle is clutching her own packet of correspondence somewhat emotionally to her bosom. Hester knows how much she misses her family and friends in Zurich, and the post has brought nothing for several weeks now. She smiles kindly at her colleague.

'Would you like me to supervise the girls' music practice so that you can read your news in peace?'

'You are too kind, Mademoiselle Dupen,' replies the Swiss woman, using the French pronunciation of Hester's name. 'Do you not wish to learn what your own family has to tell you?'

'Oh, I'm sure it's nothing urgent,' says Hester. And she makes her way to the parlour where two of the young ladies in their charge are playing a loud duet with a lot more enthusiasm than skill.

It is not until after supper that Hester opens Annie's letter and learns that her sister-in-law Julia has been safely delivered of a daughter.

'They will call her Elizabeth, of course,' Annie wrote, 'after Julia's sister who died last year, if you recall.' Hester does recall. Poor Lissie was only thirty and Julia was quite distraught when she came home from Devonport for the funeral. John had just come out of hospital and Julia kept telling them all how frightened she had been.

'I don't know what I would do without him,' she had repeated. 'With Lissie gone I have no one to turn to.'

And now she is obliged to do without John for the next three or four years, thinks Hester. It is six months since he was posted to the China station.

'I fear it will be a great burden on Mama,' Annie continues. 'You know what a featherbrain Julia is. We have dear little Mary with us constantly. She is such a remarkable child. She already knows her letters and can write her own name. I believe she prefers to be here rather than at home. Just the other day she turned to Mama and said, "You know, grandmamma, I can hardly love my mama as I ought. She is so very foolish." I had to bite my tongue not to agree!'

It must be hard being a sailor's wife, thinks Hester, especially if he is in the navy. By the time John comes home the new baby will be toddling and talking and she won't know her own father. She has some sympathy for silly, helpless Julia.

Annie sends news of Ernest too. He has written from Suez about his journey through the famous canal.

'Imagine,' Annie writes. 'He says that there are posts marking every mile with enamelled white letters, just like the signs they are adopting here for the names of streets. I expect the next we will hear will be from Calcutta. It will be strange for him to celebrate Christmas so far from home. I hope there will be a proper service for him to attend. We look forward to your own arrival, dear sister. We will be very few this year.'

Reading this, Hester senses Annie's excitement at Ernest's tales. She wonders if her sister has ever wished she was a boy, and able to travel the world. Annie is the only one who never leaves Hayle but she does not complain. Hester has always assumed that she doesn't mind but perhaps she is mistaken. She remembers her own first journey to Box, all those years ago. She knew then that she could not spend the rest of her life in Cornwall, but nor did she want to be a governess like Sarah, who has written from Cheltenham. Turning to this second letter, she reads:

> 'Mrs Thompson is quite frail and rarely leaves the house, but she has a constant stream of callers, mostly ladies who have also returned from India. She likes to reminisce about her life out there and she sometimes does me the courtesy of inviting me to take tea with them. (I think it is since I mentioned, rather naughtily, that my sister-in-law is a niece of General Pennefather!) I find it most interesting to compare the stories with what dear George tells us. It is such a vast country that life in the south must be very different from the north, where the army is stationed. Mrs Thompson's son, the Major General, is in the Punjab. To think that my pupil, Miss Georgina, has lived with her grandmother since she was five years old. Imagine how it must feel to be separated from one's parents for so long that you hardly know them. It is perhaps not such a tragedy for George and Jane that they have not been blessed with children. They would surely have had to send them home to mother in Hayle.
>
> I must say that Cheltenham is a most agreeable town and I have quite an easy life with just one pupil. We often

walk in the Winter Gardens, which are nearby, and
sometimes we make a longer expedition to the Royal
Well. It is a pleasant path through the churchyard and
then across a meadow to the pump, which stands under a
dome capped with a sundial. To the left is a most
handsome long room where one can promenade after
drinking from the well. I have made the acquaintance
there of a most interesting person, a Miss Beale, who is
the headmistress of the Ladies College that is situated
close to us, at the end of Rodney Terrace. She must, I
suppose, be about the same age as Annie, but she has
charge of more than one hundred girls and has great
ambitions to expand further. But the building that the
college occupies, Cambray House, is a gloomy old place,
more like a monastery in one of those gothic romances we
used to read. I could swear I have seen bats flitting about
at night! I believe she is hoping to find better
accommodation and to open a dormitory building so that
she can take boarders as well as day girls.'

Hester considers the possibility of working in a school like
Miss Beale's in a bigger town like Cheltenham, or even in
London. For now, Sherborne will have to do. Miss
Puddicombe is a generous employer and Hester counts
herself lucky to have obtained a position in her
establishment. Mademoiselle Bouchard and Hester are the
only teachers who are not family members. It is clearly a
source of great satisfaction to Miss Puddicombe that,
although she has never been without employment, she has
now been able, with the financial support of her cousin and
widowed sister-in-law, to rent this house and open a school
of her own. Like Annie in Hayle, she has also provided a
home for two of her nephews. The house can accommodate
a handful of boarders but most of the pupils are local girls
who attend for the day and return home at night. They
manage with just one servant and a daily woman. It is a not
so very different from life in Cornubia Cottage.

Hester has a bedroom on the attic floor with a small iron bedstead that sits under a criss-crossing framework of dark wooden beams. It feels light and spacious compared with the cramped room she used to share with her sisters, and the breeze that flutters the light muslin curtains brings no smuts or smoke from funnels and foundry chimneys. There is no clattering and banging from the quay as cargo is loaded and anchors hauled up. But nor is there a salty tang of the sea, a screeching of gulls, and the sense of a wider world just beyond the bay. Sherborne is landlocked, insular, and, Hester admits to herself, slightly dull.

Each day begins with prayers before breakfast, then the girls start to arrive and Hester is kept busy hearing lessons, supervising needlework, and playing the piano for singing practice. It is not arduous work and the girls are generally obedient, but she is pleased when evening comes and she can sit in the parlour with the Puddicombes, chatting companionably over their mending and letter-writing, or perhaps listening as one of them reads from a novel borrowed from the circulating library. Sometimes she persuades Mademoiselle Bouchard to converse in French so that she can improve her accent and vocabulary. It will stand her in good stead if she wishes to look for a better position. On Saturday afternoons she is free to take her sketchbook and stroll as far as the ruined castle with its landscaped gardens laid out by Capability Brown, the tall trees reflected in the still waters of the lake. Now that she has a little money of her own, she may go shopping for ribbon to trim a hat, or if she is feeling extravagant, a new pair of gloves. Oh, to be rich and able to afford the latest fashions. On Sundays she usually attends the Methodist chapel in Cheap Street, but occasionally she allows herself to be tempted by the magnificence of the historic abbey. She wonders if it is wrong to take pleasure in a building when you are supposed to be concentrating on repentance.

14 'Far from my native land and home'

A Strike at the Foundry

Ernest is the only one of the Dupen siblings whose voice has survived, thanks to the logbook that he bequeathed to his nephew, my grandfather. I discovered it, protected by a brown, recycled envelope and labelled by my father (who also saved oddments of string and anything else that he believed he could re-use) in black marker pen: 'E. V. Dupen 3 Voyages'. And so it made its way down the generations – a narrative of travel to foreign lands gradually transforming itself from geography into history. Within its marbled covers, in elegant handwriting now faded to sepia, Ernest recorded three years of his life in a daily journal, but first, like a schoolboy with a new exercise book, the 21-year-old engineer decorated the title page with an elaborate doodle. A swan gradually emerges from the abstract pattern, fine lines swirling and curling into a pattern of plumage, waves, and seabirds. Beneath her, like a precious egg in a nest of waves, she shelters two lines of verse:

> *Borne upon the ocean's foam*
> *Far from my native land and home*

At the foot of the page a pair of crossed quills protect the threshold to this period of his life. Perhaps Ernest hoped one day to have a son, a boy to inherit his dreams of spice islands, storms, and shipwrecks, but he left no direct descendants and the responsibility of deciphering the faded pages in order to bring him back to life has been inherited by me, a mere female. I fear he would not have approved.

Ernest is meticulous in noting weather conditions, wind direction, time, and distance, but he gives away very little

about his feelings, apart from an occasional grumpiness that
seems to belong to an older man. His prejudices are of their
time and when I decided to allow him to tell his own story, I
had to accept that his words would sometimes be offensive.
His attitude towards the men he calls 'coolies' is unacceptable
today, but if we want to understand our ancestors we cannot
endow them with twenty-first century sensibilities. I believe
Ernest's logbook has value as an authentic record of his age.
It has a truth that is of a different order to the scenes of my
own invention. But before I let him speak, I wanted to
imagine what led him to abandon the security of his home for
an uncertain life in a dark, smoky boiler room, described by
one ship's engineer as 'rather like working in a coal mine that
was on fire during an earthquake'.

Hayle, January 1872

The men walk towards the hall singly or in small groups,
hunched over as if unwilling to show their faces.
Occasionally they glance from side to side, checking to see if
they are observed. Ernest falls into step with a fellow
apprentice from the engine fitting shop who, unlike the
others, is striding out with an air of bravado. He is rumoured
to be amongst those who have called the meeting.

> **NOTICE**
> There will be a meeting held at the Copperhouse
> Public Hall this evening (Jan 10th) to take into
> consideration the best means of obtaining the 9 hour
> system. All mechanics who are interested are earnestly
> invited to attend.
> Business to commence at 7.30.

It is dark, with no moon, and a chill wind is blowing
across the Copperhouse Pool, ruffling the surface and adding
a sharp whiff of salt to the soft, sulphurous smoke from the
foundry chimneys. Ernest shivers and turns up his collar. Like
his brother John, when he began his apprenticeship at

Harvey's foundry he promised to serve his masters faithfully, 'their secrets keep, their lawful commands everywhere gladly do'. Now, he realises uneasily, he is about to rebel.

He pushes his way into the hall, already packed with men in soot-stained overalls. The room smells of sweat and coal dust. Ernest can see the Rector, the Reverend Hocken, at the front surrounded by a confused group of workers.

'But we thought you would take the chair, Reverend.'

'Not I,' replies the red-faced clergyman. 'I am here merely to observe. I would not wish my presence here to be construed as support for what I conceive to be a most wrong-headed course of action.'

There is a good deal of muttering as man after man declines to take the chair, saying that the masters have always acted very kindly and liberally by them. They can't see the difference, thinks Ernest, between treating a man with kindness and treating him with respect. But eventually a chairman is found and the invited speaker stands up to explain that in the industrial towns of the north, labourers have put pressure on their employers to reduce the working hours in factories to nine a day or 54 a week, with no reduction in pay. Harveys' men, who work a 61 hour week, are keen to see their own conditions improved in a similar way. Some of the older workers are still reluctant to risk offending their masters but the mood in the hall is against them. The men agree to draft a petition on the spot and elect a committee to submit it to management the next day. But who can find the right words?

'Where's young Dupen?' a fitter from the engine shop asks. 'He writes a fair hand and knows his grammar.'

Ernest, at just five feet tall, is hard to see amongst the crowd but he raises his hand and a path is cleared for him to the front. It is a novel experience being the centre of attention, but not an unwelcome one. At home no one would think of entrusting the baby of the family with an important job. But he was educated at Hayle Academy and here amongst the foundry workers he is respected as the brother of the Misses Dupen, proprietors of the town's most exclusive school for young ladies.

Later that night he walks home lost in thought. As he turns the corner of Commercial Road to follow the railway tracks along Penpol Terrace, he looks up at the dark mass of Brunel's great viaduct and wonders uneasily what Annie is going to say.

The next day, on his arrival at the gates of the foundry, he finds a crowd starting to gather in the square.

'What's happened?' he asks one of the fitters.

'They've only gone and dismissed the committee, that's what,' says the man grimly. 'Never even got a chance to present the petition neither.'

'I did hear tell it were Mr Hocken gave the game away,' says another man. 'He done wrote a sneaking letter to management. And him a reverend too.'

'So what are we doing out here?' asks Ernest.

'Us be on strike, young feller-me-lad. Masters'll have to think again when they see all five hundred of us have downed tools.'

The crowd is growing by the minute and Ernest can feel the anger in the air. He shares the sense of grievance. Surely it was not too much to ask to be allowed to present their case. These are not the old days, when Mr Harvey's word was law throughout the town. But before things have a chance to turn violent, a message comes from management to say that they are willing to receive a deputation, and by the end of the morning the word goes round that an agreement has been reached. All workers shall leave at midday on a Saturday and still receive a full day's pay. A great cheer goes up as the new terms are announced along with an invitation from the masters to share in a celebratory dinner. It is victory – of a sort.

Joining the *Japan*

The committee members signed an apology humbly
acknowledging that they 'would feel most obliged to Messrs
Harvey & Co. if they will look it over and reinstate [them] as
before in their employ'. Ernest, along with the other ninety
engine fitters, signed the memorandum capitulating to his
employer's terms. When I ordered up the Harvey papers from
the records' office in Truro, there was his name, in the same
hand as the logbook. But he must have started to wonder if a
job for life came at too high a price. It was an obvious choice
for him to follow in his brothers' footsteps and go to sea.
Perhaps he had heard from John about the frustrations of
being an engineer in the Royal Navy, where officers with
attitudes as stiff as their collars were still baffled about how to
treat this strange breed of men whose skills so far surpassed
their social status. Whatever the reason, Ernest chose the
more forward-thinking merchant service, signing articles as 4th
engineer on a steamer owned by the Armenian Arratoon
Apcar company, based in Calcutta. Seth, the son listed by
Lloyds as owning the *Japan*, later had the distinction of
becoming the first Armenian Sheriff of Calcutta (a ceremonial
position currently occupied by a Bollywood actor). The *Japan*
had been built specifically for the new Suez Canal trade, and
in September 1873 Ernest set off for the London docks to
board the vessel that would be his home for the next three
years. He and his brother John would be crisscrossing the
same shipping routes, although they seem never to have
encountered each other in port.

When Sharrock Dupen joined the crew of the *Herald* in
1835 there were over 19,000 sailing vessels compared with
around 550 steamships in the British merchant fleet, but by
now the balance was shifting. The change to fewer, bigger
ships meant fewer jobs for masters and mates (so George had
changed career at the right time), but a huge increase in the
need for engineers. They were well paid for their expertise.

The chief engineer on the *Japan* received £30 a month, more than double the pay of the 1st mate, while Ernest was paid £10, twice the salary of the 4th mate, and worth about around £800 today.

On his arrival Ernest would have reported to the captain, Alexander Burnett Mactavish. A Scot from Inverness, Mactavish had started as an apprentice at the age of sixteen, working his way up from boatswain to 2nd and then 1st mate, and obtaining his master's certificate in the previous February. He had done well in his first command, the *SS Arratoon Apcar*, and had now at the age of 35 been entrusted with the company's newest vessel. The first mate, an Afrikaner from Cape Town, had also transferred from the *Arratoon Apcar* and he, the other two mates, four engineers, surgeon, and purser were the only members of the crew of European descent. They were all in their twenties and thirties, some married with children and others still single, some having spent their working lives at sea, others new to life on board ship. They would have to learn to rub along together in the cramped quarters that were to be their home for the next five months. Unlike in the navy, the eighty sailors, firemen, coal trimmers and other crew, including the cook, butcher and ship's carpenter, came from across the lands of the East, from Calcutta, Sylhet, and Chittagong, from Singapore, Canton, Java and Penang. Known only by their first names, Allee, Baboo, Hassan, John or Joe, they were under the command of their *serang* or boatswain, and his assistants, the *tindals*; they had mysterious roles like *kussub* or *bandary*. It was a whole new language for Ernest to learn.

When Ernest stepped from the train at Millwall Dock station, the terminus of the new extension to the London and Blackwall railway, he would have seen before him a forest of masts and cranes, with ropes and rigging hanging like jungle creepers from the tall trunks. Single storey warehouses and open-sided timber sheds surrounded the murky water. Against the background stench of sewage from the river the smell of wood and sawdust mixed with the oily aroma of wool and the chemical stink from McDougall's fertiliser factory. Unlike the neighbouring West India Dock, with its warehouses stacked high with valuable sugar, rum, and coffee, the Millwall Dock did not need the protection of a high perimeter wall, and the policeman at the gate probably just waved him through. Ernest may have paused to examine, with professional curiosity, the hydraulic cranes that lined the wharves, before walking on towards his destination. The *Japan* occupied the dry dock alongside the engineering works. At 336 feet long she was the biggest vessel he had ever been on and more than double the length of the *Queen of the Avon*, which had carried George to New Zealand. She had recently returned from her nine-month maiden voyage to India and China and was having her hull scraped clean of the marine growth that had begun to make her sluggish. Ernest, who grew up next to a shipyard, would know that this was a disadvantage of iron ships, although they were larger, stronger, and lighter than wooden ones.

He would have quickly settled into the cupboard in the stern that was his cabin, stowing away the tin trunk containing his flannel trousers, soft shirts, and canvas overalls, along with a warm coat, his bedding and towels, and the writing case containing his new logbook. His bunk was hardly wider than a shelf and it was fortunate that he was a small man because otherwise he would not have been able to stretch out at full length. The 3rd engineer, Joseph Carrier, occupied the other bunk; it was his first ship too. Carrier, a Kentishman ten years Ernest's senior, had left a wife and two young children behind and no doubt spoke often of them in the first days. Ernest had slept alone in the bedroom at home since Sam's death, becoming accustomed to the empty space where his brother had been. Now, in the claustrophobic cabin, I wonder if he felt his loss afresh, remembering the dreams he and Sam had shared of sailing away into the unknown.

The next day the *Japan* was hauled out of the dock and
through the entrance lock. The huge gates, ten times the
height of a man, were opened and she emerged into the
Thames. She steamed round to Poplar where, in the export
dock, she took on general cargo destined for Colombo and
Calcutta: a jumble of boxes, bundles, bales and barrels
containing everything from biscuits to sewing machines. Deck
winches clattered away, dumping the cargo unceremoniously
through the hatches. Choking clouds of steam and coal dust
rose up to make Ernest cough and sneeze. He no doubt
observed with interest the muscular, brown-skinned men
known to him as 'lascars', and slight, pigtailed Chinese who
were stacking the goods in the hold. Previously he had only
seen men like these in picture books but now they would be
his constant companions. Finally the ship was fully laden and
on Friday 10th October 1873 she set out down the river for
Gravesend, where she anchored overnight. The next day, in
that dim early light that so often marks the start of a new
adventure, she steamed out of the shelter of the estuary in a
long skein of other ships heading to foreign ports.

The Bay of Biscay lived up to its reputation for bad
weather. Water crashed over the deck, smashing hen coops
and killing several of the fowl intended to provide a supply of
fresh eggs and the occasional boiled dinner. Fortunately there
was no other loss of life, but the young 4th engineer watched
carefully from the window of his cabin for an opportune
moment to come up on deck; with his short stature he was at
risk of being washed overboard by the strength of the waves.
He was starting to experience that most disagreeable
condition, sea sickness. Victuals, he wrote in his log, had
ceased to be attractive to him, but reminding himself sternly
that he was not a passenger, he fought against the malady and
managed occasionally to eat a little dry toast or biscuit
supplied by Abdool, the Indian butler.

On Monday night the chief engineer, an experienced
former naval officer in his thirties, left the youngest member

of his team in sole charge of the engines. Ernest was unaccustomed to responsibility. Although he may well have been glad to escape from the stifling care of his mother and sisters and their constant reminders to wash his hands or say his prayers, the rough, masculine world of the steamship would still have come as a shock. Unlike the foundry, there was no going home at the end of a shift. There were no women to cook, sew on buttons, or wash his clothes; no girls to play music or read aloud by the soft light of an oil lamp. I know Ernest read story books. Possibly he had grown up with the tales of Fenimore Cooper and Captain Marryat and dreamed of becoming a hero, saving people from sinking ships, quelling mutinies, and confronting hostile tribesmen. But this was real life and he would quickly be judged by his shipmates on his character and competence.

Ernest descended into the dark, steamy heat and constant, deafening noise of the huge cylinders that towered out of the depths of the hold, two decks high. That first watch must have felt like the longest four hours of his life, alone with the soot-covered gang of firemen shovelling coal to feed the insatiable red mouths of the boilers, surrounded by coils of white steam, the ash buckets clattering up to the deck with their grey, dusty load. The men crouched over in the darkness, swinging their shovels in constant rhythmic motion, protected from the fumes only by a wet rag tied across their mouths. Amidst the noise of the coal crunching underfoot, the clang of the furnace door, and the roar of the flames, the young engineer took his hourly readings of oil levels and steam pressure, alert to the slightest change in the rhythm of the engines. But during that long watch when he struggled with nausea and anxiety he must also have had time for reflection, perhaps reassuring himself with words from the poem he had chosen as his logbook motto:

Yet if wildest tempests swell,
Be thou near and all is well
Saviour! On the stormy sea
Let us find repose in thee.

By Sunday the *Japan* had passed through the Straits of
Gibraltar and was in the Mediterranean, heading towards
Malta. When Ernest wrote his next letter home, he may not
have risked the disapproval of his mother and sisters by
admitting the lack of a proper Sunday service, but he noted it
in his log:

> *Sunday 19th October 1873*
> My first Sunday at sea passed unnoticed, owing to my
> sea sickness, but today it has occurred to me that there
> is such a day. It's an old saying that there is no Sunday
> beyond 7 fathoms of water, and I'm sure such is the
> case with us. Being only 9 English on board, and a
> portion of those doing duty, it would be almost a farce
> to think of holding a service, even if any one on board
> had any inclination to do so. The men are all mustered
> on deck at 10 a.m. to see that they are all clean, and
> their clothes in order, but with this exception there is
> no difference in this and any other day of the week.

A week later, in the early hours of Sunday 26th October
the *Japan* reached the entrance to the Suez Canal.

When the canal was opened in November 1869 the map
of the oceans was redrawn overnight. It was the beginning of
the end of the seafaring life George Dupen had known. The
average journey from London to Calcutta or Hong Kong was
cut by about 3,500 miles, shortening the journey time by at
least ten days, and allowing travellers to avoid the dangerous
passage round the Cape of Good Hope or the uncomfortable
journey by land across the isthmus from Alexandria to the
Red Sea. The canal authority was a joint venture between
Egypt and France and a French pilot came on board the *Japan*
to see her safely into Port Said. The harbour, formed by large

blocks of cement dropped from barges, was still under construction and Ernest found the town lacking in natural beauty, although the offices of the agents for the different lines of steamers were 'very prettily designed' and the large lighthouse at the entrance was also 'a very fine specimen'. 'Of course,' he commented disparagingly, 'the lively French-man cannot do without the café & the music hall, which in most instances are combined, for there are several although it is such a small place.'

The navigable channel was just 72 feet wide and every six miles a siding was provided where ships could anchor to allow traffic to pass in the opposite direction. The offices in Port Said, Ismailia, and Suez each kept a narrow trough about fifteen feet long representing their section of canal and on a shelf above it a set of model ships bearing different national flags. In response to telegraph signals the staff moved these models in and out of the trough so that the exact position of every ship was always known and the traffic could be regulated. It is an image that reminds me of hours spent pushing my brother's collection of miniature ships across a sea-green plastic sheet that did duty as the Atlantic Ocean, but this was no child's game – a mistake would have potentially deadly consequences. The *Japan* travelled just thirty miles in seven hours before mooring up for the night. The next morning after passing through a narrow cutting with high banks, they stopped at Ismailia, 'the city of the desert', to change pilots. They anchored that evening at the 62 mile siding and by 9.30 the next morning they had arrived in Suez and were clear of the canal.

After a stiflingly hot voyage through the Red Sea and a clear run across the Indian Ocean, by the middle of November the *Japan* arrived off Colombo. There was no harbour so the cargo was discharged into a fleet of small boats manned by half-naked labourers, who worked all day and into the night with nothing but a little water to drink. At midnight, when they were counted off the ship, one man was so overcome with exhaustion that he fell asleep with his head resting on the rail and could not be roused, even when a hot lamp was held to his side. He was eventually carried away still sleeping.

From Colombo the *Japan* made her way up the east coast of India, tumbling about in the heavy sea after leaving half her cargo in Ceylon. At the mouth of the Hooghly a pilot came on board to take her up the river to Calcutta, the family home of the Apcars. Ernest was unimpressed by the city:

Saturday 22nd December

"Calcutta" is rather too large for me here to attempt a detailed description of it. It has been called the City of Palaces, but for my part I could see but little to admire, most of the buildings except those quite new having a dark & decayed appearance, this may be owing to the stone they are built of, like the Bath stone. Many of the buildings are very large & boast of a good deal of architectural beauty. The post-office, Paper-Currency-Office, New Law Courts & several other public buildings are very fine. The drainage seems anything but good, the smells in most parts of the city being very offensive. The public gardens are very nicely laid out & are visited about 6 p.m. (when the band of one of the regiments plays for about 2 hours) by a large number of people, many of them driving there in grand style. The river is now kept much purer than it was some years ago, the river-police always keeping a look out above the town for dead bodies and sinking them before they reach the town. There is very little wind even on the river & towards night, even at this time of the year it gets but little cooler, always the same sultry kind of weather day after day. I shall not be at all sorry to leave it.

The ship took on cargo for her return journey via Marseilles and the engineers got up steam to check the running of the engines. All seemed well until at about eleven o'clock one December night a cry of 'fire' was heard from the engine room. The wooden casing of the boilers was in flames. The crew were all ashore so the engineers had to call on other ships for help. Fortunately, enough sailors were mustered to man the pumps and after about two hours the worst was over, with no damage to any other part of the ship. Such fires were apparently a regular hazard. The river fire engine, observed Ernest drily, arrived as usual after the fire had been extinguished.

By then it was nearly Christmas. On 24ᵗʰ December Ernest went ashore and found the English families of Calcutta strolling past shops decorated with evergreens, admiring the windows full of toys, but he was not to be allowed to celebrate in the traditional way. Although Arratoon Apcar was a notable Christian philanthropist, nothing was allowed to interfere with business and on Christmas Day the *Japan* set off down the Hooghly. They anchored at about one o'clock with instructions to get their dinner over with as quickly as possible and then continued on their way.

New Year's Eve was no better, although Ernest was awake to see the new year in. 'Perhaps this is no credit to me,' he pointed out, 'it being my watch from 8 to 12 p.m.' Then as now, the merchant service relied on routine, schedules, and procedure to manage a hazardous world that exists in parallel to our own. The same calendars and clocks acquire a different significance at sea; life on board ship alternates with precision between work and rest, leaving no space for spontaneous celebration. After three months on the *Japan* Ernest was attuned to the rhythm of his new life.

For All the Tea in China

In February 1874, while John was cruising Chinese waters, Ernest was back in London. But by the end of March the *Japan* was preparing to set sail again from the West India

Docks, bound this time for the Far East. She had a new
captain. Forty-five year old Henry De Smidt from Cape Town
had first gone to sea as a fifteen-year-old midshipman and had
been a ship's master since 1865. Despite these years of
experience, Ernest was slow to trust him. In his logbook the
4th engineer wrote that he was concerned about the quantity
of heavy cargo stowed in the bottom of the hold, speculating
that had any Lloyds surveyor known how she was loaded,
they would have objected to her going to sea. He is referring
to the tables drawn up for the safe loading of ships registered
with Lloyds. It was not until two years later that a successful
campaign led by the MP Samuel Plimsoll resulted in the
Merchant Shipping Act that made load lines compulsory for
British ships (and the *Japan* of course was not British).

Ernest's comment is his first acknowledgement of the
danger that has accompanied seamen for as long as they have
entrusted their lives to the oceans. It is not something they
discuss with friends and family, who would not understand.
The risks are not just storm, shipwreck, and piracy, but also
shifting cargo that can capsize a vessel, and fire – bales of
cotton and wool for example, were known to overheat and
combust. Seamen have been described as living in a kind of
constant limbo between life and death, but they quickly learn
a contradictory mix of insecurity and confidence that allows
them to recognise danger and deal with it calmly. Ernest
noted the problem and said nothing; he recognised that in a
profit-driven business Captain De Smidt was taking a
calculated risk.

The *Japan* made her way once more through the Suez
Canal and on to Singapore. The port was an important
coaling station that supplied as much as 15,000 tons to
passing steamers every month. Ernest observed that the
Chinese did all the work there, with pairs of labourers
carrying heavy baskets of coal slung on bamboo canes at a
speed that allowed a ship in a hurry to take on about 100 tons
per hour and be away in seven or eight hours. Ernest escaped

briefly for a drive along a pleasant tree-shaded promenade where pineapples and bananas could be bought at bargain prices. Given the restricted diet on board ship, his interest in food and its cost is perhaps unsurprising.

Two weeks later the *Japan* was moored to the company's private buoy in Hong Kong. Ernest described the town with approval:

> *Friday 22nd May*
>
> The town of "Hong-Kong" presents by far the prettiest appearance of any other I've seen in the east. It is built on the side of a very steep hill or almost a mountain, Victoria Peak (where there is a signalling station) being 1500 feet above the sea level. Most of the towns I've seen in the east are very deceptive with regard to appearance, when viewed from a distance they have more or less a decayed appearance but such is not the case with "Hong-Kong". Everything looks fresh and new, and the trees that are planted on both sides of the street give it a very pleasant appearance besides the pleasant shade during the heat of the day. The town hall is well worth a visit. One can pass an afternoon there without feeling weary. On the upper storey there is a Ball-room, Dining-room, Chamber of Commerce with their respective anterooms. Below them is the Theatre, Museum and Library, which is open to the public, who can by signing their name take any book out but it must be read here and returned before leaving. The Governmental Dockyard is a small but very compact place well found in everything necessary for fitting out a large number of ships. The Military-barracks are very large, there being a great number of the military of different descriptions stationed there. Most of the small shops are kept by Chinamen, the English only doing business in a large way. The Public-Gardens are very beautifully laid out. Flowers and plants that would require care and

attention in a greenhouse in England growing in the
open air. This is a favorite resort between 5 and 7 in
the summer evenings. The Cathedral is a very
substantial building & is attended by a large & genteel
congregation.

Ernest was intrigued by the lifestyle of the boat people
who lived aboard the junks in the harbour:

There being only one wharf at which ships can
discharge their cargo, there are a large number of boats
of different sizes employed in landing cargo. Some of
the junks carry about 100 tons. All boats are numbered
& licensed & to judge from their numbers, there must
be thousands of people living afloat, the boats being
their home, no doubt there are many children years old
before they put foot on land. The boy seemed to be
most important of the two sexes for when very young
they have a buoy fastened to their backs, in order that
they may float, in case they fall overboard. The children
of both sexes are taught to swim as soon as they have
sense to work their arms and legs right. I've frequently
seen the father putting the children overboard on a bit
of wood.

Ernest was himself a keen swimmer, taking every
opportunity to bathe, but it occurs to me that I have no idea
if his sisters ever learned to swim.

On 27th May the *Japan* set off on a short voyage of about
four days to Shanghai, where the captain was hoping to pick
up a cargo of tea. Since the opening of the Suez Canal,
steamships were better able to challenge swift clippers like the
Cutty Sark. Previously, although iron ships had thinner sides
and therefore more hold capacity than wooden sailing vessels,
they had been handicapped by the amount of space that had
to be given up to coal. But now a steamer like the *Japan* could
go in search of the highly prized 'first chop' tea that reached
the ports in late May or June. She would be competing with

the forty or so sailing ships that were still engaged in the tea trade but she would have speed on her side. While the *Cutty Sark*'s fastest passage took 107 days, steamship records were being set and broken each year and the run to London from Shanghai would be cut from 41 days in 1876 to 27 in 1883. These were the last glory days of the trade, for China tea was losing its hold on the market as Assam and Ceylon took over. The new teas were cheaper, less likely to be adulterated, and generally better processed and packed.

The port of Shanghai was growing in importance. It had only been opened up to foreigners since the end of the Second Opium War and the four 'towns' – American, British, French, and the walled Chinatown – were each guarded by their own man of war. To the disappointment of the crew of the *Japan*, there was no tea to be had there, nor any prospect of a crop being sent down river for some considerable time, so they took in ballast and made their way to Hankow, about 640 miles up the Yangtze Kiang. In the safe hands of an experienced pilot who knew every inch of the banks and shoals, Ernest relaxed. He admired the flooded rice paddies and vivid green of the tea plantations, although the weather was 'simply boiling' and 'not at all healthy, a sort of low fever being very prevalent'. At Hankow lead-lined wooden chests containing millions of pounds of tea were loaded into the hold by bare-chested labourers in conical hats, one box to each yoked pair, the bamboo pole sagging under its weight. Pigtailed supervisors in long robes looked on as the cargo was stacked tightly to avoid movement that would unbalance the ship in heavy seas. The *Japan* then steamed down river to Kunkiang, where the crew spent a frustrating few weeks waiting for more tea, but by the end of June they were fully laden and homeward bound.

The chief engineer on this voyage was a 43-year-old Scot called James Laing, a hard-drinking character who was paid significantly less than his predecessor. From Singapore they headed south to try and avoid the worst of the monsoons but

in late July they found themselves in the middle of a gale. All
was well as long as they could keep moving, although men
were being washed off their feet by the waves and had to hold
tightly to the ropes to prevent themselves from pitching into
the ocean. Ernest for the first time allows himself a subtle dig
at his superior:

> *Sunday 26th July*
> As ill luck would have it we had to stop the engines at
> 4.30 a.m. to make good a defect. When I heard that we
> were going to stop I made everything secure in the
> cabin, knowing too well what we might expect, in a
> ship so large with so little canvas. The engines
> stopping, my worst fears were realised for no sooner
> had the engines stopped than the sea broke over the
> ship, like it would over a half-tide rock. All the time the
> weather was getting worse, standing on the iron plates
> in the engine room being almost impossible. Through
> bad management and a bottle of brandy, instead of the
> work being hurried forward for some hours worse than
> nothing was done, and but for the interference of the
> captain, no one knows how long we should have
> continued in the same condition, but he took it upon
> himself to remove the <u>obstacle</u> not the brandy to our
> progress, & in about 4 hours the ship was again under
> steam.

I take it that Mr Laing was escorted to his bunk to sleep
off his indisposition.

A month later they were waiting impatiently off
Gravesend for the evening tide to allow them up the river and
home to London.

Human Traffic

Both Ernest's voyages to date had lasted about five months but when he set sail again, it was to be a year and a half before he saw England again. After a few short weeks at home, in October 1874 the *Japan* set sail for India and this time came to anchor off Madras, where Ernest decided to visit the local railway works. In his backhanded compliment to the workers, he shows himself once more to be a man of his time:

> *Wednesday 18th November 1874*
> Having finished my work, thought I should like to take a run ashore. Got away from the ship at 1 p.m., landed with some difficulty at the Pier. Drove to the Post-office, then went about 4 miles into the country to visit the "Permabore"-Railway-Works. Had a very pleasant drive, the country being very beautiful, the road being shaded by beautiful palm-trees nearly all the way. The Works are far superior in size and construction to what I expected. The machinery was remarkably good and of modern construction. All the work is done by natives, who are looked after by English-Foremen. I had no idea that the Hindus were capable of doing such nice work, for those I've seen in "Calcutta" are most inferior workmen, and wanting constant attention if you wish anything done right.

He returned to Madras that evening by the same railway line that had taken George to Coimbatore and like his brother before him, experienced the drama of flying through the surf, an experience that the young man from Hayle took in his stride:

> By this time the Pier-boatmen had left so I had to look out for any one in want of a fare. In a short time a fellow came and said he had a crew at hand, who soon mustered on the beach, and commenced with any quantity of shouting to get the boat near the water.

They then stopped, the owner of the boat then came and demanded the modest sum of 10 rupees or 1£ for our passage. I didn't think it well to appear at all anxious about going off as he might then stick to the price, so I said all right I'll go off to another mooring. He soon made a dutch-auction of it and in a short time came down to a shilling over the day fare. This I promised to give. Then came the work of getting the boat through the surf which was very heavy. The boats are made of thin wood stitched together and are remarkably light, and carrying a crew of about 17 men, who almost carry the boat to where the sea has receded, then jump in and take to their oars, when the next sea comes and floats the boat they commence rowing, in this way getting a boat away in an incredibly short time. When once fairly out of the surf we were soon alongside the ship. Should I land at "Madras" again I should prefer going on to the beach through the surf, to landing at the pier, the latter being a work of some difficulty, owing to the heavy swell, while they run the boats through the surf on the beach as easily as possible, the boat being left high & dry so one has nothing to do but step out on the land.

From Madras they made their way up the coast to Calcutta but by Christmas Day they were in Penang, where Ernest remarked gloomily on yet another holiday passed without celebration:

Christmas-Day

I've passed one of the great holidays since I've been at sea without knowing it, and would rather I could pass them all in the same way, for it only makes one dissatisfied with his lot to be compelled to work, but must grin and bear it, the ship is ready for sea and must go, so once again I leave "Penang" without going ashore.

Their route took them to Singapore and on to the land known as Cochin China, or present day Vietnam, in time to celebrate the new year with a festive dinner, although Ernest had further scathing words to say about the French:

1st January 1875

At one p.m. French pilot came & took the ship up the river to "Saigon" or at least as near as the ship could go being too long to swing should she go nearer the town, this was rather more than a mile from the town. "Saigon" is about 45 miles up a winding river with very low banks, at high water the trees are almost under water & look like a flooded forest, it also overflows into the rice-fields but of course being fresh water it is the thing required for rice growing, which is carried on on a very large scale. "Saigon" is a "French" possession so there are very few English people. It is a most unhealthy place, as anyone might soon learn by the appearance of the soldiers, and sailors employed by the French Government on the several small gunboats there stationed. Everything is carried on in the French style. Cafes with small marble tables outside under the trees, all kinds of games ready at hand for gambling purposes. I dined at the Hotel d'Universe, such a dinner might suit the soup-sucking Frenchman, but an Englishman wants a more substantial meal than was here laid out. Although there were sixteen courses, the whole would scarcely make one good dish. The claret was very good, everyone being allowed a pint bottle with the dinner, and coffee and brandy to finish with.

A month later an incident occurred that was nearly the end of the *Japan*, and Ernest with her. He was, I have decided, of an exceptionally phlegmatic character – or perhaps he just wished to appear so:

5th February

Since our arrival this time the weather has been so hot
I've had no inclination to leave the ship, except to have
a swim from the jolly-boat which amusement I've
indulged in every day. Finished taking in a cargo of
rice, left Saigon 12 o.c. noon, clearing the river at
6 p.m. Strong head wind and heavy sea. Weather
continued much the same until 10th when we were
getting under cover of the land, sea almost smooth.
About 8.30 a.m. it got rather hazy, but we continued at
full speed, having a Chinese pilot in charge. At 9.23 the
Captain thought it advisable to go slower, the pilot
agreed and the Engines were slowed. Going on deck
just then I could see we were very close to the land &
that there was a rock close alongside, but thought it all
right, but in as little time as has been taken to write
from the time I got on deck, the ship struck with a
terrible crash, falling very heavily over to port as if she
was going down at once. For some seconds all was
confusion, but order being regained some ran to the
boats, others to see if the ship was making much water,
being satisfied that such was not the case things soon
reassumed their usual aspect. The ship was found to be
fairly afloat and the engines were reversed, and shortly
after, the ship was again under weigh at full speed, the
fog having cleared shortly after the accident.

They made for Hong Kong, where the *Japan* could put in
for repairs. It was only when I visited Brunel's *Great Britain,*
a ship of comparable size and construction 'afloat' on her solid
glass dock in Bristol, and was able to walk right under the vast
iron keel, that I appreciated the force needed to do the
damage described in Ernest's log:

Wednesday 24th February

Sufficient water out of the dock to see the damage
done to the boat. What is termed the fore-foot was

knocked at a complete right-angle to the side of the bows, the keel being very nearly broken in two, the plates up about 5 feet being turned back like dogs ears. Fortunately all the forward portion of the ship had been filled in with Portland-cement, which maintained its form after the plates had been torn from it, this accounted for the ship not making more water. It was estimated at the time that the repairs could be completed in a month, but before half that time had expired, it was found that the keel was broken in about 6 places, extending back 75 feet from the bows, where the last crack was situated. Owing to this discovery about 100 feet of keel had to be taken out. Extra hands were at once put on & the work was carried on night and day without intermission for six weeks when the ship was again ready for going out of the dock.

After the *Japan* had been repaired, Ernest learned that she had been chartered to take 1,018 Chinese emigrants to Cooktown in Australia. He was undismayed. He had now been working alongside Chinese firemen for nearly eighteen months and derived a good deal of amusement from learning to speak to them in pidgin, 'which is pronounced like pigeon, being the Chinese word for business'. He had seen enough 'Chinamen' at sea to know that 'they never cause any confusion however great their number,' and these passengers were not labourers but tradesmen, who would 'no doubt know how to behave themselves'. Even when he is being relatively complimentary about foreigners, he cannot help adopting a patronising air.

The *Japan* was adapted to carry passengers by an army of carpenters who added an extra deck below the main one. The Chinese workers, attracted by rumours of gold nuggets of fabulous size, paid $50 (£10) each for their passage, the equivalent of Ernest's monthly salary but much harder for them to accumulate. It was money that they hoped to earn back quickly in the recently discovered Palmer goldfield in

Queensland. Crowds of pigtailed men swarmed onto the ship, dressed in loose belted shirts, short, wide trousers and light boots. On their heads they wore flat straw hats. They brought with them pots and pans and baskets of provisions, rice, preserved ducks, and rice spirit, as well as knick knacks including silk and preserved ginger that they hoped to sell in Australia.

Large numbers of Chinese miners had been attracted to the early diggings in Victoria, with around 33,000 established there by 1858. They were unpopular with the Europeans, who resented the competition and accused them of being dirty in their habits and of spoiling the water. This hostility led to major riots and looting of Chinese property in the 1860s. Now, in an atmosphere of menace, the Chinese were setting out for the new fields in tropical north Queensland, which were not only difficult to access and work, but presented the additional danger of attack by hostile Aborigines. A newspaper article claimed that Cantonese miners were better suited to the climate, yet another reminder of their status as a different species:

> *Northern Territory Times and Gazette, 28th August 1875*
> To him the heat that thins the blood and fevers the brain and unstrings the nerve of the inhabitants of a colder climate is but an accustomed and genial warmth. He is not choked by the dust – has he not learned to endure it in the stifling streets of Canton? The burning sun does not dry his skin, and parch his throat, and sap his strength; but invigorates his tropic nature, and enables him to toil on.

It was estimated that by this time some 5,000 Chinese had landed in Cooktown.

The route to Australia took the *Japan* through the narrow and perilous Torres Straits and inside the Great Barrier Reef. It was not safe to travel by night so progress was slow but by 3rd May they were anchored off Cooktown:

Two small sailing vessels came alongside to take away
the passengers, who were not at all sorry to get away.
Each one brought his luggage on deck and in about 4
hours the vessels were away & we were relieved of our
heathen friends, who I must confess were far less
trouble on board than the same number of "English"
would have been.

After the Chinese had paid an exorbitant fee to be taken
off and dumped in the shallows, Ernest himself went ashore
and took a walk through the town. The first shops had been
set up in tents on plots pegged out along the main street, and
since all sorts of ruffians and petty criminals had flocked from
Brisbane, Sydney and Melbourne, robbery was an everyday
occurrence. Ernest's account makes me long to know what
books he had read:

> *Saturday 8th*
> I have omitted to say that soon after our arrival we
> were visited by numbers of diggers, some of whom
> were exactly of the description one sees in story book
> pictures. Their dress consisting of a broad brimmed
> straw hat, white or colored shirt, coarse cloth trousers,
> with leathern girdle to which the purse is attached, and
> rather heavy boots. Most of them seemed to have
> plenty of money, and were anxious to buy any Chinese
> curios we possessed, offering any price we liked to fix.
> In spite of the rough exterior of these men, most of
> them were remarkably well spoken & good mannered.
> Today for the first time I've had an opportunity of
> going ashore. Got away from the ship about 2 p.m., got
> ashore about 2.30. Took a walk through the town,
> which is about 2 miles long, but as yet quite in a crude
> state, having been lately too far from any place of
> importance for ships to visit, but since the Palmer
> diggings have been worked it has become a landing
> place for all stores for the diggings, and a place of

recreation for the miners who have known nothing but
hard work for months. Most of the miners who come
here are single men, so the majority of the houses are
boarding-houses, and unfortunately public-houses as
well. There are 52 of these taverns, and to judge from
the empty bottles under the houses (which by the way
are wood built on piles) I should say that they do a
remarkably good trade. In the evening I visited the
theatre, a building capable of holding about 200
people. Being Saturday night the place was well filled,
in fact there was scarcely room to form a ring for two
men to settle a dispute, as usual a woman was in the
case. During this part of the performance the curtain
was dropped until the affair was over. One or two little
affairs of this sort nearly had a like termination, but the
parties chose to go outside & do the more active part,
so as not to stop the performance on the stage.

From Cooktown they proceeded down the east coast to
Stockton, near Newcastle, to collect a cargo of coal to take
back to Hong Kong. Here Ernest was offended by the failure
of the Australians to maintain a proper sense of social
hierarchy:

Monday 16th
The ship being too long to anchor in the harbour
without getting aground, or coming in contact with
other ships, we were moored to another ship who was
made fast to a small wharf, on the opposite side of the
harbour to that on which the town is built. There is no
town here, only a few houses inhabited by people
employed at a repairing slip for ships. Here we had to
wait until the ship could be put under a crane to take in
coal. During my stay at "Stockton" I made several
visits to "Newcastle". It is not a very large town, but it
was a treat to be amongst English people again, just
like being at home. Found the people very hearty, not

the least stiffness existing, but on the other hand rather too much of the equality notion prevailing to suit my tastes.

But he clearly enjoyed being the centre of attention:

Wednesday 26th
Moved across the harbour and commenced taking coal at once. Finished taking in coal on Saturday but the pilot didn't think it safe to take the ship out unless it was perfectly smooth water. Through this we had the pleasure of spending another Sunday in "Newcastle" & were visited by nearly all the inhabitants of "Newcastle", who were anxious to have a look at the largest ship that had ever visited the port. The ship was crowded from end to end all the afternoon.

After she had discharged her cargo of coal in Hong Kong, the *Japan* was advertised in July 1875 as awaiting freight and charter. But trade, as in all the Chinese ports, was very slow, with large numbers of steamers waiting for commissions. By the end of the month Captain De Smidt had managed to put together half a load and set off for Singapore and Penang, hoping to pick up more business on the way. But after unloading the items destined for Singapore it became apparent that what remained was not enough to keep the ship safely in ballast. Rather than waste time waiting for more cargo he cancelled the rest of the voyage and had his customers' goods put into storage to await the next ship. The entrepreneurial captain then advertised his ship as open to any reasonable offer and by the middle of August was considering two possible charters: one to transport bullocks to Aceh in Sumatra, the other to take Muslim pilgrims to Jeddah, the nearest sea port to Mecca. Much to Ernest's dismay the latter was chosen – it was probably the most lucrative. The ship was fitted up to accommodate 1,250 passengers, the maximum number allowed by the Straits Settlements Passenger Act of 1858. The comparison with a cattle truck is unavoidable and

Ernest confided to his logbook that he would indeed rather have been in the Irish pig and cattle trade.

It would be another five years before the abandonment of the *SS Jeddah* inspired Conrad to write *Lord Jim*, but Ernest describes a business identical to the one so deplored in British newspapers at the time. The *Jeddah*, a steamship of about the same size as the *Japan*, set out from Penang with a cargo of 992 pilgrims bound for Mecca and on 10th August 1880 was reported as having foundered in the Red Sea. The only survivors, the captain and his wife, the chief officer, two engineers, and 16 'natives' were picked up by the steamer *Scindia* and landed at Aden. To everyone's astonishment the next day a second telegram from Aden reported that the *Jeddah* had been found drifting and towed safely into port with all her passengers. Captain Clark was universally condemned for his cowardice and inhumanity and had his master's certificate suspended by the court of inquiry.

A question was tabled in parliament about the shocking nature of the trade and the columns of the *Times* soon filled with accusations and counter-accusations. In an echo of the modern debate about Islamic extremism, the pilgrims were either accused of being 'wretched fanatics' or defended as 'decent and quiet Mahomedans' at the mercy of 'avaricious Britishers'. According to a Captain Henry Carter:

> *Times 14th August 1880*
> There are horrors on board such a ship which no Christian has ever dreamt of, and none but those who grow rich from such wickedness can form any idea of what goes on in these vessels under the British flag – wickedness worse, by far, than was ever found on board a slaver.

Nearly all the steamers engaged in this dreadful trade were owned by 'native' firms that made large profits – like Arratoon Apcar of Calcutta. An anonymous Singapore merchant stated firmly that no vessel was allowed to sail until the harbour master had counted the pilgrims to see that the maximum number was not exceeded. Ernest, however, later noted that when the quarantine doctor came aboard he made a pretence of counting while really 'drinking sundry glasses of grog'. But having signed articles that bound him to the *Japan* until the following year, he had no choice but to stay with the ship. In Singapore he watched the passengers arrive:

Tuesday 24th August
All cargo being on board the passengers commenced coming on board this morning. And a more miserable looking a lot of creatures it was never my lot to cast eyes on. Scores were very old, and in an advanced state of decrepitude, one old woman being a perfect skeleton and brought on board bound to the back of a young man, many of them being too old to walk by themselves requiring support from their juniors. There were also several women, with children too young to walk. I believe they came mostly from the Malay peninsula, Java, Corea and other small islands about 4 weeks' run from "Singapore". All going to visit the Birthplace (at Mecca) and Shrine (at Medina) of "Mahomet" their prophet. "Jeddah" being the nearest sea-port they go there by ship, and then have 2 days journey across the desert to Mecca, either on camels or on foot according to their means. After remaining at "Mecca" a short time they go on to "Medina" which is 21 days journey. When they have accomplished this they consider their most important religious duty discharged, one that is only required once in a lifetime. I've been told that the pilgrims from "Singapore" must have at least 200 dollars or about 42£ before starting, and no doubt to many this must be the savings of many years (I won't say of toil as they are all too lazy to work hard) of spice growing or tilling the ground, in different ways.

I am appalled but fascinated by Ernest's inability to see beyond racial stereotypes, even when confronted with

contrary evidence. These people have managed to save
enough money to come on the pilgrimage, but it cannot
possibly be the result of hard labour.

As the pilgrims settled themselves on deck for the month's
voyage, it was difficult to distinguish between the rags of their
clothing and their bedding. They brought with them what
food they could afford, and the more fortunate had a tea or
coffee pot. In Penang they took on board more passengers:

> *Sunday 29th*
> Ready to start at noon. Got away soon after, our
> passengers now numbering 1220, or counting every
> child under 12 years of age as one - 1367. A goodly
> number to stow in one ship beside a crew of about 80.
> I sincerely hope we shall be favoured with fair winds,
> to shorten the passage, for already the ship is in a
> beastly mess from the rinds and offal of fruit (which
> they eat in large quantities), for they never think of
> throwing anything overboard. I thought the Chinese
> bad enough, but the decks were never the worse for
> their being on board.

They called first at Al Mukalla in Yemen, as lawless then as
it is now:

> *Saturday 18th September*
> Arrived at "Macullah" about 6 a.m. today. Came to an
> anchor about a mile from the shore. This place looks
> quite as dreary as any place I've seen, and has far less
> traces of civilisation, being one of the places in
> "Arabia" that no other country has thought worth
> taking possession of. Consequently, a wretched state of
> anarchy prevails. Everyone has to be his own
> protector, being armed to the teeth in the every day
> walks of life. Nearly every man that came on board had
> two or three short daggers placed in a most convenient
> situation for immediate use & are by no means
> neglected should the slightest difference of opinion

occur. I saw one or two instances of drawing on board
our ship on a very slight provocation. In a very friendly
way I examined some of the daggers worn by those
who visited the ship, and from their dark colour, and
the constant sharpening they had received, I should see
they had done some service. The captain was the only
one from the ship that went on shore. He went to see
about getting water for the ship, and when going to see
the well, was escorted by four soldiers, two on each
side. Things at this time are in an unusually unsettled
state, the "Macullahites" being at war with a
neighbouring tribe. The captain called to see the
"Governor", and found him at the topmost story of his
house, going there to be as far away from his enemies,
up no less than sixteen flights of steps. At the landing
of each there was an iron door guarded by a soldier
with a gun and fixed bayonet.

The town is built on the rocks, the sea washing
against the houses nearest the water at high water. At
the back there are almost perpendicular cliffs of
immense height, on the top of which there are four
tumble down looking forts, of the guns they contained
I could form but little idea, being too great a distance
from them. The appearance of the town reminded me
very strongly of the pictures in Scriptural story books.
The flat roofs and plain fronts of the houses being just
like those printed in such books. We've made a much
longer stay than we expected, there being only five
small cargo-boats and the men engaged in working
them not being the most industrious. I was not at all
sorry when we were ready for a start. The smell of fish
which the pilgrims had been buying in large quantities
being enough to breed a plague.

After this brief halt, they continued on to Jeddah:

Sunday 26th

Guns got ready this morning for firing as a signal for a
pilot, but were not required as a pilot came off to us
when we were some miles from "Jeddah". The ship
was going pretty fast as the pilot came alongside & he
seeing that he wouldn't be able to bring his boat to a
standstill alongside, jumped into the water, swimming
to the ladder that was hanging over the side, and came
on the bridge with the water running out of his clothes
which were very thin and light so would take but a
short time to dry in the blazing hot sun. As we got
nearer the reefs outside "Jeddah" they presented a
most formidable appearance, running in all directions
in front of the town, but our pilot didn't seem at all
afraid of taking such a large ship in, he couldn't speak a
word of English, but his looks were sufficient to show
that he considered his task a very easy one. To the
relief of all on board the ship was anchored in the
natural harbour, by 12.30 p.m., having come through
places where one might almost jump on from the
ship's side. Immediately the ship had anchored, she
was surrounded by small boats, come to take away our
living freight & to the satisfaction of all on board, by
evening the wretched pilgrims (with very few
exceptions) had landed. There were only 14 deaths
during the voyage & those that died were nearly all very
old people. This is very unusual on such runs, as it is
the rule & not the exception to have a very high death
rate. One ship I heard of, had cholera and smallpox on
board at the same time, no less than two hundred dying
out of seven hundred. When first I saw our crowd, I
quite expected something of the same sort. I was told
by several on shore at "Singapore" that no doubt we
should bury at least a hundred, but fortunately we fared
better, no doubt owing in a great measure to our large

> hatchways & the continual current of air created by
> fine wind-sails.

Ernest found Jeddah to be less lawless than Al Mukalla,
which he attributed to it being under Turkish control,
although savage dogs roamed the streets and he had problems
avoiding the large number of camels awaiting hire,
complaining that, 'it is no uncommon thing to find oneself
(especially any one as small as myself) under a camel's nose,
or very soon getting between its legs'. He went ashore only
once and whiled away the time when he was not working by
fishing and boating in the cool of the evening.

Eventually the *Japan* was ordered back to Aden to await
instructions. On his arrival there the captain telegraphed
Calcutta and was directed to proceed to Bussorah (Basra) on
the Persian Gulf to collect another batch of passengers. In
those days before the destruction of the ancient marshlands
of Mesopotamia, Ernest could still travel the two miles up the
creek to the town by boat, enjoying the shade of the many
fine date palms loaded with fruit. Here too it was perfectly
safe at night because the Turks were in control, but he was
sorry to see the soldiers who had been Britain's loyal allies in
the Crimean War reduced by lack of money to living in
grubby mud huts.

The *Japan* had to wait nearly a month in Bussorah for
passengers but the weather was pleasant and with his usual
keen attention to his stomach, Ernest noted that beef and
mutton were to be had at very low prices. He was quite
comfortable there until on 13th November he woke up with a
fever and headache. He was soon delirious. As he lay in his
cabin sweating and calling out in confusion, he was unaware
that he had succumbed to a severe attack of the malaria that
infested the marshes and so often proved fatal. A doctor
came from the barracks and administered a massive dose of
quinine – much stronger than an English practitioner would
have risked – and after about six days his patient started to get
better. The after effects were to remain with him, however,

and Ernest would succumb periodically to attacks of fever for the rest of his life.

At the end of November the *Japan* set sail again with a cargo of grain and about 300 pilgrims. They made their way down the Persian Gulf to Bushehr, where they picked up more passengers who, hoping to 'combine business with their religious duty', were carrying numerous items for sale. The next port of call was Bandar Abbas, where they collected another fifty pilgrims, and then they made their way back to Jeddah. The Persians sat quietly on their boxes and scarcely moved but the Arabs proved to be a troublesome lot. Noisy and agitated by day, they would appear on deck at night making 'unreasonable demands'. I imagine a scene similar to one described in the *Times* by Captain Carter (who had made the comparison with the slave trade). He believed he had removed all the swords, daggers and firearms brought on board by the ferocious Bedouins but when he attempted to move some luggage that was obstructing the steering gear he found himself confronted by 150 'cut-throat Arabs', who were still in possession of enough weapons to make his task impossible. Being one of only four Europeans on board and fearing for his life, he gave in. Captain De Schmidt was made of sterner stuff and on more than one occasion threatened to shoot his unruly passengers in order to maintain order. But Ernest recognised the shocking conditions that the pilgrims had to endure:

> *Sunday 12th December*
> As on our arrival here [Jeddah] last time, there were any quantity of boats ready to take the pilgrims on shore & in about 3 hours after our arrival, they had all cleared out. Then came the task for the sailors of washing decks and cleaning the ship, which was no easy one, for she was in an indescribable mess, this lot of pilgrims being much dirtier in their habits than the "Malays". We've another dose before us and after that I trust I've done with the pilgrim traffic, which is very

little better than the African slave-trade, with regard to the arrangements made for the comfort of the poor wretches. If they are sick they must remain where they are, there being no hospital or even a doctor to attend to them, or I may go farther & say no physic, that might in many complaints be administered by unskilled hands. The water supply is not what it ought to be, water should be taken on board sufficient for the whole run, instead of which about 6 days water is taken on board, and for the rest we have to trust to a distilling apparatus making about 1 ½ days water in twenty four hours. Should this break down in mid-ocean the results must be too horrible to contemplate. Why such a state of things is overlooked in an English-possession I cannot understand, the bulk of the pilgrims going to "Jeddah" being shipped at "Singapore".

Ernest acknowledged that the amount of money earned through the business, however, was immense, calculating that some 34,000 pilgrims had been landed so far that year. To judge by the number of shops closed in the bazaar, he assumed that many residents of Jeddah were intending to join the trains of camels being loaded for the onward journey to Mecca.

It was the festive season once more and as usual Ernest was resentful:

1ˢᵗ January 1876
Xmas has passed once more, and another year commenced. I'm always glad when these seasons are past, for it only takes one back to the pleasant holidays one enjoys at home & then comes the contrast between the different ways in which each have been spent. The only difference one can make on board ship is a little extra eating and drinking, and to those who get sufficient of each every day, this is no great novelty.

But he was soon to be free. After offloading some of her
passengers in Penang and the rest in Singapore, the *Japan*
continued to Calcutta, where she arrived at the company's
private moorings in the middle of March. The articles signed
in England by the European crew were now about to expire
so Ernest and his British shipmates made enquiries about
being sent home. A couple of weeks later they were informed
that passages had been taken for them all – four engineers,
the 2nd mate and the purser – on board the steamship
Yorkshire. Ernest took his leave of the ship that had been his
home for the past two and a half years, 'not without some
little regret for she was as near perfection as a ship could be'.

While his brother John was escorting Sultan Ismail to
Johore, Ernest was enjoying his voyage home. In Colombo he
went ashore to relax in the gardens of the Galle Face hotel
and in Malta, with his customary thirst for knowledge, he
visited the cathedral and the governor's palace. His air of
middle-aged sobriety never falters and I have to keep
reminding myself that he is still only 25. At 10 a.m. on 13th
May 1876 the *Yorkshire* arrived off Gravesend but the tide was
not right for proceeding up the river. Ernest decided to
disembark and catch a train to London. He was home at last.

The Importance of Being Ernest

On board the *Yorkshire*, Ernest had found himself frequently
looking at his watch, thinking it was time to go on duty. But
soon the pleasant thought struck him that he was a passenger,
and six weeks' idleness, he told himself in a pedantic tone,
would do no harm, 'after 18 months hard work in the worst
of climates, subject to extreme changes of temperature'. He
went on to reflect that he had seen a good deal of the world,
'and to most people, especially the young, this is a great
satisfaction'. He already seems to have put his own youth
behind him and to be commenting from the perspective of an
older self. 'Should it be my lot to remain in England,' he

concludes, 'I should feel no regrets at not being able to see more strange lands'. Yet after spending just four months in England, on 6th September 1876 Ernest took passage for Madras on the *SS Merkara* of the British India Steam Navigation Company. He didn't like Madras; it was hot and dirty; he had not gone ashore from the *Yorkshire* because, he said, his previous experience had been quite enough. What on earth did he think he was doing?

He was in fact on his way to join George in the Nelliampathy Hills. It was a time of economic depression and Ernest may have had difficulty obtaining a suitable engineering job back at home, when most engine fitters remained with the company where they had served their apprenticeship and other openings were limited. He would have found Cornubia Cottage crowded with womenfolk and stifling to a young man who had seen so much of the world. Perhaps George, who had finally been home for a visit the previous year, wrote a persuasive letter about the money to be made in coffee planting. Living in a company hut with no rent to pay and no shops to tempt you, it was possible to live comfortably on £10 a month and save enough to purchase land of one's own. Whatever his reasons, Ernest overcame his dislike of life in a hot climate sufficiently to make his way to Madras and from there to Palghaut and on to the Polyampara estate, where George was established in a comfortable white bungalow overlooking a bright green quilted landscape of mature coffee plants.

But the peaceful scene was hiding an underbelly of terrible human suffering. I am ashamed to say that I knew nothing of the great Indian famines of the nineteenth century. In 1866, a catastrophic drought caused a crop failure worse than the Irish potato famine. A million people, or one in three of the population of Orissa, starved to death even while supplies of rice were being exported to Britain. Ten years later, in the Madras presidency, four or five million people died of hunger after the monsoon failed in 1876 and again in 1877.

Deforestation and drought combined to turn much of southern India into a dustbowl while a hands-off government offered totally inadequate relief that required hard labour in return for minimal rations. The economic doctrine of free trade combined with a Malthusian view that famine was nature's way of correcting over-population was used to justify a policy of non-intervention, which even at the time was seen by some as wrong-headed.

Edwin Arnold was one writer who recognised the damage brought about by the chopping down of trees and the failure to dig enough wells. But I experienced mixed emotions when I read his account of a visit to George Dupen's plantation, where food and medicine were provided to those whose desperate plight had driven them up into the hills. The two Englishmen made their way to the hospital shed where George pushed at a piece of matting *with the point of his umbrella* 'and disclosed a poor little native child, about six months old, screwed up into a tight knot'. I was confronted with the reality of the past. George was of the opinion that the child might live but could never recover 'so we covered it up', wrote Arnold, 'and went on with our walk'. I realised that I had been viewing George through the blurred lens of nostalgia, idealising a family that existed only in my imagination. I could still admire his achievements but he could never have been my favourite uncle; the gap in our understanding of the world was too great.

Arnold thought highly of George but was less impressed by Ernest, who he describes in vivid if not entirely complimentary terms as being in build and stature not unlike the Gurkhas of northern India 'five feet nothing in height, by three feet broad'. As Arnold gets to know him better he concludes that his companion is:

> a hard-working and well-meaning Cornishman, but he kept a remarkably sharp look-out for the interests of what is vulgarly called 'number one' and considered

everyone else Egyptians whom it was quite lawful to despoil.

I can see why Ernest, the youngest of a long family, might have learned to fight for his rights from an early age and I entertained myself by imagining what his own view of Edwin Arnold might have been.

Nelliampathy Hills, 1877

Ernest is feeling put out. He is being sent to mind some young gentleman amateur who has come out to try his hand at planting for a year or two before returning to a life of comfort in London. This chap, Edwin Arnold, was supposed to be an assistant to old Reid at Pardagherry but Reid has been taken sick and has gone down to the lowlands to restore his strength. His son Charlie is only sixteen and cannot be expected to manage the workers with only Arnold to help him, so it has been decided that Ernest will go over to lend a hand.

He has been in India for nearly a year now and has experienced most stages of coffee planting, but conditions have become particularly difficult. More and more people are making their way down from Mysore and every estate has been transformed into a relief camp. The poor wretches are nothing but skin and bone, after refusing to brave the evil spirits that are known to inhabit the jungle until they are half dead of starvation. They have diarrhoea from eating weeds and green coffee beans and can hardly believe that they have reached a place where they will be given food and medicine instead of being left to die. For some it is already too late. Tiny children with huge eyes and wrinkled skin gaze out from under the threadbare *cumblie* that binds them to their mother's back. But as George says, it makes financial sense to feed these people up until they are fit to work. There is always a need for more labour. Ernest hopes that there will not be so many of the poor devils over at his new home. He lacks George's confidence in dealing with the sick, especially the women.

Early one November morning, clad in his planter's uniform of white linen jacket and trousers, polished top boots and pith helmet, Ernest sets out to walk across to Pardagherry, accompanied by his manservant and a long string of women carrying his pots, pans and bedding. His destination is the southernmost of the dozen estates that have been opened up in the hills. It consists of over 2,000 acres of virgin forest inhabited only by bison and elephants, granted by the Raja of Cochin to the Oriental Coffee Company. In the previous two years some 130 acres have been cleared and planted in four separate sites. It is bounded by the Manalora river and a three hundred foot wall of sheer rock that is the Pardagherry mountain. Beyond is unclaimed jungle as far as Cape Cormorin on the very southernmost tip of India, while away to the north east the Neilgherry mountains tower on the horizon. Ernest is however uninterested in the majesty of his surroundings, being chiefly engaged in watching his feet to make sure he does not trip over a bamboo root or stand on one of the grey and white snakes known as *tic polong* that infest this land. Although it is nearly the dry season, it has started to rain again. Sometimes, thinks Ernest, the weather here is as bad as being caught in a gale on the dear old *Japan*, but George just laughs and says,

'You were all right in your warm, cosy engine room. Imagine being up the mizzen mast in that kind of weather.'

Sometimes Ernest feels so tired of being the youngest. None of his brothers has ever taken him seriously, and yet George wouldn't know how to fix the pulping machinery when it breaks down. On reflection, perhaps it is no bad thing that he is on his way to a situation where he will be the expert. He rehearses his command of the figures to himself. A bushel of seed yields 30,000 plants and to plant ten acres you need 22,000 plants, spacing them at intervals of six feet apart. It's quite simple really.

Suddenly he is distracted by the chattering of monkeys above his head. Yes, there they are, high up in the forest canopy, great black beasts the size of a retriever. It is said that when they eat the ripe berries the excreted seed makes the best coffee. The local people enjoy eating monkey flesh when they can get it. Meat is a rare enough treat for most of them. Ernest considers whether he should get out his gun but decides that he needs to keep going if he is to make Pardagherry in time for midday breakfast. There will be time enough for hunting expeditions. Ernest considers himself a decent enough shot but George, of course, is a famous marksman who has more than once brought down one of the pretty, spotted deer that can be cooked up into a tasty venison stew.

When he arrives at the planters' hut, young Charlie is there to greet him with a tall man of about Ernest's own age, who puts out a confident hand.

'I'm Arnold,' he says. 'Very pleased you've been able to come and help us out.'

'Dupen' replies Ernest. 'I think I may account myself pretty knowledgeable after nearly a year with my brother. I shall be glad to instruct you to the best of my ability.' That, he thinks to himself, should put him in his place. 'Help us out' indeed.

The hut is of new construction, with a thatched roof of lemon grass that comes within four feet of the ground. Inside there is a distinct odour of damp hay and bilge water. It is about twelve feet wide and perhaps twice as long, with a floor of beaten earth. There is no furniture to speak of, just a collection of packing cases. In one corner is a pile of picks, billhooks, and spades, while on the walls hang guns, animal skins, and a collection of battered hats. A stove with its chimney sticking through the wall in a way guaranteed to allow the rain in, and a large iron safe, complete the furnishings. There are two ill-fitting glass windows and mats have been hung to separate off the sleeping area, where a total of four beds made of unplaned teak boards laid on biscuit boxes are set up within touching distance of each other. The fourth bed is for Lister, the assistant at Varlavachen, who has come to break new land to the south for another of the big companies. The young Englishmen will have to rub along as best they can, for they are five or six miles from any other estate, which puts paid to any wider evening socialising.

While they are breakfasting the *tapal*, or running postman, arrives from Wallenghay with his a wicker basket balanced on his head. As well as their letters and papers, he brings supplies of eggs, white butter made from buffalo milk, and the weekly supply of cash to pay the workers. He waits for their return correspondence and then speeds off again. From Wallenghay another man will take the basket to Palghaut in time to catch the early morning post to Madras the next day. Ernest has been pleasantly surprised by the efficient communication. Luxuries such as sugar, cheese, tea and coffee can be shipped from Calicut or Madras by train, along with generous supplies of beer, wine and brandy. All the planters' bungalows have heaps of empty bottles piled up behind them, a permanent legacy of their presence.

A few days later they are at work pegging out the land that has been recently cleared. Ernest crawls into a thicket pulling the long rope tagged with strips of coloured cloth that will show the workers where to place the wooden pegs that mark the planting positions. There is a heavy thud immediately behind him and he looks up, startled, to see Arnold standing over the long, grey body of a deadly *tic polong*, its broad head crushed by a blow from a thick stick that he has snatched from a labourer. The men around him are gazing open-mouthed in horror at his narrow escape.

'Sorry about that, old man,' says Arnold, 'but I couldn't call out to warn you or the beast would have struck out.'

'My dear chap,' replies Ernest. 'What can I say? Thank you very much. I am more grateful than I can possibly say.' He puts out a hand and the two men shake. Ernest turns to the workmen and chivvies them back to work.

'You can't afford to be soft with them,' he tells Arnold. 'They'll cheat you if they can.' But his tone is more cordial than it was.

He repeats his advice in the evening when they prepare to pay their workers for the week. Ernest helps Arnold decipher the long list of names, in Tamil, Canarese, Hindustani and Malayalam. The men are due five *annas* a day, the women three, and the children one, but there are arguments aplenty over the hours checked off in the daybook or coins that are deemed to be bad. At last they have finished and all the tools have been counted back into the storehouse. They eat dinner by the light of a paraffin lamp but it is cold and a light drizzle is falling so they decide they will be warmer in bed. Lying in the darkness wrapped in thick grey blankets, they puff on fragrant cheroots as they exchange edited versions of their life histories. When Ernest tells them about the *Japan*, Arnold chuckles and says,

'We'll have to call you the stoker then.'

Ernest starts to explain the difference between a stoker and a qualified engineer but realises he is just sounding like a bad sport and changes the subject, to ask about Arnold's family. It turns out that his father is the editor of the *Daily Telegraph* and a noted poet. The family spent time in Poona, where he was principal of a college, and he maintains a strong interest in Indian affairs. When her gracious Majesty was proclaimed Empress at the start of the year, Arnold's father was made a companion in the Order of the Star of India. Unable to compete with such splendid achievements, Ernest takes out his accordion and offers to entertain his companions with a song or two before they settle down to sleep. After a couple of false starts he plays a slow and painstaking melody that the others think they recognise. They begin singing along until Ernest stops and says,

'I say, can't you chaps hold a tune? Here's one you should be able to manage.'

And he launches into *God Save the Queen*. His companions make a half-hearted move to get to their feet but think the better of it and content themselves with sitting up straight while they chorus the words of the national anthem.

The next day they are up at five o'clock to resume pegging and the routine of life goes on, broken only by the occasional Sunday visit to one of the other isolated bungalows that dot the hills. A favoured destination is the well-established domain of Varlavachen, where the manager has planted an English garden with roses and geraniums and his wife presides over a tea table resplendent with a white cloth and silver teapot. It is at moments like this that Ernest is hopeful of a future where he too may have a wife and a comfortable home (although his imagination stops short of a picture that includes a cluster of fair-haired children like the ones at play on the lawn). With this end in view he volunteers to take charge of the estate on Christmas Day while his companions enjoy lunch with a group of local planters. In return, Ernest will be relieved of duty on New Year's Day to join a picnic in Palghaut, where it is rumoured there are two young ladies newly arrived from England.

On Christmas Eve the young men at Pardagherry stick candles in beer bottles, hang shrubs from the roof to look like holly, and mix punch in a washbasin. After a few glasses of this powerful mixture Ernest is moved to suggest they go outside for a snowball fight, but when they stagger outside they find it is a hot, humid night sprinkled with fireflies, the stillness broken only by the croaking of frogs and the barking of deer.

'Oh well,' says Ernest ruefully, 'I suppose I'd better get out the old accordion. I'm sure I can manage Mr Wesley's *Hark the Herald Angels Sing*.'

CENSUS 1881

The census of 1881 was the first one where housewives were reclassified as 'unoccupied' and so the column for 'occupation' next to Johanna Dupen's name is blank. She is simply a widow, while Annie and Salome are described as private teachers. No fewer than five grandchildren have joined the household: Clara, Dora and Vivian Dupen, and Florence and Agnes Price. The first three are the children of Johanna's oldest son Sharrock, and the others are Kate's twin daughters, taking the place of their older sisters, who have returned home to Bristol where their parents are now keeping the White Lion hotel. Sharrock, who filed for bankruptcy in 1871, also has a hotel, the Guildhall, in the centre of Bristol. Julia, named for her mother, is the only one of his children to be living with him. The death in 1875 of Sharrock's wife, Julia Pennefather Dupen, left seven motherless children aged between fourteen and three. Their grandmother and aunts scooped them up and brought them back to Cornubia Cottage, where Vivian seems to have become a favourite of Salome and Annie. I imagine them soothing the bewildered toddler when he woke sobbing in the night, showing a patience that might have surprised their younger brothers. But in the way of small children he soon forgot the events of his third year and Hayle became his home, the only one that he remembered. He was to tell his own children that his mother died when he was born, one of the many half-truths that are passed down through the generations to ambush unwary genealogists.

The landscape of Hayle had changed dramatically by that time: the Copperhouse foundry was gone, demolished in 1875 after the rest of the business went under the hammer at the Cornubia Hotel. Harveys' foundry had found a new lease of life after winning a contract to supply engines to drain the tunnel that was being opened up under the river Severn for

the Great Western Railway, but it was the shipyard that had
become the biggest employer. Penpol Terrace was changing
too, and not for the better. The Dupens' neighbours were no
longer engine fitters and blacksmiths; the monopoly that
forced everyone to shop at Harvey's emporium was over and
the residents had started to lower the tone of the
neighbourhood by building shops in their front gardens.

Ernest, of course, is in India in 1881, and John with his
ship, *HMS Serapis*, while his wife is living in Hayle in
Commercial Road with their four remaining children. George
has brought his wife Jane to England for a visit and they are
lodging in west London. It was this entry describing him as a
planter that first put me on the trail of his Indian life. Ellen is
listed at her school in Tregenna Place, St Ives, where the
oldest of Sharrock and Julia's children, Anna, has joined her
as an assistant. There is one young lady boarder, Agnes
Baxter, who I identify as my great-grandmother Hester's
stepdaughter. Hester has recently married and is living in
Shepherd's Bush with her new husband, George Baxter, and
four more stepchildren, one of them a baby girl just six
months old. Her sister Sarah is nearby, in Brooklyn Road.
Three years earlier Sarah had married Henry Sanders, a
widower from Bristol ten years her senior, and she too has a
stepdaughter, Annie Lilian, aged ten.

We worry today about the divorce rate and the number of
broken families that result, forgetting how many children
were deprived of their parents in an earlier age by death. If
they were not sent to live with grandparents or other relatives,
they often acquired a new mother or father. Sarah and Hester
were not unusual in taking on ready-made families, but that
does not mean it was easy. Elizabeth Gaskell, in *Wives and
Daughters*, wrote from the point of view of a girl saddled with
a manipulative and selfish stepmother, while Charlotte Yonge,
in *The Young Stepmother*, described the tribulations of a naïve
young woman who marries a remote, older widower with
three badly brought up children. I am of course inclined to

imagine my great-grandparents as much better suited and happier than either of these fictional couples, but Hester must have thought very seriously before taking on another woman's baby. As the youngest girl in a long family she can hardly have had the experience of toddlers that her sisters had. And while her stepson Gilbert, at seven, might be easy for an experienced governess to manage, his three older sisters were of an age to resent a stranger taking the place of their mother. It is perhaps not surprising that sixteen-year-old Agnes was packed off to St Ives and Blanche, aged thirteen, to a girls' school in Stoke Newington. Only seventeen-year-old Eleanor remained at home.

15 A New Family

A small roll of felted brown cloth containing half a dozen rusted needles, capped by an even rustier thimble, is all that remains of the tools of George Baxter's trade. A story that began with domestic embroidery will end with professional stitching. I found these relics of my great-grandfather's skill in the same envelope as the stiff, faded pages of his will, suggesting that they represented something precious. It is said that Bernard Weatherill, the Speaker of the House of Commons and a former tailor, kept a thimble in his waistcoat pocket to remind himself of his humble origins. I like to think that George Baxter, who died a wealthy man, did the same. But when I first set out to trace his life, I did not realise that we were not his first family and that others might have a stronger claim to the small package of fabric.

It is, in many ways, a Dickensian story. George's father, who was also a tailor, died when his youngest son was a baby and by the age of thirteen, like the young Charles Dickens, George was put to work. He was apprenticed to his stepfather, a cordwainer or maker of new leather shoes. It was not until after his mother and stepfather died that he turned, like his four much older brothers, to tailoring, which was at that time, along with shoemaking, the largest single artisan trade. There were more than 21,000 tailors at work in the middle of the nineteenth century. A young apprentice would learn from a sewing tailor who specialised in one type of garment – coat, trousers, waistcoat – and if fortunate would learn more than one item, but when he became an 'improver' he would himself become a specialist. Once he was working fast enough to produce clothes at an economic rate he would qualify as a journeyman. If the opportunity arose, he could then train as a cutter, and potentially an organising foreman. Only after this was he allowed anywhere near the customers, learning the art of measuring and pattern cutting to fit, and eventually qualifying as one of the élite, a master tailor.

All garments other than shirts and underclothes were at that time made by tailors, with much of the fine stitching done by women. A complete outfit of evening coat, trousers, and waistcoat from a fashionable workshop cost £7 (rather more than the £6 earned annually by a maid of all work). The profit margin would however depend on how the suit was produced. It was that campaigner for social justice Charles Kingsley who, well before he tackled the evils of chimney sweeping in the more famous *Water Babies*, set out in the preface to his 1849 novel *Alton Locke* the terrible reality of 'cheap clothes and nasty'. There were two types of trade, the honourable, which was 'almost confined to the West End, and rapidly dying out there', and the 'dishonourable trade of the show-shops and slop-shops'. In respectable shops journeymen worked on the premises for good wages, but disreputable tailors handed out piecework to so-called 'sweaters', or middle men, who took their cut and then passed on the work to be done at home by the unfortunate 'dungs' and their wives and daughters. It is hardly surprising that Alton Locke, the tailor of the title, allied himself to the Chartists and came to an untimely end.

Once I was aware of this distinction, I wanted to find out what kind of businessman my great-grandfather George Baxter had been. My research led me to a quietly intimidating shop in Savile Row, where I sat on an aristocratically shabby buttoned leather sofa with Mr Keith Levett, Managing Director of Henry Poole & Co. 'There is only one Poole – all the rest are puddles', so people used to say. Mr Levett picked up my great-grandfather's thimble and put it on his finger, where it fitted perfectly. It was open-ended, he explained, because unlike dressmakers, tailors did not use the tip to push the needle through the cloth, and oval rather than circular because George will have bent it between his teeth to fit his finger. He must have had slender craftsman's hands like those

of Mr Levett, who now turned his attention to the cloth that
held the needles. It was, he said, a piece of fine quality
broadcloth, so called because it starts off very wide and
shrinks as it is felted. My great-grandfather was undoubtedly a
craftsman who worked with the best materials.

It was a rare privilege to be able to see for myself how
clothing is still made by hand, in a way that has hardly
changed in a hundred years. I was shown a jacket that was
part way to completion. Woollen cloth was layered with
horsehair and duster fabric to give shape to the shoulders and
it was basted in white thread so that the complex detail of the
construction was very visible. The firm of Henry Poole & Co.
still makes ceremonial court dress and I coveted a dramatic
inky blue velvet High Sheriff's outfit lined with delicately
stitched black silk. This was Mr Levett's own work. To ask
the price seemed sordid and irrelevant.

I did, however, want to know about the economics of the
nineteenth century business. An old ledger fell open at
Cornelius Vanderbilt but any page would have given us an
equally famous name. A customer was often a customer for
life and would run up a bill for many hundreds of pounds, so
even when a business was flourishing, cash flow could be a
problem. Poole was owed a substantial amount by Charles
Dickens's oldest son but Dickens paid off the debt. I was
pleased that I could share with Mr Levett my own connection
with the great novelist. The 'Dickens letter' was, according to
family myth, written by Charles Dickens to George Baxter
himself, but when I examined it properly I realised that it was
in fact directed to a Mr Maltby. The obvious explanation for
it being in George's possession is that he was working for
Henry Bristow Maltby, a tailor with a shop at 41 Marylebone
Road, close to Sherborne Street, where the census tells me
George was lodging in 1861. The letter, on black-edged
mourning paper following the death of Dickens's son Walter
in Calcutta on 31st December 1863, is signed with Dickens's
usual flourish and reads succinctly:

Gads Hill
Higham by Rochester
Saturday Ninth January 1864
Please make master Harry and master Edward, each
two suits of clothes,
Charles Dickens

Maltby was still providing clothes for the boys of the
family in 1865, when Dickens ordered a list of items to be
supplied for his son Alfred, who was being sent out to
Australia to take up sheep farming, and I feel justified in
imagining that he made garments for Sydney, John Dupen's
ill-fated shipmate who died on board *HMS Topaze*.

The tailoring business offered an opportunity to make a
good living, possibly as much as £1,000 a year; in comparison
the young Anthony Trollope earned just £140 as a clerk. It
has been suggested that as a money maker it can be compared
to witchcraft, but one obvious way in which men like Henry
Poole became rich was by supplying livery. Servants' uniforms
were big business and those that could afford to do so spent a
fortune on distinctive outfits for their footmen, who
blossomed in the park, so it was said, like a bed of tulips.
When George Baxter died he was worth over £62,000,
equivalent to at least £3.5 million today, but there is no
evidence that he made livery. I was worried that he may have
been one of those who exploited his workforce and was
relieved to discover from his will that the origin of his wealth
lay not in sweatshops but in houses. He had a property
portfolio in Shepherd's Bush and one grey autumn day I set
off to see it for myself.

The 1881 census had George and Hester living at
3 Thornfield Road. In the Hammersmith archives I pieced
together what I could from the electoral registers. George was
at 68 Thornfield Road in 1883, then moved to number 70,
which is where my grandfather Harold must have grown up,
and in 1910 I hit the jackpot. In the 1910 register George
Baxter was eligible to vote in both council and parliamentary

elections by virtue of the six houses he owned in Thornfield
Road (numbers 48, 50, 68, 70) and nearby Warbeck Road
(numbers 2 and 4). The chairman of the local history society,
who had been assisting me with the microfiche, was polite
enough to pretend to share my excitement. It is so satisfying,
he murmured, when people find what they are looking for.

It was getting dark as I hurried along the Uxbridge Road. I
passed an enormous Lebanese supermarket and turned by the
Babylon Pharmacy into Warbeck Road. It was a mixed area of
family homes and rented property in multiple occupancy. The
typically Victorian houses had grimy hedges, greyish net
curtains, and a few incongruous satellite dishes; there were
dainty flower-patterned tiles above some of the bay windows
while others had ugly security grilles; I spotted at least one
Porsche parked in the road. Numbers 2 and 4 were a pair of
houses four storeys high and wide enough for three windows
on the first floor; they must have brought in substantial
income. I turned into Thornfield Road. Number 3 was an
undistinguished two storey terraced cottage and, when new,
must have been a suitable home for a lower-middle class
family with a single maidservant. The investment properties at
48 and 50 were three storeys high, with bay windows on the
ground and first floors. They too were big solid houses that
would have generated a good return. I expected numbers 68
and 70 to be similar but as I counted off the numbers, I
reached 60 and was faced with the railings of the Miles
Coverdale Primary School. My carefully sewn fabric was
starting to fray around the edges. Had the street been
renumbered? It seemed unlikely when the numbering still
runs consecutively, accounting for all the houses on this side
of the road. When I consulted the old ordnance survey maps
later it looked as if some five homes must have been pulled
down to make way for the school in 1916. It was frustrating
that I could not follow my grandfather Harold to his
childhood home at number 70, but I had seen the house his

mother must have come to as a new bride and that would
have to do.

I have inherited no anecdotes about how my great-
grandparents met, but I suspect it was through Hester's sister
Sarah and her husband Henry Sanders, who was a commercial
traveller in woollens. There was a constant to-ing and fro-ing
between the cloth merchants based in Soho and the London
tailors, and widowed George Baxter may well have been one
of Henry's customers. In another Dickensian twist, it was just
three days before Christmas 1879 that George's wife
Charlotte died, leaving him with a son and four daughters, the
youngest still a baby. Like the Sanders, he lived in west
London, in Wood Lane on the other side of Shepherd's Bush
station. This rural area of market gardens and brickworks had
recently been invaded by developers who were building
seemingly endless streets of houses for those Londoners who
wanted to move out of town but still have easy access to their
place of work. George would have travelled every day by the
Metropolitan railway or the new horse tram to his workshop
at 56 Mortimer Street, just north of Oxford Street. It is
possible that like many widowers of the time, George was
looking for a suitable woman to combine the roles of
governess and housekeeper and care for his orphaned
children when Henry Sanders introduced him to his wife's
sister, Hester Dupen. If so, my great-grandmother would not
be the first governess to end up marrying the master of the
house, if in decidedly less dramatic circumstances than Jane
Eyre. Whatever the story of their courtship, as soon as his
year of mourning was up, Hester became George Baxter's
second wife. After a series of voyages taking the Dupen
siblings away from Hayle, this was an opportunity to follow
one of them as she returned home for her wedding.

Hayle and London, February 1881

It is a cold, grey winter's day when Hester Dupen gets ready
to travel home to Cornwall for her wedding to George Baxter.
She counts herself fortunate that they have not had to
postpone the ceremony after January brought the worst
snowstorm that Britain had seen in a generation. From across
the country came reports of people frozen to death or badly
injured in boiler explosions, while in London the hurricane
force winds that accompanied the intense cold sank one
hundred barges on the river. Passengers on the Great
Western Railway travelling from Penzance to the capital
were delayed by a full day on their journey. It is with some
trepidation that Hester buttons herself into her warm, velvet
trimmed pelisse, skewers her hat firmly with several long
pins, and picks up her fur muff.

George's daughters, Agnes and Blanche, will be travelling
with them. Agnes, it has been decided, will stay on as a pupil
with Ellen in St Ives. She is sixteen and it will do her good to
test her wings a little, away from her domineering older
sister. Baby Maude is too young to make such a long journey
and has been left at home with the maidservant, together
with her seven-year-old brother Gilbert (who has
understandably no interest in weddings), and seventeen-year-
old Eleanor, who has so far refused to put off her mourning
and responded with icy scorn to Hester's invitation.

'No, I won't come. Why would I want to watch my
mother being replaced? It's scarcely a year since she went to
her grave. Indecent, I call it.'

Hester had to bite her tongue. The girl was clearly still
grieving.

They climb into a cab lined with the usual dirty blue
velvet, the driver stows their luggage on the roof, and the
elderly nag sets off at a cautious pace for Paddington,
through streets still slippery with melting snow. The train is
due to leave at nine, but they must get there in good time to
be sure of a compartment together. To Hester's relief they

arrive with half an hour to spare and while George deals with the luggage she settles the girls into an empty carriage and tucks warm rugs around them. The other seats soon fill up and they are on their way. Hester's anxiety recedes as she points out the sights to her stepdaughters.

'Look, there's Windsor Castle,' she says.

'What an enormous tower,' cries Blanche excitedly. 'It's just like a fairy tale. Do you think there's a princess locked inside?'

'I don't know which one it could be,' laughs Hester. 'They're all married apart from Princess Beatrice, and I'm sure her mother wouldn't want to lock her away.'

The girls seem increasingly at ease with her and Hester begins to hope that they are becoming a proper family. At Didcot she leans out to buy Banbury cakes from the boy on the platform.

'Eleanor doesn't know what she is missing,' says Agnes through a mouthful of raisins.

At Swindon they take advantage of the ten-minute stop to consume hot soup, warming their chilled fingers on the bowls, and then the next excitement is the darkness that descends as they steam through the tunnel at Box. It is a chance for Hester to tell them about her visit to Ellen, all those years ago.

'Tell us again,' says Blanche, 'about your family. You were the baby, weren't you? Like Maude. Did you mind being the youngest? Were your sisters very strict with you?'

'Well don't forget there were two more after me, poor Sam, and then Ernest. He was the baby, not me,' Hester replies. 'Annie and Ellen were strict with us all, but I can't imagine Salome ever scolding anyone. She's much too soft-hearted. And I never saw very much of Kate after she got married.'

'I can't imagine Eleanor getting married,' says Agnes thoughtfully.

Bristol is all noise and confusion but their fellow passengers have reached their destination and from now on, the family will have the carriage to themselves. Hester takes out the lunch basket. It seems like no time at all before they are pulling into Exeter, and after that comes the run along the shore.

'It's so wonderful to see the sea again,' says Hester, taking a deep breath. 'Can you smell the salt in the air? I think if I'd been a boy, I would have been a sailor like my brothers.'

She sees Blanche glance warily across at her and she smiles reassuringly.

'But of course I'm not a boy and I'm very happy with the way my life has turned out. I am lucky to have such prettily behaved daughters!'

At Plymouth they change to the local service and soon they are crossing the great span of the Albert Bridge.

'Welcome to Cornwall,' says Hester proudly. 'I hope you are going to like my home. It is quite the most beautiful place in the world.'

When they arrive in Hayle Hester's mother greets them on the doorstep of Cornubia Cottage.

'Come in by the fire. You must be chilled to the bone. Thank goodness you're safe! I have never seen anything like this weather, not even when I was a girl. Did you hear about the people who were caught overnight near Didcot? They climbed out into the snowdrifts to throw snowballs! But your father would have been pleased by one piece of news – they put on a special train to transport the broccoli to London!'

'Good gracious!' says Hester, 'I'm sure he never thought how the trade would grow. It's good to see you, mama, and looking so well. Now, this is Mr Baxter, and here are my new daughters.'

The girls bob shy curtseys while George shakes hands with his future mother-in-law and is presented to Annie, Salome, and Ellen, who has come across from St Ives for a few days. A room has been reserved for him at the White Hart and it is Hester's brother George who will escort him there. George Dupen is making his first visit home in twenty years, and he and his wife are staying at the hotel too. Hester barely remembers her big brother; she was only a small child when he first went to sea. But it is wonderful to see how happy her mother is.

'I thank the Good Lord every day that I have been spared to see my boy again,' she says emotionally.

'Really mother,' says Annie. 'Spared indeed. You will outlast us all.'

George's wife Jane looks older than they had expected, although perhaps it is the Indian sun that has made her so sallow and wrinkled, and her clothes are very outmoded. Wrapped in layers of fine cashmere shawls, she complains of the cold all the time, which is hardly surprising since she has never before travelled further than Madras. There are gifts for everyone, wide silver bracelets for all of the sisters, engraved brass cups, and a tiny ivory elephant. Each morning the aroma of coffee fills the house, although Annie turns up her nose and complains that the brew that Jane demonstrates to them is too strong.

George Baxter, curious to see a working port and full of questions about life at sea, strolls around Hayle with his new brother-in-law, who remarks constantly on how much the town has changed. Hester is struck by how alike the two men are but how different in life experience. Of a similar age, both sport the customary moustache and neatly trimmed beard. But her brother is muscular and leathery from days spent toiling in the unforgiving heat of southern India while her future husband has the pale complexion of one who spends long hours indoors. She is filled with admiration for the strength of character that has enabled each of them in their own way to overcome adversity and make a success of their life.

Sarah and Henry have come from London but the house is so full that they are sent to stay with Julia and her four children in Hayle Terrace. John is of course away at sea again, somewhere in the Mediterranean or passing through the Suez Canal. No one seems quite sure. Sharrock claims to be unable to leave his business and his daughters are briefly

disappointed, but they have Blanche and Agnes to take care
of and are soon listening wide-eyed to stories of London life.
Their aunt Kate also is too busy to leave her hotel in Bristol
but two of her daughters are boarding with their aunts in
Penpol Terrace, and like their cousins are an eager audience
for tales of horse-drawn trams, men on velocipedes, and
dancing bears. The Baxter girls have been to the West End to
see their father's shop, and have walked down Regent Street
admiring the array of fashionable goods set out in the plate
glass windows, ranging from rose-patterned china to hats
trimmed with feathers. They have visited the gardens at Kew
and on one never to be forgotten day sailed on a steamer all
the way to Greenwich and back.

'Stepmama said she was homesick and wanted us to
know what it was like to travel by water.'

Annie and Ellen have set aside their differences to help
put the finishing touches to Hester's modest trousseau and
interrogate her as only older sisters can.

'I suppose you think you can bribe your new daughters
with treats,' says Annie as they trim the hats they will wear to
the wedding. 'Just you wait and see. You won't remember
our sister Hannah. "Sister" was what we were told to call her,
though she wasn't mama's child. I remember she used to
pinch me when she thought no one was looking. She didn't
like her papa having so many new children.'

'You were fond of Lizzie, though, weren't you?' asks
Hester.

'Lizzie was younger so I don't suppose she remembered
her mother so well. She was very quiet,' says Annie, 'but
quick-witted. I remember Kate saying how fast she could tot
up the amount of ribbon needed to trim a gown. We were
quite sad when she upped and married her engineer, for we
never saw her again.'

'It must have been hard for mama to have two growing
girls to care for as well as her own babies. Are you quite sure
you know what you're doing?' Ellen asks.

Hester feels the hot colour rising in her cheeks at the implication behind Ellen's words. Her sister has always been very forthright. But she answers calmly.

'Yes I am,' replies Hester. 'I'm not like you, Ellen. I don't want to live my life teaching other people's children and worrying every month about paying the bills. I want a family of my own and a man I can trust to take care of us.'

'I had my chances,' snorts Ellen, 'as you well know. But I prefer to be my own mistress.'

'So your tailor is the right man for you?' enquires Annie in a neutral tone.

'Just because he's different, is no reason to doubt him,' Hester says, hearing the criticism behind the question, 'You should see his shop. It's so well situated, in a most fashionable area, and it has quite enormous windows.'

She can see her sister is looking quizzical but she ploughs on.

'You have to be very diplomatic to be a successful tailor. Gentlemen can be so sensitive about their measurements. George counts Sir John Tenniel, the illustrator of Alice in Wonderland you know, amongst his customers. In fact he told me rather a funny story about him.'

Annie raises her eyebrows as her sister continues,

'George was working for a while in partnership with his brother Alfred, who is quite elderly. Anyway, Sir John wrote a note recommending them to one of his friends but he said to be sure to ask for the young Mr Baxter because the other is 'an hold hass'! The friend showed the note to George and he asked if he could keep it because it was so entertaining.'

Having a brother with the intelligence of a donkey hardly seems like a recommendation, but Hester's future husband certainly seems more respectable than their own oldest brother, so no more is said on that count. Hester's final argument is in any case unanswerable.

'I have prayed for guidance and I know it is my Christian duty to care for George's poor orphaned children, as mama

and Annie have done with Sharrock's brood. And see how
well they have turned out.'

The wedding takes place on 21st February in the church at
Phillack and the next day in the darkness of the early
morning the newly married couple set off for the station for
the day-long journey home to London. Agnes seems happy to
be going to St Ives with Ellen, and Blanche will come home
later with her newly acquired aunt Sarah. George and Jane
will also be making their way to London where they intend
to spend a few weeks before travelling home to India.

That evening Hester peers from the grimy window of the
cab as it makes its way through the dark streets towards
Thornfield Road. The occasional yellow glow of a gas lamp
pierces the murky gloom of the February evening but does
little to illuminate the close-packed rows of terraced houses.
It is not exactly raining but there is a damp chill in the air
that penetrates her woollen pelisse and makes her shiver. For
a moment she wonders if she has made a terrible mistake.
But then she turns her head to look at the man seated beside
her. He smiles his gentle smile and touches her lightly on the
arm.

'Nearly home,' he says. 'Are you very fatigued, my dear?'

'No, not at all,' she replies. And it is true. She feels a wave
of gratitude for the combination of circumstances that has
brought her, at the age of 33, a respectable marriage to a
good man. Her husband is quiet and self-contained, but over
the months of their acquaintance she has come to understand
that he is also driven to succeed, not in the reckless fashion
of her brother Sharrock but in a methodical way that brings
results. He has promised that she will be secure and she
believes him sufficiently to give up her independence.

George has told her a little about his childhood. Ten years
younger than the last of his brothers, he never knew his
father. He is fortunate, or so he says, not to remember how
he was fostered out while his mother desperately looked for
employment. He has never known what it was like not to
work. He cannot speak too highly of his old master, Mr

Maltby, who gave him his start in life. And now he has a business of his own that brings in sufficient income that he can start putting aside money to invest in property. There is a boom going on in west London since the District Line and the horse tram followed the opening of the Metropolitan Railway. Streets of new houses are going up all the time. If he can purchase one or two to rent out it will bring in extra money, and why stop there? With the rental income he could buy another, and then another. He has it all planned out.

But meanwhile here they are. The cab stops in front of the modest redbrick cottage squeezed between its neighbours that is to be their home. It seemed best, George had said, to leave Wood Lane and its unhappy memories behind, and make a fresh start. Hester takes a deep breath as he hands her down and unlocks the front door. Eleanor will be waiting for them, with Gilbert and little Maude. A ready-made family. She will try to love them as she should but she hopes, blushing in the darkness, that before too long she may be blessed with a baby of her own.

CENSUS 1891

By 1891, Annie has become the head of the household in Penpol Terrace. Her profession is given as school teacher and she is assisted by Salome and their niece Dora. Vivian is now old enough to contribute to the household budget and is working as an ironmonger's assistant. Johanna Dupen died in 1885 at the age of 79, leaving Cornubia Cottage no doubt strangely empty without her steady, guiding hand. It is disconcerting to think that Annie, the one daughter who never left home, was in her fifties when she first found herself cast adrift from the anchor of her mother's presence. Johanna lived one third of her life as a widow; she gave birth to thirteen babies and lost two; in her sixties she found herself responsible for half a dozen orphaned grandchildren. But throughout her long life she had her Wesleyan faith to sustain her. She brought up her children to be self-sufficient, to work hard, and to better themselves. With perhaps one exception, they did not disappoint her.

Sarah in Shepherd's Bush is also running a seminary from her home, with three teachers, while Ellen's private school in St Ives is flourishing. The sisters were all in their own way entrepreneurs, women who earned their own living, set aside enough money to ensure a comfortable retirement (an abiding source of anxiety for governesses), and provided education and employment for their nieces. Theirs would be the last generation to run the kind of small, unregulated establishment that had flourished for the past hundred years or more. New high schools were being founded, under the auspices of the Girls Public Day Schools Company or the Church of England, to provide a good, inexpensive education for girls above the elementary level. Teachers were becoming better qualified as training colleges were set up and ambitious women, the daughters and sisters of professional men, started to argue for (and win) the right to attend university and take degrees. The Dupen sisters were not part of this movement, but nor did they answer to a board of male shareholders (unlike Dorothea Beale in Cheltenham) and they showed themselves to be as capable of managing a business as their father and brothers.

Ellen seems to have been the most successful. In 1880, the new Elementary Education Act made attendance at a certified school compulsory. The traditional dame schools, which had for so long acted as glorified child-minding services, teaching basic reading, occasionally writing, and practical skills like knitting, were unlikely to qualify for certification. Private school owners like Annie and Ellen seem not even to have applied. School boards started to summon those parents who appeared to be flouting the law by using uncertified schools. Some pleaded poverty while others complained of poor standards and mistreatment at the board schools. At St Ives in February 1883, a certain John Care said in his defence that he could not afford shoes for his child; Mrs Betsy Martin claimed that she had stopped sending her son because he was beaten by the other boys and the master, while Mrs Trevorrow said her boy had been locked in a dark room and she feared this would bring on fits. The Board refused to accept any of these excuses and ordered all the parents to send their children to a certified school. (Mr Care was advised to apply to the relief officer for shoes.) But when Alderman Hosking was summoned on a charge of failing to send his three children to a certificated elementary school, it was a different story. His daughter Eliza attended Miss Dupen's school and was, he claimed, receiving a thoroughly efficient education for which he paid the sum of 9d per week. The fee was judged to be irrelevant but the Bench ruled in favour of the defendant. A second case was brought against a Mr Best, himself a Justice of the Peace, who also had two children at Miss Dupen's and stated that:

> He was in favour of compulsory education but his reason for not sending his children to Board Schools was his belief that

they were each receiving a superior education to that they
would get at the rate-supported schools, and he was quite
satisfied with the results of their training.

His case too was dismissed. Ellen was further defended by
a clergyman, the Reverend Tyacke, former incumbent of St
Ives, who wrote to the editor of the *Cornishman* on 15th March
1883 in robust terms:

> Miss Dupen instructed my daughters when I lived in St Ives,
> and I have no hesitation in stating that she is a most excellent
> teacher, quite taking the place as schoolmistress in St Ives,
> which Mr Rowe [also prosecuted] holds as schoolmaster.
> I hope, sir, what I have said will satisfy everyone that it would
> be a gross insult to class with "dames' schools" either of the
> schools I have named.

At a meeting of the School Board in April, recriminations
flew as a result of this fiasco, but Ellen's school went from
strength to strength, in spite of, or perhaps in part because of,
the publicity generated by the court cases. In 1884 the musical
end of term entertainment was reported in enthusiastic terms:

> On Thursday last the young people attending Miss Dupen's
> school held their "breaking up" party. This school has for
> twenty years held the position of the best in the town, and the
> intellectual character of the pastimes indulged in by the pupils
> on Thursday shows that education in its truest sense – that
> which promotes self-development – is that which the teachers
> have strived to impart; for all unaided the pupils got up among
> themselves a series of theatrical representations or charades,
> the acting in which showed them to be worthy sisters-in-art of
> the great Irving, whose birthplace, by-the-bye, is but about a
> mile from here.

But while the Dupen sisters flourished, their brothers were
starting to pay the price for years of hard physical work in
fever-ridden climates.

Cornish Telegraph 10th April 1884

SAD NEWS. We regret to announce the death in Madras of Mr George Dupen, formerly of Hayle, brother of Mr John Dupen, of H.M.S. Serapis, which occurred recently after a short illness. He had been suffering from bronchitis and congestion of the lungs for two or three months, and had gone to Madras to consult a physician, and had also made preparations for a voyage to Australia for a change of air. His death was almost sudden, as he was out driving the day before. Mr Dupen was owner of a coffee plantation, and was assisted by his brother, Mr E. Dupen.

George was 42 years old. In his will he left everything to his wife Jane, apart from a legacy of £100 to his mother.

Sharrock, like his father before him, was a risk taker. After his first bankruptcy he took on the management of the Royal Hotel in Portishead. It should have been a splendid business opportunity. The hotel was situated by the pier at the mouth of the Avon, where every Saturday afternoon the steamers from Bristol brought crowds of day trippers eager to pay the shilling return fare (no luggage allowed, children half price) and if they were feeling flush, the extra penny to promenade on the pier or tuppence for a boating ticket. On Monday mornings too, excursion trains ran with the added attraction of a band playing on the pier and sixpenny trips out to the naval training ship *HMS Formidable* at anchor in the bay. But after his wife's death, Sharrock returned to Bristol and was declared bankrupt for a second time in 1882. He appeared to bounce back with his usual insouciance, marrying his housekeeper two years later and moving to Weston-super-mare, where he was soon advertising his latest venture:

By an ingenious contrivance, Mr Dupen, the enterprising proprietor of the Claremont Hotel, has just fitted up a grotto adjacent to the rocks at Anchor-head, where non-intoxicants "steaming hot or icy cold" are dispensed to thirsty souls in a novel and highly enjoyable fashion.

Unfortunately his new business success was short-lived for he too died, in December 1886, at the age of 51.

In 1882 John was posted once more to the China station, to the screw sloop *Albatross*. Julia, who had by now given birth to three more children, must have found it hard to say farewell to him for another four-year tour of duty. But he returned with his reputation enhanced. A note on his service record from the officers at the Chatham dockyard stated that 'the machinery and boilers of Albatross as regards general order and cleanliness reflects the greatest credit on the officer who has had charge of the same during the commission'. John was promoted once more, to staff engineer, and stationed back in Portsmouth. His record states that he was posted to the collection of floating hulks known as *HMS Vernon*, recently detached from the gunnery school *HMS Excellent*, 'for torpedo and hydraulic instruction', meaning that he would have been working with the new science of electricity. But in January 1888 John died at just 46 years old. He had been suspended from active duty in the previous November, suffering from pleuritis and pericarditis. His body was brought back to Hayle to be buried in the churchyard at Phillack, where his beloved daughter Mary was at rest. His oldest son Arthur was by now also training to be a naval engineer. At the bottom of John's service record is a note refusing his widow's request to have Arthur's fees reduced because of her straitened circumstances.

One of the pleasures of writing about maritime history is the support you receive from the community of researchers. On the same trip to Portsmouth when I visited *HMS Warrior*, I was privileged to be given a guided tour of the naval headquarters on Whale Island, which would have been under development in John's time. Over the course of the nineteenth century, the soil excavated to build the docks was used to enlarge the island to more than double its original size. Barracks accommodation and redbrick mess buildings were erected, and a parade ground laid out. Although John

knew it as a centre for gunnery training, he would have been
delighted to discover that it now boasts a whole complex
dedicated to teaching sailors how to fight fire and flooding,
with a purpose built simulator that tilts and fills with water
just like a sinking ship. Lunch in the mess was reminiscent of
dining in an Oxford college, but with a variety of uniforms
replacing black university gowns. John would no doubt have
been surprised to see so many women, smart in white
uniform shirts with navy and white epaulettes. The site of
HMS Vernon is now buried under the Gunwharf shopping
centre, but I came away with a much stronger sense what it
must have meant to be part of the great Victorian naval
family.

By the time of the 1891 census, as well as the grievous
losses of the preceding years, there were plenty of new
additions to the family. My grandfather Harold makes his first
appearance at the age of six. He is living in Hammersmith
with his parents, his two sisters and a new baby brother. An
early photograph shows him dressed in a sailor suit, clutching
a model ship. It would be wrong to read any particular
significance into the outfit; parents had been dressing their
children like this throughout the second half of the century,
ever since Queen Victoria had chosen to have the five-year-
old Prince of Wales painted by Winterhalter wearing a
miniature white linen version of a naval uniform. But I like to
think that Hester was already thinking of her son as a
seafaring Dupen.

16 A Final Inventory

Ten years later, in January 1901, Queen Victoria died at Osborne. Many of her subjects in Britain and across the empire had never known a time when she was not their monarch. The royal yacht *Alberta*, so proudly guarded by young assistant engineer John Dupen all those years before, carried her body across the Solent to Gosport, while the new king, Edward VII, followed on board the *Victoria and Albert*. As the coffin passed, a line of warships fired salutes and their bands played funeral marches.

The end of one era was soon followed by another. The Hayle foundry was dying too, making annual losses that would lead to its closure in 1903. Instead of manufacturing boilers, Richard Trevithick's grandson had gone into partnership with a miller and was making Cornubia biscuits – a well-regarded product but hardly a technical revolution. In 1902 an advertisement offered reduced rail fares from Hayle to Liverpool for anyone who wanted to emigrate to America. When Harveys closed their doors for the last time nearly 600 jobs disappeared and there were few alternatives in the local area. Cornwall had by then lost around one third of its population to emigration and was, so it was said, surviving on remittances from overseas.

After disease destroyed the Indian coffee plantations, Ernest Dupen set up a successful civil engineering business. But like his older brothers, he was in poor health. In June 1902 he arrived on the *SS Derbyshire* from Colombo and this time it appeared that he was home to stay. Despite his efforts to meet eligible young women he had never married and he moved back into Cornubia Cottage with his sisters, who had by then retired. After thirty years of complaining about his liver, in November 1905 he died, not of the recurrent fever that so often laid him low, but of a stroke. At the age of 54, the last of the Dupen brothers was gone. Amongst the photographs I have inherited is one taken of Ernest in the uniform of a Captain in the Malabar Volunteer Rifles, a small, plump, balding man with a dapper moustache. He left an estate worth £1,700 (more than any of his brothers) to his unmarried nieces.

Annie Dupen lived on until 1910. When she died, her sister Sarah was appointed as the executor of her will. Sarah, the custodian of the family history, whose careful inscription ensured that the origin of her mother's New Testament was preserved, was the sister everyone turned to when something needed organising. Widowed in 1903, she left London and returned home to live with Annie and Salome in Cornubia Cottage, together with Hester's youngest stepdaughter, Maude, who was destined to live out her life in other people's houses. A group portrait shows Sarah standing in the garden with a huge fluffy cat in her arms, her chin tilted confidently upwards. Annie, in a dark, high-necked gown, and Salome, in a lighter patterned one with a ruffled hem, sit with their arms defensively folded, unsure that they want to be photographed. It is, I'm afraid, almost entirely because of this image that I have characterised Annie as a sharp-tongued businesswoman and Salome as gentle and affectionate. Just because they chose two different dress fabrics and Annie continued to dress her hair in the severe fashion of an earlier time.

I may have been unfair, but there is other evidence. Annie's will is meticulous in its detail and pointed in its omissions. The house that Harold will eventually inherit is left to Salome for her lifetime, along with the furniture. Hester and Sarah are to receive jewellery and her gold spectacles, Kate, who will die two years later in 1912, gets her 'wearing apparel', but Ellen is to have nothing. I feel sure that I am right to see them as two strong-willed women who fell out. Hester's daughters get a gold-framed brooch and a gold ring, while Kate's two oldest are to have Annie's gold watch and her Indian silver bracelet, and John's second daughter is left a gold brooch. Vivian, beloved by his aunts, is to receive the proceeds from the sale of two pianos and a velvet-backed rocking chair, while his sister Clare and two of her children are also remembered, with a ring, a writing desk and a gold chain. Annie had a lot of gold and a clear set of favourites.

Salome died in March 1918 and her will confirms my belief in her more kindly nature. She leaves money to the British and Foreign Sailors' Society, the Bible Society and the Wesleyan Missionary Society. Her list of bequests is even longer than Annie's and there is something for each of the nephews and nieces, including Maude, who is strictly speaking no relation. Even her sister Ellen, who dies later that year in Bristol, gets a pair of gold eyeglasses. There is nothing for Harold, but then he was going to get the house. What my grandfather did to deserve Cornubia Cottage I will never know. Perhaps it was simply that unlike most of his male cousins, he didn't emigrate.

The next generation of Dupens too was scattering, never to return. I have chosen to draw a line under my story at the end of Victoria's reign but I could have continued with the tale of many more voyages. Sharrock and Julia's oldest son, John Lysaght, travelled to Douglas, Wisconsin. Like Laura Ingalls Wilder and her family, he later headed west, leaving behind the big woods and crossing the prairie, making his way to Arizona before eventually settling in Los Angeles with his wife and a total of twelve children. The next son, Sharrock Perceval (known as Percy), became a sea captain, sailing between Liverpool and Africa. When he obtained his master's certificate in 1890 he gave his permanent address as that of his aunt Sarah in Hammersmith. I wonder if it was she and her kindly husband Henry who had paid for his apprenticeship. His sister Clare followed her mining engineer husband to Tilt Cove in Newfoundland, while their brother Vivian's future lay in India after he joined his uncle in Palghaut in 1892. He would still be sailing to and fro on P & O steamers between England and India well into his eighties.

Kate's oldest son, Sharrock Dupen Price, emigrated to
Montreal. He too would make his way west, to Minnesota and
eventually to the state of Washington. His younger brother
Walter obtained his mate's certificate and, like his cousin
Percy, qualified as a master mariner. Later he settled in South
Africa, returning to serve as one of the early aviators of World
War I.

John Dupen's second son George made a voyage to
Australia before he too headed for India to join his uncle
Ernest. He was appointed Assistant Commissioner of the
Palghaut Circle, recruiting Indian labourers to work on the
plantations of Sri Lanka. In this capacity he travelled
thousands of miles by motorbike in the most basic conditions
and like his uncles, ruined his health. Two of his brothers
became the war heroes their father had never had the chance
to be. Cuthbert, known as Bertie, who seems to have run off
to Australia to become a farmhand, signed up for active
service with the 11th Australian battalion and was killed at
Gallipoli. Arthur benefited from Admiral Fisher's reforms of
1905 and reached the rank of engineer captain, excelling in
the upper class pursuits of fencing and polo. (In a fascinating
example of the snakes and ladders of social mobility, his
children were not allowed to mix with their less well-off
cousins, the grandchildren of Sharrock and the aristocratic
Julia Pennefather.) He survived the war, only to die in Malta
on Christmas day 1918, as a result of a fall from his polo
pony.

In 1903, as the Hayle foundry was closing its doors for the
last time, my grandfather Harold went to sea as 4th engineer
on the tramp steamer *Tregantle*, part of the 'Tre' fleet owned
by a family from St Ives and manned by Cornish officers.
Like his uncle Ernest, Harold kept a logbook, which begins
with his packing list. In his wooden box were his shoes and
socks, a supply of magazines and books, a pack of cards, two
boxes of biscuits and four tins of milk. In his tin box he
packed his clothes and bedding, a bag of oatmeal, and his

sewing case, as well as his precious photographic supplies: 8 dozen glass plates, his dark room lamp, and bottle of developer with a measuring glass. This time there is a pictorial record to go with the logbook: photographs of the ship and her crew, including the youthful 4th engineer in his grimy suit of white duck, images of camels and date palms, feluccas on the Nile, a paddle steamer on the Bosphorus, and what looks like a double decker Egyptian train.

On 21st July the *Tregantle* sailed from Cardiff, past St Ives and out into the Bay of Biscay where, like his Uncle Ernest before him, Harold was ill for two days but managed to eat the occasional biscuit. On his first Sunday he noted that the crew spent their time washing and mending clothes, a routine not so very different from the one his Uncle George would have known. They witnessed a glorious sunset as they passed Gibraltar and then made their way into the Mediterranean and along the African coast. After calling at Alexandria, where Harold enjoyed tea with a missionary in Aboukir, they sailed through the Dardanelles to Constantinople and by 18th August they were in the Black Sea. On arriving at Theodosia, on the Crimean peninsula, the crew were draped in white cloaks and examined for bubonic plague while their dirty clothes were steamed, the young engineer recorded, for 45 minutes at a pressure of 160lbs per square inch. Apart from that, it seems to have been an uneventful voyage, with no dramatic incidents to rival the adventures of Uncle Ernest. The *Tregantle* carried Russian barley to Hamburg without being holed below the waterline; the chief engineer was never made incapable by drink; and no ferocious passengers threatened the crew with daggers.

Whether my grandfather was disappointed or not, I have no idea. Like Ernest, he gives no clue to his emotions in the diary of his travels. It has not turned out to be a way for me to get to know him. But after that one voyage, he settled back home in London, later travelling to install an electric plant in a mansion in Aberdeenshire, where he met my grandmother.

By the time he inherited Cornubia Cottage in 1918, he was married and living in London with a newborn son, my father. He would have had no use for a home in Cornwall and I doubt if there was any room for sentiment in a world turned upside down by war. The last surviving aunt, Sarah, moved back to London and I imagine the house was sold. By the end of the year, the Armistice had been signed and the only Dupens left in Hayle lay in the churchyard at Phillack. I wish now that I had asked my grandmother more about her husband Harold, but the stories she preferred to tell were of her own childhood, before she lost so many of those closest to her. My granddaughter, born as this book nears completion, will also grow up without her grandfather. I have made a promise that she will know who he was.

I first went to Hayle to look for my grandfather's family nearly a hundred years after his aunt Annie's death, hardly knowing what to expect. It was March, and like any out-of-season holiday resort it felt grey and desolate. The B & B where I stayed had slippery nylon sheets and smelled of sickly-sweet pot pourri and stale bacon fat. Penpol Terrace was dominated by a row of shops displaying half-hearted offerings of beach toys, ice cream, and random items of hardware. The air smelled of vinegary fish and chips. Number 35 turned out to be a plain, flat-fronted house with sash windows and a modern, glassed-in porch, painted a cheerful Mediterranean pink under a slate roof. Was the Dupen home pink in 1918? Surely not. Standing with my back to the house, in front of the overgrown bushes that filled the front garden, I could see the replacement for Brunel's viaduct soaring over the muddy creek where small pleasure craft and fishing boats lay beached by the tide. No more railway tracks or paddle steamers, no smoking chimneys or hammering from the foundry. Just a few melancholy seagulls wheeling overhead. If this was Cornubia Cottage, it did not feel familiar.

When I began my quest for the Dupens, I was thinking about what we lose when we no longer have a home to return

to, the house where we grew up, one that has been in the
family for more than a single generation. But it turns out that
you can't manufacture your past. Cornubia Cottage was never
my grandfather's home, nor my father's, and it isn't mine. I
will always feel the pull of the sea, but not enough to move to
Hayle. In exploring my seafaring heritage I have become a
maritime historian of sorts, but not a mariner.

Now that I am reaching the end of the story, I have
started to consider graveyards. They too are places that we
have lost. Most of us will be cremated, our ashes scattered in
some meaningful place, a cliff top or a meadow, our only
memorial perhaps a bench with a plaque. Or not even that.
My parents' ashes stayed in the grounds of the crematorium
in Exeter. We couldn't think what else to do. I don't visit
them; the people they once were are no longer there and the
soft air of south Devon does nothing to soothe my sense of
loss. My Scottish grandmother, in death as in life, has wrested
control of the family history. In a small village cemetery, set
amidst farmland in the shadow of an Iron Age fort not far
from Aberdeen, is the family memorial. There are the names
of my grandmother Jean, her parents, brothers and sister, her
husband Harold and son Malcolm. She herself is not there,
her ashes scattered by the RAF over the North Sea, as close
as possible to where Malcolm's bomber went missing in 1943.
When it came to carving the name of her older son, my
father, in stone, the only possible choice was here on Scottish
granite. There is not much space left and I'm not sure it's
where I want to be when my time comes. But I don't belong
in Phillack either. I know that now.

I would quite like to be scattered amongst the fritillaries by
the river here in Oxford. They are Oxfordshire's flower and at
the end of all this sifting through history I have come to the
conclusion that this is my place. It is not my childhood home
but I have made a community here, of friends and
neighbours. It is my present, not my ancestral past, and will
be my future too. The streets are full of people I have shared

experiences with for thirty years. When I go travelling now, I have an answer to the question that baffled my younger self, 'Where are you from?' But mine is not an insular community and I do not think of myself as English. I am Cornish and Scottish by inheritance, Canadian by adoption; I have two passports and three languages. The same is true of many of my friends, connected by our status as outsiders.

I am sitting under my plum trees to write this, my little calico cat curled up by my chair. Red kites wheel overhead, calling in eerie voices that belong to the chalk uplands, not a suburban back garden. This in the end is where I belong. Not in historic Oxford with its golden stone quadrangles and flocks of cawing students, but this borderland that is not the university city and not quite industrial Cowley either, although the church William Morris commissioned for his workers stands at the end of my road. When my house was built in 1890 the area was all market gardens. The stone walls and fruit trees survive, although the goats, pigs, and chickens have gone. I planted a quince ten years ago and each year I harvest the aromatic golden globes to make preserves. It has put down strong roots and so have I. My house has a past and eventually I too will become part of its history.

I have been back to Hayle since my first visit and observed the progress that has been made in regenerating the town as a World Heritage site, using Lottery funding to restore buildings for community use and establish a heritage centre in Harveys' old offices. The town trail takes you along a woodland path that was once the ropewalk, to a tranquil lake where ducks carefully escort their ducklings past the water lilies and into the rushes. The pool that Henry Harvey created to flush the silt from the harbour has become a haven for wildlife. You can still drink in Jane Trevithick's White Hart hotel but the Wesleyan chapel where Kate and Sarah Dupen were both married has been transformed into the Foundry shopping village, a jumble sale of knitting wool, postcards, and second-hand books. In the opposite direction, the

George V Memorial walk leads you between manicured
flower beds along the shore of the Copperhouse Pool
towards Phillack Hill. If you turn left here and keep straight
on up, you will reach the dunes where the children of Hayle,
in their best Sunday suits and white pinafores, came to picnic.
A series of caravan parks now overlook the vast expanse of
turquoise sea. The surf thunders in, children fly kites, and
seals bask on the rocks.

Before you reach the dunes you can visit the church where
my great-grandmother Hester was married. Here, the past is
suddenly present again. In the rough turf scattered with
primroses lies four-year-old Mary Leslie, dearly beloved child
of John and Julia Dupen, together with her parents. Here too
is Mary's brother George, the motor-biking district
commissioner from south India. Her other brothers, the war
heroes, Trooper Cuthbert Dupen and Engineer Captain
Arthur Dupen, although buried far away, are listed on the
wood panel of the war memorial, as well as on the stone
outside. Great-great-grandfather Sharrock is hard to find, a
long, low, ridged stone half hidden by the uncut grass, and the
lost babies have no markers, but the last resting place of his
older children stands tall, surmounted by a Cornish cross.
Ernest's name is on the pillar and on three sides of the base
are his sisters, any differences forgiven: Salome, Ellen, and
Joanna – for the purposes of eternity no longer Annie.

My journey of discovery began with an embroidered verse
and ends with a chiselled epitaph. The original poem has an
extra, penultimate line, 'Life's victory won', but I somehow
feel Annie would have considered that too grandiose a claim.
I have imagined her as clever, prickly, and independent, but
also conscientious and modest. It seems fitting that the child
whose neat stitching decorates my home is remembered in
these simple words:

Life's race well run
Life's work well done
Then cometh rest

Acknowledgements

This book began life as part of a PhD thesis about the boundaries between fiction and nonfiction. I am grateful for the support and supervision I received through Oxford Brookes University, and in particular would like to thank Emma Darwin, Nicole Pohl, Nigel Cliff, and Alysa Levene. Chapter 14 is based on my MA dissertation at the University of East Anglia, where I benefited from the comments and advice of my fellow MA students, especially Rob Atkinson, Gill Blanchard, Lisa Eveleigh, Ann Kennedy-Smith and Deborah Spring. Also at UEA, Frances Wilson encouraged me to write the story told in Chapter 15. I am grateful to her and my other tutors, Rebecca Stott and Ian Thomson. Simon Wenham at OUDCE gave me an excellent grounding in the Victorian period and read an early version of Chapter 5. I am grateful to Keith Levett at Henry Poole & Co., who was so generous with his time and knowledge, and to family and friends for the introduction. I would particularly like to thank Commander Mark Barton RN, who answered all my naval queries with good humour and patience; any remaining errors are mine.

I owe a great deal to the friends and family members who have read and commented on various drafts: Andy Baxter, Debra Emmett, Rebecca Goddard, Chris Lindop (thanks also for the tour of Bristol), Sarah Massey, Sorrel Pitts, Carly Schabowski, Paul Sullivan, and Henry Warren; and to those who provided a listening ear when I needed it: Needra Copley, Claire Thacker, and Morven Wilkie (with thanks also for medical expertise). And always remembering Patch, who helped with the typing all the way through but is sadly no longer here to place her paw print on the final version.

Printed in Great Britain
by Amazon